STYLE WRITS
FOR THE
SHERIFF COURT

Second Edition

*To the memory of
Fleur S Bennett*

STYLE WRITS
FOR THE
SHERIFF COURT

Second Edition

S A Bennett
LLB, Advocate

Edinburgh
Butterworths
1994

United Kingdom	Butterworth & Co (Publishers) Ltd, 4 Hill Street, EDINBURGH EH2 3JZ and Halsbury House, 35 Chancery Lane, LONDON WC2A 1EL
Australia	Butterworths Pty Ltd, SYDNEY, MELBOURNE, BRISBANE, ADELAIDE, PERTH, CANBERRA and HOBART
Canada	Butterworths Canada Ltd, TORONTO and VANCOUVER
Ireland	Butterworth (Ireland) Ltd, DUBLIN
Malaysia	Malayan Law Journal Sdn Bhd, KUALA LUMPUR
New Zealand	Butterworths of New Zealand Ltd, WELLINGTON and AUCKLAND
Puerto Rico	Butterworth of Puerto Rico, Inc, SAN JUAN
Singapore	Butterworths Asia, SINGAPORE
South Africa	Butterworth Publishers (Pty) Ltd, DURBAN
USA	Butterworth Legal Publishers, CARLSBAD, California, and SALEM, New Hampshire

All rights reserved. No part of this publication may be reproduced in any material form (including photocopying or storing it in any medium by electronic means and whether or not transiently or incidentally to some other use of this publication) without the written permission of the copyright owner except in accordance with the provisions of the Copyright, Designs and Patents Act 1988 or under the terms of a licence issued by the Copyright Licensing Agency Ltd, 90 Tottenham Court Road, London, England W1P 9HE. Applications for the copyright owner's written permission to reproduce any part of this publication should be addressed to the publisher.

Warning: The doing of an unauthorised act in relation to a copyright work may result in both a civil claim for damages and criminal proceedings.

© S A Bennett 1994

A CIP Catalogue record for this book is available from the British Library.

ISBN 0 406 02052 3

Typeset by Phoenix Photosetting, Chatham, Kent
Printed and bound in Great Britain by Clays Ltd, St Ives plc

FOREWORD

by THE RIGHT HONOURABLE LORD HOPE,
LORD PRESIDENT OF THE COURT OF SESSION

The aim of good pleading is to express one's meaning with clarity in as few words as possible. A collection of styles is a means to this end, and the expert pleader is always on the lookout for styles of pleadings, minutes or motions which meet this requirement. Recourse to such styles will save time in a busy day, but it will also assist continuity and uniformity of practice which is in itself desirable. No style should be followed slavishly, but consistency of pleading practice reduces the risk of misunderstanding. It helps to ensure that justice is done with the minimum of expense and delay.

Mr Bennett has brought together in this collection an impressive array of style writs drawn from almost every kind of action and proceeding likely to be encountered in the sheriff court. In doing so he has done a service both to the expert and to the beginner in the pleader's art. The expert will recognise the quality of the pleading exemplified by these styles, and he or she will welcome the assistance which they provide in cases which may be less familiar. The beginner will find here a collection of examples which, without this assistance, it would have taken years to build up. For my part I am happy to acknowledge the care with which Mr Bennett has put together this second edition of his book and the benefits which will follow from regular recourse to it in daily practice in the sheriff courts throughout Scotland.

David Hope
Edinburgh
August 1994

PREFACE

'The general standard of written pleading in the sheriff court today is, to put it mildly, low.' (Professor Robert Black QC, *An Introduction to Written Pleading* (1982)).

This book is intended to assist in laying such a perception to rest, and that by providing a visual aid for the draftsman. The styles that follow are designed to illustrate written pleading in general and the possible form and content of writs and motions commonly encountered in sheriff court practice (not including summary causes and small claims) in particular. Styles have been compiled with the Ordinary Cause Rules 1993 specifically in mind. Petitions, summary applications and motions are new to this edition.

The writs are drawn from fictitious processes in mid to late 1994. All parties to these imaginary actions are fictitious.

I wish to thank Craig Paterson for preparing the index, Selina Rae for typing the script and Alan Johnston, Sheriff Clerk Depute at Glasgow, Ian Baillie and Joseph Moyes, his counterparts at Edinburgh Sheriff Court, and Brenda Thomson of Messrs Robin Thompson & Partners for their generous assistance. Ronald Clancy and Paul Cullen, Advocates, expertly reviewed the text.

Siggi Bennett
Edinburgh
August 1994

CONTENTS

Foreword v
Preface vii

I   Declaratory Actions   1
II   Petitory Actions   13
III Family Proceedings   201
IV   Heritage Proceedings   285
V   Miscellaneous Proceedings   297

Index   363

I DECLARATORY ACTIONS

1. MUIR v ROBERTSON

Declarator of servitude

a. Initial writ

2. ALLAN v HEATH

Declarator and dissolution of partnership

a. Initial writ

3. LANE v LANE

Declarator of death

a. Initial writ
b. Motion for order for proof (OCR 37.4(1))

4. RAMSAY v RAMSAY

Declarator of death (seven years disappearance)

a. Initial writ

1. MUIR v ROBERTSON

Declarator of servitude

a. Initial writ

SHERIFFDOM OF NORTH STRATHCLYDE AT DUNOON

INITIAL WRIT

in the cause

PAUL JOHN MUIR, residing at Annandale Farm, Dunoon

PURSUER

against

RONALD ROBERTSON, residing at Carrbridge Farm, Dunoon

DEFENDER

The pursuer craves the court:

1. To find and declare that there exists over the heritable subjects All and Whole the lands and estate of Carrbridge Farm in the County of Dunoon described in the disposition by Thomas Thomson in favour of Alexander Craxton dated 10 May 1931 and recorded in the Division of the General Register of Sasines for the County of Dunoon on 12 July 1931, belonging to the defender, a servitude right of way for pedestrian and vehicular traffic in favour of the heritable subjects All and Whole the lands and estate of Annandale Farm in the County of Dunoon described in the disposition by George Clark in favour of Peter John Andrew Marsden dated 10 July 1951 and recorded in the Division of the General Register of Sasines for the County of Dunoon on 19 July 1951, belonging to the pursuer, and that on or about the line marked A B C D E on the Ordnance Survey plan annexed hereto leading from the said lands and estate of Annandale Farm to the public road between Semple and Dunoon marked on the plan aforesaid.

2. To find the defender liable in the expenses of the action.

CONDESCENDENCE

1. The pursuer resides at Annandale Farm, Dunoon. The defender resides at Carrbridge Farm, Dunoon. This action has as its object rights *in rem* in the heritable subjects (hereinafter referred to as 'Carrbridge Farm')

in which the defender resides aforesaid, which are situated within the territory of this court. This court accordingly has jurisdiction.

2. The pursuer is the proprietor of the heritable subjects (hereinafter referred to as 'Annandale Farm') in which he resides aforesaid, which are more fully described in the crave. Annandale Farm is adjacent to Carrbridge Farm, which is also more fully described in the crave, conform to Ordnance Survey plan annexed hereto.

3. There exists a servitude right of way for pedestrian and vehicular traffic over Carrbridge Farm in favour of Annandale Farm and that on or about the line marked A B C D E on the said plan leading from Annandale Farm to the public road between Semple and Dunoon marked on the plan aforesaid. Said servitude has been possessed since about 1960, and in any event for a continuous period of twenty years, openly, peaceably and without judicial interruption, as the proprietors from time to time of Carrbridge Farm knew or ought to have known. The defender has recently disputed the existence of the said servitude right. This action is therefore necessary.

PLEA-IN-LAW

A servitude right of way for pedestrian and vehicular traffic over the defender's subjects in favour of the pursuer's subjects having been possessed for a continuous period of twenty years openly, peaceably and without judicial interruption, decree of declarator should be granted as craved.

IN RESPECT WHEREOF

Enrolled solicitor
20 Blacket Street
Dunoon
Solicitor for the pursuer

2. ALLAN v HEATH

Declarator and dissolution of partnership

a. Initial writ

SHERIFFDOM OF TAYSIDE, CENTRAL AND FIFE AT FALKIRK

INITIAL WRIT

in the cause

FRANCIS ALLAN, residing at 1 Halbeath Drive, Falkirk

PURSUER

against

PETER NIGEL HEATH, residing at 2 Plant Hill, Falkirk

DEFENDER

The pursuer craves the court:

1. To find and declare that the business of the partnership between the pursuer and the defender trading under the name of 'Groovee Sounds' can only be carried on at a loss; and to decree a dissolution of the said partnership.

2. To find the defender liable in the expenses of the action.

CONDESCENDENCE

1. The pursuer resides at 1 Halbeath Drive, Falkirk. The defender resides at 2 Plant Hill, Falkirk. These proceedings have as their object the dissolution of the partnership between the pursuer and the defender trading under the name of 'Groovee Sounds'. The said partnership was formed under the law of Scotland. Its central management and control is exercised in Scotland. It has its place of business at 291 Main Street, Falkirk. This court has jurisdiction.

2. The said partnership was constituted by Minute of Agreement executed by the parties on 1 July 1991 and has a term of five years. It has traded since that date at the said place of business without making profits. Reference is made to the partnership books and accounts produced

herewith. There is no prospect of the business of the partnership becoming profitable. It can only be carried on at a loss. The defender however refuses to agree the dissolution of the partnership. The pursuer is therefore under necessity of bringing this action.

PLEA-IN-LAW

The business of the partnership being capable only of being carried on at a loss, decree of declarator and dissolution should be granted as craved.

IN RESPECT WHEREOF

Enrolled solicitor
15 Charlotte Place
Falkirk
Solicitor for the pursuer

3. LANE v LANE

Declarator of death

a. Initial writ

SHERIFFDOM OF TAYSIDE, CENTRAL AND FIFE
AT KIRKCALDY

INITIAL WRIT

in the cause

JOAN LANE (Assisted Person), residing at 14 Appleby Court, London

PURSUER

against

GEORGE ARMOUR LANE, whose whereabouts are not known

DEFENDER

The pursuer craves the court:

1. To find and declare that the defender, whose last known place of residence was at 19 Dee Street, Kirkcaldy, died on 15 July 1994 at 7 pm.

2. To grant warrant for citation of the defender by the publication of an advertisement in Form P1 in the Kirkcaldy Times.

3. To grant warrant for intimation to Mrs Miranda Lane, presently an in-patient at Dunfermline Royal Infirmary, Dunfermline, as wife; to Margaret Rodgers, residing at 619 Delgado Avenue, Shotts, as daughter; and to The Friends Mutual Life Assurance Company, 16 James Square, Edinburgh, as persons having an interest in the presumed death, of George Armour Lane, whose last known place of residence was at 19 Dee Street, Kirkcaldy; and to the Lord Advocate.

4. To appoint John Henry Smith, Chartered Accountant, 612 High Street, Kirkcaldy, or such other person as the court shall think proper, to be judicial factor on the estate of the defender.

5. To find any person offering opposition hereto liable in the expenses of the action.

CONDESCENDENCE

1. The pursuer resides at 14 Appleby Court, London. She is the daughter of the defender, George Armour Lane, whose whereabouts are

not known and cannot reasonably be ascertained. The pursuer has sought without success to locate him by personal enquiries and by advertisement in the national press. At the material date, the defender was domiciled in Scotland, having been born in Scotland of Scottish parents and having lived his whole life in Scotland. His last known place of residence was within the Sheriffdom of Tayside, Central and Fife at Kirkcaldy, namely at 19 Dee Street, Kirkcaldy. This court has jurisdiction. The defender has a wife, namely Mrs Miranda Lane, and one other child, namely Mrs Margaret Rodgers, each designed in the third crave. The only person who so far as known to the pursuer has an interest in the presumed death of the defender is The Friends Mutual Life Assurance Company, designed in the third crave, with whom the defender has a policy of life insurance, number 1296431.

2. The defender was born in Glasgow on 24 December 1937. After his marriage to the said Mrs Miranda Lane on 15 June 1967, he lived at the said place of residence until about 15 July 1994. On that date, he left home in the morning and drove to work. He spent the day in his office, tending his business affairs. For some time prior to that date, he had exhibited signs of anxiety and tension concerning his business affairs. He was frequently depressed and worried about money. On the said date, he left his office at about 6.30 pm. His car was subsequently found parked near the Forth Road Bridge. A shoe identified as belonging to him was later found washed up on the banks of the River Forth. His body has not however been located. In these circumstances the pursuer believes and avers that the defender drove from his office to the Forth Road Bridge on the said date and jumped therefrom, taking his own life. She seeks declarator as first craved. The pursuer also seeks the appointment of a judicial factor on the estate of the defender, in terms of the fourth crave. The defender has a business which requires to be wound up. It is expedient in the circumstances that such an appointment be made.

PLEAS-IN-LAW

1. The defender having died on 15 July 1994 at 7 pm, decree of declarator should be pronounced as first craved.

2. It being expedient that a judicial factor should be appointed to the estate of the defender, decree should be pronounced in terms of the fourth crave.

IN RESPECT WHEREOF

Enrolled solicitor
14 Bank Street
Kirkcaldy
Solicitor for the pursuer

b. Motion for order for proof (OCR 37.4(1))

SHERIFFDOM OF TAYSIDE, CENTRAL AND FIFE
AT KIRKCALDY

Court ref no A629/1994

MOTION FOR THE PURSUER

in the cause

JOAN LANE (Assisted Person), residing at 14 Appleby Court, London

PURSUER

against

GEORGE ARMOUR LANE, whose whereabouts are not known

DEFENDER

The pursuer moves the court to grant an order for proof.

16 December 1994   IN RESPECT WHEREOF

Enrolled solicitor
41 Bank Square
Kirkcaldy
Solicitor for the pursuer

4. RAMSAY v RAMSAY

Declarator of death (seven years disappearance)

a. Initial writ

SHERIFFDOM OF LOTHIAN AND BORDERS AT EDINBURGH

INITIAL WRIT

in the cause

MRS IVY BRUCE or RAMSAY (Assisted Person), residing at 12 Tower Road, Edinburgh

PURSUER

against

GEORGE RAMSAY, whose whereabouts are not known

DEFENDER

The pursuer craves the court:

1. To find and declare that the defender, whose last known place of residence was at 12 Tower Road, Edinburgh, has not been known to have been alive for a period of in excess of seven years and that he died at midnight on 5 July 1993.

2. To grant warrant for citation of the defender by the publication of an advertisement in Form P1 in the Scotsman newspaper.

3. To grant warrant for intimation to Alison May Ramsay, residing at 157 Marchfield Drive, Penicuik, as nearest relative; and The Life Provident Insurance Company, 197 George Street, Glasgow, as person having an interest in the presumed death of George Ramsay, whose last known place of residence was at 12 Tower Road, Edinburgh; and to the Lord Advocate.

4. To find any person offering opposition hereto liable in the expenses of the action.

CONDESCENDENCE

1. The pursuer resides at 12 Tower Road, Edinburgh. She is the wife of the defender, George Ramsay, whose whereabouts are not known and cannot reasonably be ascertained. The pursuer has sought without

success to locate him, as hereinafter condescended upon. The pursuer has been habitually resident in Scotland throughout the period of 12 months immediately preceding the raising of this action. She has been resident in the Sheriffdom of Lothian and Borders for a period of not less than 40 days ending with the date of the raising of this action. This court has jurisdiction. The defender has no children. His nearest relative known to the pursuer is his sister, Alison May Ramsay, designed in the third crave. The only person who so far as known to the pursuer has an interest in the presumed death of the defender is The Life Provident Insurance Company, designed in the third crave, with whom the defender had a policy of life insurance number 4355021.

2. The defender was born in Edinburgh on 24 October 1956. After their marriage, the parties lived together until 5 July 1986. On that date, the defender left the parties' matrimonial home and went missing. He has not been seen since by the pursuer or to her knowledge anyone else. The pursuer attempted to trace him with the assistance of the police but without success. No government agencies have any knowledge of him. None of his family or friends has seen or heard from him. So far as the pursuer is aware, the defender has not been known to be alive since 5 July 1986.

3. In these circumstances, the pursuer seeks declarator that the defender has not been known to have been alive for a period of in excess of seven years, and that he died at midnight on 5 July 1993.

PLEA-IN-LAW

The defender having gone missing on 5 July 1986 and not being known to have been alive since the said date, decree of declarator should be pronounced as craved.

IN RESPECT WHEREOF

Enrolled solicitor
123 More Street
Edinburgh
Solicitor for the pursuer

II PETITORY ACTIONS

1. SCHULTZ & BRAUN v WHITE & CO

Payment—Debt—Hire of services—Implied contract—Foreign currency

a. Initial writ
b. Motion for pursuers to be ordained to sist mandatary
c. Minute of sist (mandatary)
d. Motion for sist of mandatary

2. INDUSTRIAL SUPPLIES LTD v PLUMBING MATERIALS LTD

Payment—Debt—Sale of goods—Damages—Breach of contract—Merchantable quality and fitness for purpose—Plea of retention

a. Initial writ
b. Reponing note (OCR 8.1)
c. Defences and counterclaim (OCR 19.1)
d. Motion for pursuers to be ordained to find caution (OCR 27.2)
e. Motion for recall of arrestment

3. THE IMPERIAL BANK PLC v HAMILTON

Payment—Debt—Loan from bank—Guarantee—Joint and several liability—Interest from prior to citation at variable rate—Plea to relevancy of defences—Defenders' whereabouts not known

a. Initial writ
b. Minute of amendment (instance)
c. Motion for amendment in terms of minute of amendment
d. Note of adjustments
e. Motion for summary decree in terms of craves (OCR 17.2)

4. DANSON v BOGGS

Payment—Debt—IOU—Interest from prior to citation—Plea of writ or oath

a. Initial writ
b. Defences
c. Note of adjustments
d. Record (OCR 9.11)

e. Motion for reference to oath (OCR 29.1(1))
f. Minute of sist (representative) (OCR 25.2)
g. Motion for sist of minuter as pursuer
h. Minute of withdrawal of defences

5. HUGHES v BARRETT

Payment—Damages—Fatal case—Road traffic accident—Negligence—Personal services to deceased's relatives—Plea of apportionment

a. Initial writ
b. Defences
c. Motion for order for service of third party notice (OCR 20.1)
d. Third party notice
e. Answers for third party (OCR 20.5)
f. Minute of sist, adoption and amendment (OCR 36.6)
g. Motion for minute of sist, adoption and amendment to be received
h. Minute of tender (Williamson tender)

6. HALL v AIRDRIE DISTRICT COUNCIL

Payment—Damages—Personal injuries—Accident in tenement—Negligence—Occupiers' liability—System of inspection

a. Initial writ
b. Joint minute of agreement
c. Minute of abandonment (OCR 23.1(a))
d. Joint motion for decree of absolvitor and expenses against pursuer as assisted person
e. Motion for modification of assisted person's liability for expenses

7. BROWN v TARMACADAM (ROADS) LTD

Payment—Damages—Personal injuries—Accident at work—Negligence—Safe plant and equipment—Breach of statutory duty—Provision and use of work equipment—Work of engineering construction—Provisional damages

a. Initial writ
b. Motion for summary decree disposing of merits (OCR 17.2)
c. Motion for pursuer to be ordained to submit himself for medical examination
d. Motion for interim payment of damages (OCR 36.9)
e. Joint minute of settlement (extra-judicial) (including certification of skilled witnesses and sanction for employment of counsel)
f. Joint motion for decree in terms of joint minute of settlement

8. BLACK v INVERCLYDE METALS LTD

Payment—Damages—Personal injuries—Accident at work—Negligence—Safe system of work—Breach of statutory duty—Manual handling operation—Necessary services to injured person—Plea to relevancy of defences

a. Initial writ
b. Note of adjustments
c. Minute of admission of liability
d. Specification of documents (OCR 28.2(2))
e. Motion for commission and diligence to recover documents
f. Joint minute of admissions

9. ANDERSON v PRESS (UK) LTD

Payment—Damages—Personal injuries—Accident at work—Negligence—Safe place of work—Breach of statutory duty—Workplace safety—Plea of contributory negligence—Plea of time bar

a. Initial writ
b. Defences
c. Specification of property (OCR 28.2(2))
d. Motion for order for inspection and photographing of property
e. List of witnesses (OCR 9.14(1))
f. Motion for document to be admitted as evidence without calling maker as witness (OCR 29.3(2))
g. Motion for commission to examine a witness (OCR 28.10)
h. Motion for discharge of diet of proof

10. HUGHES v AMEX ENGINEERING LTD (IN LIQUIDATION)

Payment—Damages—Personal injuries—Occupational disease—Asbestosis—Negligence—Plea of apportionment—Plea of indemnity

a. Initial writ
b. Defences
c. Third party notice
d. Notice to admit (document) (OCR 29.14(1)(b))
e. Specification of matters (OCR 28.2(2))
f. Motion for defenders to be ordained to disclose information anent identity of potential witness
g. Minute of tender (Houston tender)
h. Minute of withdrawal of tender

11. SMITH v LANARKSHIRE REGIONAL COUNCIL

Payment—Damages—Personal injuries—Occupational disease—Dermatitis—Negligence—Safe plant and equipment—Breach of statutory duty—Control of substances hazardous to health

a. Initial writ
   b. Motion for evidence of witness to be received by way of affidavit (OCR 29.3(1))
   c. Affidavit
   d. Minute of amendment
   e. Motion for minute of amendment to be received and answered
   f. Motion for prorogation of time to lodge answers
   g. Answers
   h. Motion for amendment in terms of minute of amendment and answers

12. HOGG v MAXWELL & CO

Payment—Damages—Breach of contract—Negligence—Professional negligence—Interest from prior to citation at different rates

   a. Initial writ
   b. Motion for sist for negotiation
   c. Motion for recall of sist

13. JONES v MIDLOTHIAN HEALTH BOARD

Payment—Damages—Negligence—Professional negligence—Vicarious liability

   a. Initial writ
   b. Minute of tender
   c. Minute of acceptance of tender
   d. Motion for decree in terms of minutes of tender and acceptance of tender
   e. Note of objections to Auditor's report (OCR 32.4)

14. ANDREWS v THOMPSON

Payment—Count reckoning and payment (partnership)

   a. Initial writ
   b. Motion for pursuer to be ordained to find caution (OCR 27.2)

15. CARGILL v CARGILL'S EXECUTOR

Payment—Count reckoning and payment (executry)

   a. Initial writ
   b. Defences
   c. Note of objections to accounts

16. JOHNSON'S TRUSTEES v DUNS BUILDING SOCIETY

Payment—Furthcoming—Arrested funds—Defender's whereabouts not known

a. Initial writ

17. PETE'S GARAGE LTD v HARRISON

Payment—Multiplepoinding (raised by party holding fund in medio)

a. Initial writ
b. Condescendence and claim (OCR 25.11(1))
c. Minute of transference (OCR 35.2)
d. Motion for transference of cause against representative of defender's estate

18. KUMAR v RASHID

Payment—Multiplepoinding (raised by party not holding fund in medio)

a. Initial writ
b. Condescendence and list (OCR 35.4(2))
c. Motion for approval of condescendence of fund (OCR 35.13(2))

19. JENKINS v YOUNG

Ad factum praestandum—Implement—Missives for sale of heritage (seller pursuing action)—Plea to competency—Plea of exception

a. Initial writ
b. Defences
c. Minute of amendment (crave)

20. BLACKWOOD PROPERTIES LTD (IN RECEIVERSHIP) v DUNN

Ad factum praestandum—Implement—Missives for sale of heritage (buyer pursuing action)

a. Initial writ

21. EAZEE CREDIT LTD v KHAN

Ad factum praestandum—Delivery—Damages—Debt—Hire purchase—Interest from prior to citation

a. Initial writ

22. ENGINEERING ACCESSORIES LTD v ROSS

Interdict—Breach of contract—Restrictive covenant

a. Initial writ

23. BARTON v LONGSTONE GOLF CLUB

Interdict—Nuisance—Plea of prescription

a. Initial writ
b. Motion for defences to be received late
c. Defences
d. Motion for pursuer whose solicitor has withdrawn from acting to appear or be represented at specified diet (OCR 24.2)
e. Note of adjustments
f. Record

24. THE BREAD-BASKET v BREAD-BASKET LTD

Interdict—Passing off

a. Initial writ

1. SCHULTZ & BRAUN v WHITE & CO

Payment—Debt—Hire of services—Implied contract—Foreign currency

a. Initial writ

SHERIFFDOM OF GLASGOW AND STRATHKELVIN
AT GLASGOW

INITIAL WRIT

in the cause

SCHULTZ & BRAUN Liederstrasse 421, Bremen, Germany

PURSUERS

against

WHITE & CO, a firm with a place of business at 231 Govan Road, Glasgow and JOHN WHITE and MRS MARY WHITE, both residing at 'Fairlie', Blythswood Road. Milngavie, the partners of the said firm, as such partners and as individuals

DEFENDERS

The pursuers crave the court:

1. To grant decree against the defenders jointly and severally for payment to the pursuers of the sum of EIGHT THOUSAND SEVEN HUNDRED AND THREE DEUTSCHMARKS (8,703 DM), with interest thereon at the rate of eight *per centum per annum* from the date of citation until payment, or the sterling equivalent thereof at the date of payment or the date of extract, whichever is the earlier.

2. To find the defenders liable in the expenses of the action.

CONDESCENDENCE

1. The pursuers are a firm of surveyors formed under the law of Germany with a place of business at Liederstrasse 421, Bremen, Germany. The

first named defenders are a partnership formed under the law of Scotland, where their central management and control is exercised. They have a place of business at 231 Govan Road, Glasgow. They are domiciled there. This court has jurisdiction. The second and third named defenders are the partners of the said firm. They reside at 'Fairlie', Blythswood Road, Milngavie. To the knowledge of the pursuers, no proceedings are pending before any other court involving the present cause of action and between the parties hereto. To the knowledge of the pursuers no agreement exists between the parties prorogating jurisdiction over the subject-matter of the present cause to another court.

2. In about March 1992, the defenders instructed the pursuers to survey certain commercial properties in Bremen, Germany. The pursuers duly carried out their instructions. The value of their services is 8,703 Deutschmarks, conform to the applicable professional table of fees. Said sum is a reasonable charge but remains unpaid, despite requests. This action is therefore necessary.

PLEA-IN-LAW

The pursuers having rendered services to the defenders are entitled to payment at a reasonable rate therefor, as craved.

IN RESPECT WHEREOF

Enrolled solicitor
23 Johnston Street
Glasgow
Solicitor for the pursuers

b. Motion for pursuers to be ordained to sist mandatary

SHERIFFDOM OF GLASGOW AND STRATHKELVIN
AT GLASGOW

Court ref no A105/1994

MOTION FOR THE
DEFENDERS

in the cause

SCHULTZ & BRAUN, Liederstrasse 421, Bremen, Germany

PURSUERS

against

WHITE & CO, a firm with a place of business at 231 Govan Road, Glasgow and **JOHN WHITE** and **MRS MARY WHITE**, both residing at 'Fairlie', Blythswood Road, Milngavie, the partners of the said firm, as such partners and as individuals

DEFENDERS

The defenders move the court to ordain the pursuers to sist a mandatary within 28 days.

14 November 1994   IN RESPECT WHEREOF

Enrolled solicitor
6 Queen's Drive
Glasgow
Solicitor for the defenders

c. Minute of sist (mandatary)

SHERIFFDOM OF GLASGOW AND STRATHKELVIN
AT GLASGOW

MINUTE OF SIST

for JOHN ARTHUR MAXWELL, residing at 41 Largs Road, Glasgow

in the cause

SCHULTZ & BRAUN, Liederstrasse 421, Bremen, Germany

PURSUERS

against

WHITE & CO, a firm with a place of business at 231 Govan Road, Glasgow and JOHN WHITE and MRS MARY WHITE, both residing at 'Fairlie', Blythswood Road, Milngavie, the partners of the said firm, as partners and as individuals

DEFENDERS

The minuter craves the court:

To grant him leave to be sisted as mandatary for the pursuers in this action.

IN RESPECT WHEREOF

Enrolled solicitor
23 Johnston Street
Glasgow
Solicitor for the minuter

d. Motion for sist of mandatary

SHERIFFDOM OF GLASGOW AND STRATHKELVIN
AT GLASGOW

Court ref no A105/1994

MOTION FOR THE MINUTER

in the cause

SCHULTZ & BRAUN, Liederstrasse 421, Bremen, Germany

PURSUERS

against

WHITE & CO, a firm with a place of business at 231 Govan Road, Glasgow and JOHN WHITE and MRS MARY WHITE, both residing at 'Fairlie', Blythswood Road, Milngavie, the partners of the said firm, as such partners and as individuals

DEFENDERS

The minuter moves the court to grant the crave of the minute.

Part of process lodged with the motion:

Minute of sist

5 December 1994   IN RESPECT WHEREOF

Enrolled solicitor
23 Johnston Street
Glasgow
Solicitor for the minuter

2. INDUSTRIAL SUPPLIES LTD v PLUMBING MATERIALS LTD

Payment—Debt—Sale of goods—Damages—Breach of contract—Merchantable quality and fitness for purpose—Plea of retention

a. Initial writ

SHERIFFDOM OF GLASGOW AND STRATHKELVIN
AT GLASGOW

INITIAL WRIT

in the cause

INDUSTRIAL SUPPLIES LIMITED, a company with a place of business at 35 Buccleuch Street, Glasgow

PURSUERS

against

PLUMBING MATERIALS LIMITED, a company with a place of business at 41 Devlin Street, Glasgow

DEFENDERS

The pursuers crave the court:

1. To grant decree against the defenders for payment to the pursuers of the sum of SIX THOUSAND NINE HUNDRED AND EIGHTY FIVE POUNDS, FOURTEEN PENCE (£6,985.14) with interest thereon at the rate of eight *per centum per annum* from the date of citation until payment.
2. To grant warrant to arrest on the dependence of the action.
3. To find the defenders liable in the expenses of the action.

CONDESCENDENCE

1. The pursuers are a company incorporated under the Companies Acts with a place of business at 35 Buccleuch Street, Glasgow. The

defenders are a company incorporated under the Companies Acts with a place of business at 41 Devlin Street, Glasgow. The defenders are domiciled there. This court accordingly has jurisdiction. To the knowledge of the pursuers, no proceedings are pending before any other court involving the present cause of action and between the parties hereto. To the knowledge of the pursuers, no agreement exists between the parties prorogating jurisdiction over the subject-matter of the present cause to another court.

2. On or about 4 September 1991, the pursuers sold to the defenders various goods to a total value of £6,985.14, conform to pursuers' invoice number 120192, produced herewith and its terms adopted and held as repeated herein *brevitatis causa*. The said sum remains unpaid. The defenders have refused or at least delayed to make payment. This action is accordingly necessary.

PLEA-IN-LAW

The pursuers having sold and delivered goods to the defenders as condescended upon, are entitled to payment of the price thereof.

IN RESPECT WHEREOF

Enrolled solicitor
2 George Square
Glasgow
Solicitor for the pursuers

b. Reponing note (OCR 8.1(1))

SHERIFFDOM OF GLASGOW AND STRATHKELVIN
AT GLASGOW

REPONING NOTE

for the defenders

in the cause

INDUSTRIAL SUPPLIES LIMITED, a company with a place of business at 35 Buccleuch Street, Glasgow

PURSUERS

against

PLUMBING MATERIALS LIMITED, a company with a place of business at 41 Devlin Street, Glasgow

DEFENDERS

The defenders apply to be reponed, under reference to the following:

The proposed defence
The defenders propose to defend this action on the ground that the goods sold to them by the pursuers were not of merchantable quality nor fit for the purpose for which they were purchased, all as more particularly detailed in the defences and counterclaim produced herewith, and that therefore the pursuers were in material breach of contract; that that breach has caused the defenders to sustain loss and damage, as set forth in the defences and counterclaim aforesaid; and that the defenders are entitled to retain any sum due to the pursuers pending resolution of the counterclaim.

The explanation for the failure to appear
Decree in absence passed on 15 August 1994. Service of the initial writ was effected upon the defenders by the recorded delivery postal service on

18 July 1994. The writ was signed for by an employee of the defenders whose employment was terminated that same day for reasons unconnected with the present proceedings. Said employee left the writ in a desk drawer where it was discovered by chance on 16 August 1994. Steps were then taken without delay to make this application to be reponed.

IN RESPECT WHEREOF

Enrolled solicitor
95 St James Street
Glasgow
Solicitor for the defenders

c. Defences and counterclaim (OCR 19.1)

SHERIFFDOM OF GLASGOW AND STRATHKELVIN
AT GLASGOW

DEFENCES AND
COUNTERCLAIM

in the cause

INDUSTRIAL SUPPLIES LIMITED, a company with a place of business at 35 Buccleuch Street, Glasgow

PURSUERS

against

PLUMBING MATERIALS LIMITED, a company with a place of business at 41 Devlin Street, Glasgow

DEFENDERS

Warrant for arrestment on the dependence applied for.

The defenders crave the court:

To grant decree against the pursuers for payment to the defenders of the sum of TWELVE THOUSAND EIGHT HUNDRED AND EIGHTY FOUR POUNDS, TWENTY SIX PENCE (£12,884.26), with interest thereon at the rate of eight *per centum per annum* from 1 April 1993 until payment; and to find the pursuers liable in the expenses of the counterclaim.

ANSWERS TO CONDESCENDENCE

1. The averments relating to the defenders and jurisdiction are admitted. *Quoad ultra* not known and not admitted.
2. Admitted that on the said date the pursuers sold to the defenders the

said goods. Admitted that the said sum remains unpaid. The said invoice is referred to for its terms. *Quoad ultra* denied. Explained and averred that the goods detailed in the said invoice were 50-gallon cisterns. To the pursuers' knowledge, they were to be installed in the workplaces of certain of the defenders' customers for the storage of water there. It was an implied term of the parties' contract that the said cisterns should be of merchantable quality and, further, that they should be reasonably fit for the purpose of storing water in the workplaces. In the event, the said cisterns were neither of merchantable quality nor reasonably fit for such use by reason of the defects more fully condescended on in the statement of facts hereunder, the terms of which are adopted and held as repeated herein *brevitatis causa*. The pursuers are accordingly in material breach of contract. As a result of the pursuers' said breach, the defenders have suffered loss and damage as more fully condescended on in the statement of facts aforesaid. Accordingly, the defenders are entitled to retain the sum sued for pending resolution of the counterclaim.

STATEMENT OF FACTS

1. The defenders contracted with the pursuers for the sale by the pursuers to the defenders of certain cisterns specified in the pursuers' invoice number 120192, all as more particularly condescended upon in the answers to the condescendence, which answers are held as repeated herein *brevitatis causa*. It was an implied term of the contract that the cisterns should be of merchantable quality and that they should be reasonably fit for the storage of water in workplaces. Accordingly, the cisterns required to be free from any defects which might cause them to leak.

2. The said cisterns were duly delivered by the pursuers to the defenders. The defenders thereafter sold them to a number of their customers in whose workplaces they were installed. Thereafter, each cistern sprang a leak at the point of its junction with the premises' pipework. The cause of the leakages was the defective manufacture of the cisterns. The internal profile of each cistern was found to be of varying and irregular thickness. According to the specification issued by the manufacturers, the walls and base of the said cisterns should have had a consistent thickness of 4 mm. In the event, the thickness of the walls thereof varied from 3 mm to 3.5 mm and the thickness of the base from 3 mm to 4.75 mm. The said variations occurred randomly over small areas, the profile thereof being irregular and 'hilly'. The said irregularities exceeded normal manufacturing tolerances. As a result, it was impossible to achieve a watertight union of pipes with the cisterns. Consequently, the cisterns leaked.

3. In the foregoing circumstances, the pursuers were in breach of the said implied terms. The cisterns were not of merchantable quality. They were not reasonably fit for the storage of water in workplaces. They had present in them defects which rendered them liable to leak when pipes were connected to them. The pursuers were accordingly in material breach of contract. As a result, the defenders suffered the loss and damage hereinafter condescended upon.

4. As a result of the pursuers' material breach of contract, the defenders have suffered loss and damage. As a consequence of the said leakages, damage was caused to the defenders' said customers' premises. The cisterns required to be repaired. The costs of remedying the damage and repairing the cisterns totalled £12,884.26, which is the sum sued for in this counterclaim. The costs were incurred by the defenders on or about 1 April 1993.

5. The defenders have repeatedly asked the pursuers to make reparation to them for the said loss and damage. This they refuse, or at any rate delay, to do. The present counterclaim is accordingly necessary.

PLEAS-IN-LAW

1. The defenders having suffered loss and damage through the pursuers' material breach of contract and being entitled to reparation therefor, are entitled to retain any sum due to the pursuers pending resolution of the counterclaim for the defenders.

2. The defenders having suffered loss and damage through the pursuers' material breach of contract, are entitled to reparation therefor as counterclaimed.

3. The sum sued for being a reasonable estimate of the defenders' loss and damage, decree should be pronounced as counterclaimed.

IN RESPECT WHEREOF

Enrolled solicitor
95 St James Street
Glasgow
Solicitor for the defenders

d. Motion for pursuers to be ordained to find caution (OCR 27.2)

SHERIFFDOM OF GLASGOW AND STRATHKELVIN AT GLASGOW

Court ref no A291/1994

MOTION FOR THE DEFENDERS

in the cause

INDUSTRIAL SUPPLIES LIMITED, a company with a place of business at 35 Buccleuch Street, Glasgow

PURSUERS

against

PLUMBING MATERIALS LIMITED, a company with a place of business at Devlin Street, Glasgow

DEFENDERS

The defenders move the court to ordain the pursuers to find caution in the sum of £10,000 or such other sum as the court thinks fit and to sist the proceedings until caution is found; all on the ground that it appears by credible testimony that there is reason to believe that the pursuers will be unable to pay the defenders' expenses if successful in their defence.

Documents lodged with the motion:-
Companies Office documentation.
Extract decree for payment.

14 October 1994   IN RESPECT WHEREOF

Enrolled solicitor
95 St James Street
Glasgow
Solicitor for the defenders

e. Motion for recall of arrestment

SHERIFFDOM OF GLASGOW AND STRATHKELVIN
AT GLASGOW

Court ref no A291/1994

MOTION FOR THE
DEFENDERS

in the cause

INDUSTRIAL SUPPLIES LIMITED, a company with a place of business at 35 Buccleuch Street, Glasgow

PURSUERS

against

PLUMBING MATERIALS LIMITED, a company with a place of business at 41 Devlin Street, Glasgow

DEFENDERS

The defenders move the court to recall the arrestment on the dependence of this action served by the pursuers upon New Bank plc, 121 East George Street, Glasgow on 9 September 1994.

14 October 1994   IN RESPECT WHEREOF

Enrolled solicitor
95 St James Street
Glasgow
Solicitor for the defenders

3. THE IMPERIAL BANK PLC v HAMILTON

Payment—Debt—Loan from bank—Guarantee—Joint and several liability—Interest from prior to citation at variable rate—Plea to relevancy of defences—Defenders' whereabouts not known

a. Initial writ

SHERIFFDOM OF TAYSIDE, CENTRAL AND FIFE AT DUNDEE

INITIAL WRIT

in the cause

THE IMPERIAL BANK PLC, a company with its registered office at 16 The Mall, London

PURSUERS

against

GEORGE HAMILTON and MRS AUDREY HAMILTON, whose whereabouts are not known

DEFENDERS

The pursuers crave the court:

1. To grant decree against the defenders jointly and severally for payment to the pursuers of the sum of SIX THOUSAND FOUR HUNDRED AND TWELVE POUNDS SIXTEEN PENCE (£6,412.16), with interest thereon at the rate of two *per centum per annum* above the pursuers' base rate applicable from time to time from 13 February 1994 until payment.

2. To grant decree against the defenders jointly and severally for payment to the pursuers of the sum of NINETY SEVEN POUNDS SIX PENCE (£97.06), with interest thereon at the rate of eight *per centum per annum* from the date of decree to follow hereon until payment.

3. To grant decree against the defenders jointly and severally for payment to the pursuers of the sum of FIFTEEN THOUSAND SIX HUNDRED AND TWENTY POUNDS NINE PENCE (£15,620.09), with interest thereon at the rate of three *per centum per annum* above the pursuers' base rate applicable from time to time from 13 February 1994 until payment.

4. To grant decree against the defenders jointly and severally for payment to the pursuers of the sum of THREE HUNDRED AND ONE POUNDS (£301) with interest thereon at the rate of eight *per centum per annum* from the date of decree to follow hereon until payment.

5. To grant warrant to cite the defenders by the publication of an advertisement in Form G3 in the Dundee Express newspaper.

6. To grant warrant for arrestment on the dependence of the action.

7. To find the defenders liable in the expenses of the action.

CONDESCENDENCE

1. The pursuers are a public limited company incorporated by Royal Charter with its registered office at 16 The Mall, London. The defenders' whereabouts are not known and cannot reasonably be ascertained. Their last known residence was at 123 Alderbank Drive, Dundee. They removed therefrom in about early 1994 and left no forwarding address. Enquiry agents instructed by the pursuers have been unable to locate them. The pursuers in the present action claim payment of sums due to them by the defenders under and in terms of the contracts hereinafter condescended upon. These sums ought to have been paid by the defenders to the pursuers in Dundee. This court accordingly has jurisdiction. To the knowledge of the pursuers, no proceedings are pending before any other court involving the present cause of action and between the parties hereto. To the knowledge of the pursuers, no agreement exists between the parties prorogating jurisdiction over the subject-matter of the present cause to another court.

2. The pursuers afforded to the defenders banking facilities at their High Street, Dundee branch. The defenders opened a current account there, numbered 261 359. They borrowed money from the pursuers on the said account. Interest was exigible on sums borrowed at the rate of two *per centum per annum* above the pursuers' base rate applicable from time to time. As at 13 February 1994 the total sum borrowed by the defenders, exclusive of interest accrued but unapplied, was £6,412.16, which is the sum first craved. Interest accrued thereon but unapplied amounts to £97.06, which is the sum second craved. A certified statement of account will be produced.

3. The pursuers afforded banking facilities at their said branch to a company named George Hamilton Enterprises Ltd (hereinafter referred to as 'the company'). The company opened a current account there, numbered 461 293. It borrowed money from the pursuers on the said account. On or about 4 May 1991, the defenders guaranteed full and final payment on demand of all sums for which the company was or would become due or liable for to the pursuers. Copy guarantee of the said date is produced herewith and its terms held as repeated herein *brevitatis causa*. Interest was exigible on sums borrowed by the company at the rate of three *per centum per annum* above the pursuers' base rate applicable from time to time. As at 13 February 1994, the total sum borrowed by the company, exclusive of interest accrued but unapplied, was £15,620.09, which is the sum third craved. Interest accrued thereon but unapplied

amounts to £301, which is the sum fourth craved. A certified statement of account will be produced.

4. The pursuers have repeatedly called upon the defenders to make payment of the sums borrowed and guaranteed, respectively, by them. They refuse or at least delay to do so. This action is accordingly necessary.

PLEAS-IN-LAW

1. The defenders having borrowed money from the pursuers, the pursuers are entitled to decree in terms of the first and second craves.

2. The defenders having granted to the pursuers the guarantee condescended on, and the sums third and fourth craved being due thereunder, the pursuers are entitled to decree in terms of said craves.

IN RESPECT WHEREOF

Enrolled solicitor
1 Market Street
Dundee
Solicitor for the pursuer

b. Minute of amendment

SHERIFFDOM OF TAYSIDE, CENTRAL AND FIFE AT DUNDEE

MINUTE OF AMENDMENT

for the pursuers

in the cause

THE IMPERIAL BANK PLC, a company with its registered office at 16 The Mall, London

PURSUERS

against

GEORGE HAMILTON and MRS AUDREY HAMILTON, whose whereabouts are not known

DEFENDERS

DUNLOP for the pursuers craved and hereby craves the court to allow the initial writ to be amended by correcting the designation of the defenders in the instance to:

'both residing at 461 Alexander Place, Newcastle.'

IN RESPECT WHEREOF

Enrolled solicitor
1 Market Street
Dundee
Solicitor for the pursuers

c. Motion for minute of amendment to be received and for amendment

SHERIFFDOM OF TAYSIDE, CENTRAL AND FIFE
AT DUNDEE

Court ref no A29/1994

MOTION FOR THE
PURSUERS

in the cause

THE IMPERIAL BANK PLC, a company with its registered office at 16 The Mall, London

PURSUERS

against

GEORGE HAMILTON and MRS AUDREY HAMILTON, whose whereabouts are not known

DEFENDERS

The pursuers move the court to allow the minute of amendment, no. 7 of process, to be received and to allow amendment in terms thereof.

Part of process lodged with the motion:

Minute of amendment

4 August 1994   IN RESPECT WHEREOF

Enrolled solicitor
1 Market Street
Dundee
Solicitor for the pursuers

d. Note of adjustments

SHERIFFDOM OF TAYSIDE, CENTRAL AND FIFE
AT DUNDEE

NOTE OF ADJUSTMENTS

for the pursuers

in the cause

THE IMPERIAL BANK PLC, a company with its registered office at 16 The Mall, London

PURSUERS

against

GEORGE HAMILTON and MRS AUDREY HAMILTON, both residing at 461 Alexander Place, Newcastle

DEFENDERS

1. Add at the end of articles 2 and 3 of the condescendence the following:

'The averments in answer are denied except insofar as coinciding herewith.'

2. Add a new plea-in-law as follows:

'3. The defences being irrelevant *et separatim* lacking in specification, decree should be granted in terms of the craves *de plano*.'

e. Motion for summary decree in terms of craves (OCR 17.2)

SHERIFFDOM OF TAYSIDE, CENTRAL AND FIFE
AT DUNDEE

Court ref no A29/1994

MOTION FOR THE
PURSUERS

in the cause

THE IMPERIAL BANK PLC, a company with its registered office at 16 The Mall, London

PURSUERS

against

GEORGE HAMILTON and MRS AUDREY HAMILTON, both residing at 461 Alexander Place, Newcastle

DEFENDERS

The pursuers move the court to grant summary decree in terms of the craves of the initial writ.

14 October 1994   IN RESPECT WHEREOF

Enrolled solicitor
1 Market Street
Dundee
Solicitor for the pursuers

4. DANSON v BOGGS

Payment—Debt—IOU—Interest from prior to citation—Plea of writ or oath

a. Initial writ

SHERIFFDOM OF GRAMPIAN, HIGHLAND AND ISLANDS
AT INVERNESS

INITIAL WRIT

in the cause

EDWARD JOHN DANSON,
residing at 3 Market Square, Tain

PURSUER

against

WILLIAM BOGGS, residing at 49
New Street, Inverness

DEFENDER

The pursuer craves the court:

1. To grant decree against the defender for payment to the pursuer of the sum of ONE THOUSAND EIGHT HUNDRED POUNDS (£1,800), with interest thereon at the rate of eight *per centum per annum* from 16 May 1993 until payment.
2. To grant warrant for arrestment on the dependence of the action.
3. To find the defender liable in the expenses of the action.

CONDESCENDENCE

1. The pursuer resides at 3 Market Square, Tain. The defender resides at 49 New Street, Inverness. He has been so resident for more than three months immediately preceding the raising of this action. He is domiciled there. This court accordingly has jurisdiction. To the knowledge of the pursuer, no proceedings are pending before any other court involving the present cause of action and between the parties hereto. To the knowledge of the pursuer, no agreement exists between the parties prorogating jurisdiction over the subject-matter of the present cause to another court.

2. The defender owes to the pursuer the sum of £1,800, conform to IOU signed by the defender and dated 1 July 1992. The said IOU is produced herewith and its terms adopted and held as repeated herein *brevitatis causa*. On or about 16 May 1993 the pursuer demanded that the defender repay the said sum. This the defender has refused or at least delayed to do. This action is therefore necessary.

PLEA-IN-LAW

The defender being indebted to the pursuer in the sum sued for, decree should be granted as craved.

IN RESPECT WHEREOF

Enrolled solicitor
1 Main Street
Tain
Solicitor for the pursuer

b. Defences

SHERIFFDOM OF GRAMPIAN, HIGHLAND AND ISLANDS
AT INVERNESS

DEFENCES

in the cause

EDWARD JOHN DANSON,
residing at 3 Market Square, Tain

PURSUER

against

WILLIAM BOGGS, residing at 49 New Street, Inverness

DEFENDER

ANSWERS TO CONDESCENDENCE

1. Admitted.
2. The said IOU is admitted. Admitted that the pursuer made such a demand on the said date. *Quoad ultra* denied. Explained and averred that the defender repaid the said sum to the pursuer in 'The Quill' public bar, Inverness, on or about 17 May 1993.

PLEA-IN-LAW

The defender having repaid the said sum, is entitled to absolvitor.

IN RESPECT WHEREOF

Enrolled solicitor
3 The Square
Inverness
Solicitor for the defender

c. Note of adjustments

SHERIFFDOM OF GRAMPIAN, HIGHLAND AND ISLANDS
AT INVERNESS

NOTE OF ADJUSTMENTS

for the pursuer

in the cause

EDWARD JOHN DANSON,
residing at 3 Market Square, Tain

PURSUER

against

WILLIAM BOGGS, residing at 49 New Street, Inverness

DEFENDER

1. Add at the end of article 2 of the condescendence the following:

'The averment in answer is denied. The defender is called upon to produce any writ in the hand of the pursuer vouching such repayment.'; and

2. Add a new plea-in-law as follows:

'2. The final averment in answer 2 being provable only by the writ or oath of the pursuer, proof should be restricted accordingly.'

d. Record (OCR 9.11)

SHERIFFDOM OF GRAMPIAN, HIGHLAND AND ISLANDS
AT INVERNESS

RECORD

in the cause

EDWARD JOHN DANSON,
residing at 3 Market Square, Tain

PURSUER

against

WILLIAM BOGGS, residing at 49 New Street, Inverness

DEFENDER

The pursuer craves the court:

1. To grant decree against the defender for payment to the pursuer of the sum of ONE THOUSAND EIGHT HUNDRED POUNDS (£1,800), with interest thereon at the rate of eight *per centum per annum* from 16 May 1993 until payment.
2. To grant warrant for arrestment on the dependence of the action.
3. To find the defender liable in the expenses of the action.

CONDESCENDENCE FOR PURSUER AND ANSWERS THERETO FOR DEFENDER

COND. 1. The pursuer resides at 3 Market Square, Tain. The defender resides at 49 New Street, Inverness. He has been so resident for more than three months immediately preceding the raising of this action. He is domiciled there. This court accordingly has jurisdiction. To the knowledge of the pursuer, no proceedings are pending before any other court involving the present cause of action and between the parties hereto. To the knowledge of the pursuer, no agreement exists between the parties prorogating jurisdiction over the subject-matter of the present cause to another court.

ANS. 1 for DEFENDER. Admitted.

COND. 2. The defender owes to the pursuer the sum of £1,800 conform to IOU signed by the defender and dated 1 July 1992. The said IOU is produced herewith and its terms adopted and held as repeated herein *brevitatis causa*. On or about 16 May 1993 the pursuer demanded that the defender repay the said sum. This the defender has refused or at least delayed to do. This action is therefore necessary. The averment in answer is denied. The defender is called upon to produce any writ in the hand of the pursuer vouching such repayment.

ANS. 2 for DEFENDER. The said IOU is admitted. Admitted that the pursuer made such a demand on the said date. *Quoad ultra* denied. Explained and averred that the defender repaid the said sum to the pursuer in 'The Quill' public bar, Inverness, on or about 17 May 1993.

PLEAS-IN-LAW FOR PURSUER

1. The defender being indebted to the pursuer in the sum sued for, decree should be granted as craved.

2. The final averment in answer 2 being provable only by the writ or oath of the pursuer, proof should be restricted accordingly.

IN RESPECT WHEREOF

Enrolled solicitor
1 Main Street
Tain
Solicitor for the pursuer

PLEA-IN-LAW FOR DEFENDER

The defender having repaid the said sum, is entitled to absolvitor.

IN RESPECT WHEREOF

Enrolled solicitor
3 The Square
Inverness
Solicitor for the defender

e. Motion for reference to oath (OCR 29.1(1))

SHERIFFDOM OF GRAMPIAN, HIGHLAND AND ISLANDS
AT INVERNESS

Court ref no A21/1994

MOTION FOR THE DEFENDER

in the cause

EDWARD JOHN DANSON,
residing at 3 Market Square, Tain

PURSUER

against

WILLIAM BOGGS, residing at 49 New Street, Inverness

DEFENDER

The defender moves the court to refer the final averment in answer 2 to the oath of the pursuer.

16 June 1994   IN RESPECT WHEREOF

Enrolled solicitor
3 The Square
Inverness
Solicitor for the defender

f. Minute of sist (representative) (OCR 25.1)

SHERIFFDOM OF GRAMPIAN, HIGHLAND AND ISLANDS
AT INVERNESS

MINUTE OF SIST

for ALFRED ELLIS, 21 Newby Avenue, Inverness, executor-nominate of the late Edward John Danson, residing latterly at 3 Market Square, Tain

in the cause

EDWARD JOHN DANSON, residing at 3 Market Square, Tain

PURSUER

against

WILLIAM BOGGS, residing at 49 New Street, Inverness

DEFENDER

The minuter craves the court:

To be sisted, as executor-nominate aforesaid, as pursuer in room and in place of the late Edward John Danson.

STATEMENT OF FACTS

The pursuer, Edward John Danson, died on 15 July 1994. He left a Will, dated 1 November 1986, whereby he nominated the minuter to be his executor. The minuter duly accepted the said office. He was confirmed as executor aforesaid conform to confirmation issued by the Sheriff of Grampian, Highland and Islands at Inverness on 15 November 1994.

PLEA-IN-LAW

The pursuer having died while this cause is depending, the minuter as his executor is entitled to be sisted as pursuer in his place.

IN RESPECT WHEREOF

Enrolled solicitor
1 Main Street
Tain
Solicitor for the minuter

g. Motion for sist of minuter as pursuer

SHERIFFDOM OF GRAMPIAN, HIGHLAND AND ISLANDS
AT INVERNESS

Court ref no A21/1994

MOTION FOR THE MINUTER

in the cause

EDWARD JOHN DANSON,
residing at 3 Market Square, Tain

PURSUER

against

WILLIAM BOGGS, residing at 49 New Street, Inverness

DEFENDER

The minuter moves the court to grant the crave of the minute.

Part of process lodged with the motion:

Minute of sist

14 December 1994   IN RESPECT WHEREOF

Enrolled solicitor
1 Main Street
Tain
Solicitor for the minuter

h. Minute of withdrawal of defences

SHERIFFDOM OF GRAMPIAN, HIGHLAND AND ISLANDS AT INVERNESS

MINUTE OF
WITHDRAWAL OF
DEFENCES

in the cause

ALFRED ELLIS, 21 Newby Avenue, Inverness, executor-nominate of the late Edward John Danson, residing latterly at 3 Market Square, Tain

PURSUER

against

WILLIAM BOGGS, residing at 49 New Street, Inverness

DEFENDER

HARRISON for the defender stated to the court that the defender withdraws his defences and consents to decree against him.

IN RESPECT WHEREOF

Enrolled solicitor
3 The Square
Inverness
Solicitor for the defender

5. HUGHES v BARRETT

Payment—Damages—Fatal case—Road traffic accident—Negligence—Personal services to deceased's relatives—Plea of apportionment

a. Initial writ

SHERIFFDOM OF GLASGOW AND STRATHKELVIN
AT GLASGOW

INITIAL WRIT

in the cause

(FIRST) GEORGE GORDON HUGHES (Assisted Person), residing at 41 Tarvit Street, Glasgow, suing as an individual and as guardian of John Purdie Hughes, residing with him; and (SECOND) ELIZABETH JOAN HUGHES (Assisted Person), residing at 41 Tarvit Street, Glasgow

PURSUERS

against

HAMILTON BARRETT, residing at 219 Sharpe Street, Manchester

DEFENDER

The pursuers crave the court:

1. To grant decree against the defender for payment to the first named pursuer as an individual of the sum of FIFTY THOUSAND POUNDS (£50,000), with interest thereon at the rate of eight *per centum per annum* from the date of decree to follow hereon until payment.

2. To grant decree against the defender for payment to the first named pursuer as guardian of John Purdie Hughes of the sum of THIRTY THOUSAND POUNDS (£30,000), with interest thereon at the rate of eight *per centum per annum* from the date of decree to follow hereon until payment.

3. To grant decree against the defender for payment to the second named pursuer of the sum of THIRTY THOUSAND POUNDS (£30,000), with interest thereon at the rate of eight *per centum per annum* from the date of decree to follow hereon until payment.

4. To grant warrant for intimation to Arnold Crosby, residing at 14 John Street, Glasgow.

5. To find the defender liable in the expenses of this action.

CONDESCENDENCE

1. The first named pursuer resides at 41 Tarvit Street, Glasgow. He is aged 39 years. He is the widower of the late Alison Hughes (hereinafter referred to as 'the deceased'). The first named pursuer and the deceased had two children (hereinafter referred to as 'the children'), namely Elizabeth Joan Hughes, born 3 December 1977 (the second named pursuer) and John Purdie Hughes, born 8 August 1980. Relative extract certificates of birth, death and marriage will be produced. The defender resides at 219 Sharpe Street, Manchester, where he is believed to be domiciled. The pursuers in the present action seek reparation for loss, injury and damage sustained through the defender's negligence. The harmful event in consequence of which the pursuer suffered said loss, injury and damage occurred in Glasgow. This court accordingly has jurisdiction. To the knowledge of the pursuers, no proceedings are pending before any other court involving the present cause of action and between the parties hereto. To the knowledge of the pursuers, no agreement exists between the parties prorogating jurisdiction over the subject-matter of the present cause to another court. There is a connected person, being the person specified and designed in the fourth crave, who is the father of the deceased.

2. On or about 15 February 1992, at or about 9.30 am, the deceased was driving her Ford Fiesta motor car, registration number B293 AFG, along Annan Street in Glasgow towards Lee Drive. At a point about 100 metres from the junction of the said roads, a Volvo motor car, registration number D47 FGA, being driven by the defender in the opposite direction, suddenly and without warning drove on to the deceased's side of the road. The defender thereby caused the said cars to collide. As a result of the said collision, the deceased died instantaneously.

3. The death of the deceased was caused by the fault of the defender. It was his duty to take reasonable care for the safety of other road users, including the pursuer. It was his duty to take reasonable care to drive carefully, keep a proper look-out and keep his vehicle under proper control. It was his duty to take reasonable care to drive on the correct side of the road. It was his duty to take reasonable care to avoid causing the said cars to collide. In each and all of these duties, the defender failed and by his failures so caused the deceased's death. But for his failures in duty, the deceased would not have died.

4. As a result of the death of the deceased, the first named pursuer and the children have suffered loss, injury and damage. The first named pursuer incurred funeral expenses of £560. He and the children have

suffered grief and sorrow caused by the death of the deceased. They were all greatly attached to her. At the date of her death, the deceased was aged 35 and in good health. She lived in family with the first named pursuer and the children. Had she not died, the first named pursuer would have continued to cohabit with her in a close and loving relationship. The children would likewise have so continued, until adulthood, and throughout that time and beyond would have benefitted from her guidance. Further, the deceased rendered personal services to them. She ran the household, *inter alia* cleaning, cooking and shopping for the family. She had the primary role in the care of the children. In the whole circumstances the sums sued for are reasonable estimates of the loss, injury and damage sustained by the first pursuer and the children.

5. The defender has been called upon to make reparation to the first named pursuer and the children in respect of their said loss, injury and damage. He refuses or at least delays to do so. This action is accordingly necessary.

PLEAS-IN-LAW

1. The first named pursuer and the children having suffered loss, injury and damage through the defender's fault are entitled to reparation therefor.

2. The sums sued for being reasonable estimates of the aforesaid loss, injury and damage, decree should be granted as craved.

IN RESPECT WHEREOF

Enrolled solicitor
15 Bath Avenue
Glasgow
Solicitor for the pursuers

b. Defences

SHERIFFDOM OF GLASGOW AND STRATHKELVIN
AT GLASGOW

DEFENCES

in the cause

(FIRST) GEORGE GORDON HUGHES (Assisted Person), residing at 41 Tarvit Street, Glasgow, suing as an individual and as guardian of John Purdie Hughes, residing with him; and (SECOND) ELIZABETH JOAN HUGHES (Assisted Person), residing at 41 Tarvit Street, Glasgow

PURSUERS

against

HAMILTON BARRETT, residing at 219 Sharpe Street, Manchester

DEFENDER

ANSWERS TO CONDESCENDENCE

1. The averments regarding the defender and jurisdiction are admitted. *Quoad ultra* not known and not admitted.

2. Admitted that on 15 February 1992, at or about 9.30 am, the deceased was driving her Ford Fiesta motor car, registration number B293 AFG, along Annan Street in Glasgow towards Lee Drive. Admitted that at a point about 100 metres from the junction of the said roads, a Volvo motor car, registration number D47 FGA, being driven by the defender in the opposite direction, suddenly and without warning drove on to the deceased's side of the road. Admitted that as a result of the said collision the deceased died instantaneously. *Quoad ultra* denied. Explained and averred that the defender was caused to drive on the deceased's side of the road by the actions of Jonathan Bland, residing at 21 East Street, Greenock. At the material time, he was the driver of a Peugeot motor car, registration number K50 BWF. Immediately before the said collision he

had been parked by the side of the road. Suddenly and without warning, he pulled out from the roadside into the path of the defender's vehicle, causing the defender to swerve and drive on to the deceased's side of the road. In the circumstances, the collision was caused or at least partly caused by the actions of the said Jonathan Bland.

3. Denied. Explained and averred that the accident was caused or at least partly caused by the fault of the said Jonathan Bland. It was his duty to take reasonable care for the safety of other road users. It was his duty to take reasonable care to drive carefully, keep a proper lookout and keep his vehicle under proper control. It was his duty to take reasonable care to avoid pulling out from the roadside into the path of the defender's vehicle. It was his duty to take reasonable care to avoid causing the defender to swerve and drive on to the deceased's side of the road. In these duties, the said Jonathan Bland failed and by his said failures so caused or at least partly caused the said accident. But for his said failures in duty, the said accident would not have happened.

4. The nature, extent and consequences of any loss, injury and damage sustained by the first-named pursuer and the children are not known and not admitted. *Quoad ultra* denied. Explained and averred that the sums sued for are in any event excessive.

5. Denied that the action is necessary.

PLEAS-IN-LAW

1. The pursuer's averments being irrelevant *et separatim* being lacking in specification, the action should be dismissed.

2. The pursuer's averments so far as material being unfounded in fact, decree of absolvitor should be pronounced.

3. The first named pursuer and the children not having suffered loss, injury and damage through any fault on the part of the defender, the defender should be assoilzied.

4. The said accident having been caused by the fault of the said Jonathan Bland, the defender should be assoilzied.

5. *Separatim, esto* the said accident was caused to any extent by fault on the part of the defender (which is denied), it also having been caused by the fault of the said Jonathan Bland, any liability to the pursuers in damages and expenses should be apportioned between the defender and the said Jonathan Bland in terms of the Law Reform (Miscellaneous Provisions) (Scotland) Act 1940, s 3(2).

6. In any event, the sums sued for being excessive, decree should not be pronounced as craved.

IN RESPECT WHEREOF

Enrolled solicitor
12 Edward Street
Glasgow
Solicitor for the defender

c. Motion for order for service of third party notice (OCR 20.1)

SHERIFFDOM OF GLASGOW AND STRATHKELVIN
AT GLASGOW

Court ref no A293/1994

MOTION FOR THE
DEFENDER

in the cause

(FIRST) GEORGE GORDON HUGHES (Assisted Person), residing at 41 Tarvit Street, Glasgow, suing as an individual and as guardian of John Purdie Hughes, residing with him; and (SECOND) ELIZABETH JOAN HUGHES (Assisted Person), residing at 41 Tarvit Street, Glasgow

PURSUERS

against

HAMILTON BARRETT, residing at 219 Sharpe Street, Manchester

DEFENDER

The defender moves the court to grant an order for service of a third party notice on Jonathan Bland, residing at 21 East Street, Greenock.

Part of process lodged with the motion:

Defences

4 June 1994   IN RESPECT WHEREOF

Enrolled solicitor
12 Edward Street
Glasgow
Solicitor for the defender

d. Third party notice

SHERIFFDOM OF GLASGOW AND STRATHKELVIN
AT GLASGOW

THIRD PARTY NOTICE

in the cause

(FIRST) GEORGE GORDON HUGHES (Assisted Person), residing at 41 Tarvit Street, Glasgow, suing as an individual and as guardian of John Purdie Hughes, residing with him; and (SECOND) ELIZABETH JOAN HUGHES (Assisted Person), residing at 41 Tarvit Street, Glasgow

PURSUERS

against

HAMILTON BARRETT, residing at 219 Sharpe Street, Manchester

DEFENDER

To Jonathan Bland 21 East Street, Greenock
You are hereby given notice by Hamilton Barrett of an order granted by Sheriff N Thomson in this action in which George Gordon Hughes and Elizabeth Joan Hughes are the pursuers and Hamilton Barrett the defender. In the action the first pursuer claims against the defender the sums of £50,000 as damages for himself and £30,000 as damages for the child John Purdie Hughes and the second pursuer claims against the defender the sum of £30,000 as damages for herself, all in respect of the collision of the cars being driven by the defender and the late Alison Hughes in Annan Street, Glasgow on 15 February 1992, as more fully appears in the pleadings enclosed.

The defender denies liability to the pursuers for the death of the deceased and maintains that liability, if any, to the pursuers rests solely on you or, if there is any liability that he shares it with you, as more fully appears from the defences lodged by him in the action.

IF YOU WISH to resist either the claims of the pursuers against the defender, or the claim of the defender against you, you must lodge answers with the sheriff clerk at the above address within 28 days of 10 June 1994. You must also pay the court fee of £42.

9 June 1994   Enrolled solicitor
                                              12 Edward Street
                                              Glasgow
                                              Solicitor for the defender

Glasgow 30 June 1994
I, Arnold Thomson, hereby certify that on 9 June 1994 I duly cited Jonathan Bland, third party, to answer the foregoing notice. This I did by recorded delivery post.

'A Thomson' (Solicitor for the defender)

e. Answers for third party (OCR 20.5)

SHERIFFDOM OF GLASGOW AND STRATHKELVIN
AT GLASGOW

ANSWERS

for JONATHAN BLAND, residing at 21 East Street, Greenock, Third Party

in the cause

(FIRST) GEORGE GORDON HUGHES (Assisted Person), residing at 41 Tarvit Street, Glasgow, suing as an individual and as guardian of John Purdie Hughes, residing with him; and (SECOND) ELIZABETH JOAN HUGHES (Assisted Person), residing at 41 Tarvit Street, Glasgow

PURSUERS

against

HAMILTON BARRETT, residing at 219 Sharpe Street, Manchester

DEFENDER

ANSWERS TO CONDESCENDENCE AND ANSWERS TO AVERMENTS FOR DEFENDER

1. Not known and not admitted.
2. The pursuers' averments are not known and not admitted. With reference to the defender's averments, admitted that at the material time the third party was the driver of a Peugeot motor car, registration number

K50 BWF. *Quoad ultra* denied except insofar as coinciding herewith. Explained and averred that prior to the said collision, the third party was parked by the side of the road. He decided to move off. He checked his wing mirror. There was no traffic behind him. He thereupon pulled out and drove off. In these circumstances, *esto* the defender swerved and drove on to the deceased's side of the road as a result of any action on the part of the third party (which is denied), the third party believes and avers that the defender was driving at an excessive speed.

3. On the hypothesis of fact on which they proceed, the pursuers' averments of fault are admitted and adopted. The defender's averments are denied. Explained and averred that the accident was in any event caused or at least partly caused by the fault of the defender in driving at an excessive speed. Reference is made to the preceding answer.

4. The nature, extent and consequences of any loss, injury and damage sustained by the first named pursuer and the children are not known and not admitted. *Quoad ultra* denied. Explained and averred that the sums sued for are in any event excessive.

PLEAS-IN-LAW

1. The pursuers' averments being irrelevant *et separatim* being lacking in specification, the action should be dismissed.

2. The defender's averments, so far as directed against the third party, being irrelevant *et separatim* being lacking in specification, the action so far as directed against the third party should be dismissed.

3. The defender's averments so far as directed against the third party being unfounded in fact, the third party should be assoilzied.

4. The said accident having been caused by the fault of the defender, the third party should be assoilzied.

5. *Separatim, esto* the said accident was caused to any extent by fault on the part of the third party (which is denied), it also having been caused by the fault of the defender, any liability to the pursuers in damages and expenses should be apportioned between the defender and the third party in terms of the Law Reform (Miscellaneous Provisions) (Scotland) Act 1940, s 3(2).

6. In any event, the sum sued for is excessive.

IN RESPECT WHEREOF

Enrolled solicitor
120 Bath Place
Glasgow
Solicitor for the third party

f. Minute of sist, adoption and amendment (OCR 36.6)

SHERIFFDOM OF GLASGOW AND STRATHKELVIN
AT GLASGOW

MINUTE OF SIST,
ADOPTION AND
AMENDMENT

for ARNOLD CROSBY, residing at 14 John Street, Glasgow

in the cause

(FIRST) GEORGE GORDON HUGHES (Assisted Person), residing at 41 Tarvit Street, Glasgow, suing as an individual, and as guardian of John Purdie Hughes, residing with him; and (SECOND) ELIZABETH JOAN HUGHES (Assisted Person), residing at 41 Tarvit Street, Glasgow

PURSUERS

against

HAMILTON BARRETT, residing at 219 Sharpe Street, Manchester

DEFENDER

The minuter craves the court:

1. To grant him leave to be sisted as an additional pursuer to the action; and
2. To grant him leave to adopt the existing grounds of action and to amend the initial writ as follows:
   (i) by deleting the fourth crave and substituting therefor the following:

'4. To grant decree against the defender for payment to the third pursuer of the sum of FIVE THOUSAND POUNDS (£5,000), with interest thereon at the rate of eight *per centum per annum* from the date of decree to follow hereon until payment.';
(ii) by inserting before the fifth sentence in article 1 of the condescendence (commencing 'Relative extract . . . .') the following:
'The third named pursuer is the father of the deceased.'
(iii) by deleting the final sentence in the said article of condescendence;
(iv) by adding a new article of condescendence as follows:
'5. The third named pursuer is a widower. The deceased was his only daughter. She visited him regularly. Her death caused him immense grief and sorrow. He is entitled to a reasonable sum in respect of his grief and sorrow and the loss of society of the deceased.',
renumbering the remaining article of condescendence accordingly;
(v) by deleting in the first plea-in-law the words 'named pursuer' and substituting therefor the words 'and third named pursuers.'

IN RESPECT WHEREOF

Enrolled solicitor
14 Green Street
Glasgow
Solicitor for the minuter

g. Motion for minute of sist, adoption and amendment to be received

SHERIFFDOM OF GLASGOW AND STRATHKELVIN
AT GLASGOW

Court ref no A293/1994

MOTION FOR THE
MINUTER

in the cause

(FIRST) GEORGE GORDON HUGHES (Assisted Person), residing at 41 Tarvit Street, Glasgow, suing as an individual and as guardian of John Purdie Hughes, residing with him; and (SECOND) ELIZABETH JOAN HUGHES (Assisted Person), residing at 41 Tarvit Street, Glasgow

PURSUERS

against

HAMILTON BARRETT, residing at 219 Sharpe Street, Manchester

DEFENDER

The minuter moves the court to allow the minute to be received and to allow answers to be lodged within 14 days from the date of intimation of the minute.

Part of process lodged with the motion:

Minute of sist, adoption and amendment

14 August 1994   IN RESPECT WHEREOF

Enrolled solicitor
14 Green Street
Glasgow
Solicitor for the minuter

h. Minute of tender (Williamson tender)

SHERIFFDOM OF GLASGOW AND STRATHKELVIN AT GLASGOW

MINUTE OF TENDER

for the third party

in the cause

(FIRST) GEORGE GORDON HUGHES (Assisted Person), residing at 41 Tarvit Street, Glasgow, suing as an individual and as guardian of John Purdie Hughes residing with him; (SECOND) ELIZABETH JOAN HUGHES (Assisted Person) residing at 41 Tarvit Street, Glasgow; and (THIRD) ARNOLD CROSBY, residing at 14 John Street, Glasgow

PURSUERS

against

HAMILTON BARRETT, residing at 219 Sharpe Street, Manchester

DEFENDER

and

JONATHAN BLAND, residing at 21 East Street, Greenock

THIRD PARTY

FORD for the third party stated to the court that under reservation of his whole rights and pleas and without admission of liability, the third party tendered and hereby tenders to the defender to make reparation along with the defender to the pursuer but only upon the basis that the defender and the third party shall contribute to the amount of any award of damages and expenses to which the pursuer may be found entitled in the proportion of 60 *per centum* to the defender and 40 *per centum* to the third party.

           IN RESPECT WHEREOF

           Enrolled solicitor
           120 Bath Place
           Glasgow
           Solicitor for the third party

6. HALL v AIRDRIE DISTRICT COUNCIL

Payment—Damages—Personal injuries—Accident in tenement—Negligence—Occupiers' liability—System of inspection

a. Initial writ

SHERIFFDOM OF SOUTH STRATHCLYDE, DUMFRIES AND GALLOWAY AT AIRDRIE

INITIAL WRIT

in the cause

MARGARET HALL (Assisted Person), residing at 41A Primrose Rise, Airdrie

PURSUER

against

AIRDRIE DISTRICT COUNCIL, Town House, Main Street, Airdrie

DEFENDERS

The pursuer craves the court:

1. To grant decree against the defenders for payment to the pursuer of the sum of THIRTY THOUSAND POUNDS (£30,000), with interest thereon at the rate of eight *per centum per annum* from the date of decree to follow hereon until payment.
2. To find the defenders liable in the expenses of the action.

CONDESCENDENCE

1. The pursuer resides at 41A Primrose Rise, Airdrie. The defenders are a local authority with its headquarters at Town House, Main Street, Airdrie, where they are domiciled. This court has jurisdiction. To the knowledge of the pursuer no proceedings are pending before any other court involving the present cause of action and between the parties hereto. To the knowledge of the pursuer no agreement exists between the parties prorogating jurisdiction over the subject-matter of the present cause to another court.

2. On or about 11 December 1990, at or about 7.20 pm, the pursuer was descending the common stairs of a tenement block at Violet Rise, Airdrie (hereinafter 'the tenement block'). The tenement block was owned by the defenders and the flats therein leased to various tenants who had right of access thereto by way of the said common stairs. The defenders retained responsibility *inter alia* for the maintenance and repair of the common stairs including the illumination thereof. Immediately beforehand, the pursuer had been visiting a friend living in a top-floor flat. Night had fallen. The stairs were in darkness. For several months prior to the said date, the stair lights had been inoperative as a result of vandalism. It was a matter of public knowledge that vandals periodically damaged stair lights in the locality. The pursuer required to guide herself down the stairs by feeling the walls with her hands. She was unable to see where she was placing her feet. In the course of her descent, the pursuer stood on a slippery item or substance of a nature unknown to her. She was thereby caused to lose her footing, whereupon she fell and sustained the injuries hereinafter condescended on.

3. The said accident was caused by the defenders' fault. As occupiers of the common stairs, it was their duty to take reasonable care to see that persons entering thereon would not suffer injury by reason of dangers due to the state thereof. They knew or ought to have known that the stairs would require to be used by persons entering or leaving the tenement block during the hours of darkness. They knew or ought to have known that persons such as the pursuer using the stairs without adequate lighting during the hours of darkness were at risk of injury. They knew or ought to have known that the stair lights were subject to the attention of vandals and liable periodically to be rendered inoperative by them. It was their duty to take reasonable care to see to it that the stair lights were kept in a reasonable state of repair. It was their duty to take reasonable care to institute and maintain a system for the regular inspection of the stair lights on a weekly or at least a fortnightly basis. It was their duty to act promptly upon any such notification or inspection. In all these duties the defenders failed and by their failures so caused the accident. But for their failures in duty, the accident would not have happened.

4. As a result of the said accident, the pursuer suffered loss, injury and damage. She sustained an injury to her lower left leg, including an oblique fracture of the lower third of the tibia extending to the ankle joint and involving the posterior malleolus together with a spiral fracture of the fibula. She required in-patient and out-patient treatment at the General Hospital, Airdrie and from her general practitioner, Dr James Lovell, The Health Centre, Airdrie. She has suffered and continues to suffer pain and inconvenience. Her said left leg remains painful and has a tendency to swell. Her mobility has been reduced. Her ability to enjoy pre-accident leisure pursuits such as dancing has been significantly impaired. She required to be absent from work for a lengthy period and lost earnings, as will be vouched. In all the circumstances, the sum sued for is a reasonable estimate of the pursuer's loss, injury and damage.

5. The defenders have been called upon to make reasonable reparation to the pursuer for her said loss, injury and damage. They refuse or at least delay to do so. This action is accordingly necessary.

PLEAS-IN-LAW

1. The pursuer having suffered loss, injury and damage through the defenders' fault, is entitled to reparation from them therefor.
2. The sum sued for being a reasonable estimate of the pursuer's said loss, injury and damage, decree therefor should be pronounced as craved.

IN RESPECT WHEREOF

Enrolled solicitor
14 Charleston Street
Airdrie
Solicitor for the pursuer

b. Joint minute of agreement

SHERIFFDOM OF SOUTH STRATHCLYDE, DUMFRIES AND GALLOWAY AT AIRDRIE

JOINT MINUTE OF AGREEMENT

for the parties

in the cause

MARGARET HALL (Assisted Person), residing at 41A Primrose Rise, Airdrie

PURSUER

against

AIRDRIE DISTRICT COUNCIL, Town House, Main Street, Airdrie

DEFENDERS

WALLACE for the pursuer and JENKS for the defenders concurred in stating to the court that the parties have agreed and hereby agree that on full liability the loss, injury and damage sustained by the pursuer as a result of her accident on 11 December 1990 amounts to TWELVE THOUSAND POUNDS (£12,000), inclusive of interest to the date of any decree to follow hereon.

IN RESPECT WHEREOF

Enrolled solicitor
14 Charleston Street
Airdrie
Solicitor for the pursuer

Enrolled solicitor
Town House
Main Street
Airdrie
Solicitor for the defender

c. Minute of abandonment (OCR 23.1.(1)(a))

SHERIFFDOM OF SOUTH STRATHCLYDE, DUMFRIES AND GALLOWAY AT AIRDRIE

MINUTE OF
ABANDONMENT

for the pursuer

in the cause

MARGARET HALL (Assisted Person), residing at 41A Primrose Rise, Airdrie

PURSUER

against

AIRDRIE DISTRICT COUNCIL, Town House, Main Street, Airdrie

DEFENDERS

JONES for the pursuer stated to the court that the pursuer abandons this action.

IN RESPECT WHEREOF

Enrolled solicitor
14 Charleston Street
Airdrie
Solicitor for the pursuer

d. Joint motion for decree of absolvitor and expenses against pursuer as assisted person

SHERIFFDOM OF SOUTH STRATHCLYDE, DUMFRIES AND GALLOWAY AT AIRDRIE

Court ref no A29/1994
JOINT MOTION FOR THE PARTIES

in the cause

MARGARET HALL, (Assisted Person), residing at 41A Primrose Rise, Airdrie

PURSUER

against

AIRDRIE DISTRICT COUNCIL, Town House, Main Street, Airdrie

DEFENDERS

The parties jointly move the court to grant decree of absolvitor and to find the pursuer liable as an assisted person to the defenders for the expenses of the action.

Part of process lodged with the motion:

Minute of abandonment

16 November 1994   IN RESPECT WHEREOF

         Enrolled solicitor
         14 Charleston Street
         Airdrie
         Solicitor for the pursuer

         Enrolled solicitor
         Town House
         Main Street
         Airdrie
         Solicitor for the defenders

e. Motion for modification of assisted person's liability for expenses

SHERIFFDOM OF SOUTH STRATHCLYDE, DUMFRIES AND GALLOWAY AT AIRDRIE

Court ref no A29/1994

MOTION FOR THE PURSUER

in the cause

MARGARET HALL (Assisted Person), residing at 41A Primrose Rise, Airdrie

PURSUER

against

AIRDRIE DISTRICT COUNCIL, Town House, Main Street, Airdrie

DEFENDERS

The pursuer moves the court to assess her liability under the awards of expenses against her in this action at nil.

Documents lodged with the motion:

Statement of earnings
Statement of outgoings

16 November 1994   IN RESPECT WHEREOF

Enrolled solicitor
14 Charleston Street
Airdrie
Solicitor for the pursuer

7. BROWN v TARMACADAM (ROADS) LTD

Payment—Damages—Personal injuries—Accident at work—Negligence—Safe plant and equipment—Breach of statutory duty—Provision and use of work equipment—Work of engineering construction—Provisional damages

a. Initial writ

SHERIFFDOM OF GRAMPIAN, HIGHLAND AND ISLANDS
AT PETERHEAD

INITIAL WRIT

in the cause

GEOFFREY BROWN, residing at 46 Barbican Way, Aberdeen

PURSUER

against

TARMACADAM (ROADS) LIMITED, a company with its registered office at Aintree Road, Liverpool

DEFENDERS

The pursuer craves the court:

1. To grant decree against the defenders for payment to the pursuer of the sum of ONE HUNDRED THOUSAND POUNDS (£100,000), as provisional damages, with interest thereon at the rate of eight *per centum per annum* from the date of decree to follow hereon until payment.

2. Alternatively, to grant decree against the defenders for payment to the pursuer of the sum of ONE HUNDRED AND FIFTY THOUSAND POUNDS (£150,000), with interest thereon at the rate of eight *per centum per annum* from the date of decree to follow hereon until payment.

3. To find the defenders liable in the expenses of the action.

CONDESCENDENCE

1. The pursuer resides at 46 Barbican Way, Aberdeen. The defenders are a company incorporated under the Companies Acts with its registered

office at Aintree Road, Liverpool. The pursuer in the present action seeks reparation for loss, injury and damage sustained by him through the defenders' negligence and breach of statutory duty. The harmful event in consequence of which the pursuer suffered said loss, injury and damage occurred in Cruden, which is within the territory of this court. This court accordingly has jurisdiction. To the knowledge of the pursuer, no proceedings are pending before any other court involving the present cause of action and between the parties hereto. To the knowledge of the pursuer, no agreement exists between the parties prorogating jurisdiction over the subject-matter of the present cause to another court.

2. On or about 15 January 1993 the pursuer was working in the course of his employment with the defenders at a site in Cruden where the defenders were constructing a pipeline. At or about 11.30 am on the said date, the pursuer was detailed by his foreman to assist in the laying of a section of pipe in a deep trench. The pursuer required to stand in the trench to receive couplings for the pipe section. The said couplings were being lowered by rope in a heavy metal bucket beneath which the pursuer required to stand. Prior to the said date, the said rope had broken. It had been repaired by being spliced. As a result, it was liable to break or come apart under strain. As the bucket was being lowered, the splice suddenly gave way and the rope broke or came apart. Consequently, the bucket fell and struck the pursuer on the head, thereby causing the loss, injury and damage hereinafter condescended on.

3. The said accident was caused by the fault of the defenders. It was their duty to take reasonable care for the safety of their employees, such as the pursuer. It was their duty to take reasonable care to provide him with safe plant and equipment. It was their duty to take reasonable care to see to it that the said rope was of adequate strength. It was their duty to take reasonable care to see to it that a rope which was liable to break or come apart under strain was not used for the suspension of a heavy load. In these duties, the defenders failed and by their failures so caused the said accident. But for their said failures in duty, the said accident would not have happened.

4. Further and in any event, the said accident was caused by the defenders' breach of statutory duty. The said bucket and rope constituted work equipment in terms of the Provision and Use of Work Equipment Regulations 1992. Regulation 6 thereof requires every employer to 'ensure that work equipment is maintained in an efficient state in efficient working order and in good repair.' The said bucket and rope were not so maintained in respect that the rope was liable to break or come apart under strain, as in fact occurred. Further, the work being carried out on the said site was a work of engineering construction to which the Construction (Lifting Operations) Regulations 1961 applied. Regulation 34(1) thereof provides *inter alia*: '. . . no . . . rope . . . shall be used in . . . lowering or as a means of suspension unless (*a*) it is of . . . sound material, adequate strength, suitable quality and free from patent defect'. The said rope was not of sound material, adequate strength, nor of suitable quality. It was not free from patent defect. It had been spliced and was liable to break or come apart under strain, as in fact happened. In these circumstances, the defenders were in breach of

statutory duty. Had they performed the said statutory duties incumbent upon them, the accident would not have happened.

5. As a result of the said accident, the pursuer has suffered loss, injury and damage. He sustained a fractured skull and was rendered unconscious. He suffered a life-threatening sub-dural haematoma. He required in-patient and out-patient treatment at Aberdeen General Hospital and has continued to require to attend his general practitioner, Dr Martin, 319 Forres Road, Aberdeen. He has suffered and has continued to suffer severe headaches and stiffness and pain in the neck and shoulders. He has developed a post-traumatic syndrome. He is irritable and intolerant of noise. He suffers from insomnia, vertigo and dizziness on exertion. He requires to take painkillers daily. He is permanently unfit for his previous work. Prior to his accident, the pursuer earned a substantial wage, details of which will be produced. He has lost and will continue to lose wages and increases in wages enjoyed by persons employed in a similar capacity by the defenders. There is a risk that the pursuer will in future contract epilepsy, which is a serious disease, as a result of his said accident. At the material time, the defenders were insured. The pursuer accordingly seeks provisional damages assessed on the assumption that he will not suffer the development of the said disease. Decree should accordingly be pronounced in terms of the first crave. Failing such an award, the pursuer seeks as an alternative damages in terms of the second crave. In all the circumstances, the sums sued for are reasonable.

6. The defenders have been called upon to make reparation to the pursuer for his said loss, injury and damage. They refuse or at least delay to do so. This action is accordingly necessary.

PLEAS-IN-LAW

1. The pursuer having suffered loss, injury and damage through the fault and breach of statutory duty of the defenders, is entitled to reparation therefor.

2. The pursuer being entitled to provisional damages, which failing to damages *simpliciter*, and the sums sued for being reasonable, decree should be pronounced in terms of the first crave, which failing in terms of the second crave.

IN RESPECT WHEREOF

Enrolled solicitor
14 Bank Drive
Aberdeen
Solicitor for the pursuer

b. Motion for summary decree disposing of merits (OCR 17.2)

SHERIFFDOM OF GRAMPIAN, HIGHLAND AND ISLANDS AT PETERHEAD

Court ref no A45/1994

MOTION FOR THE PURSUER

in the cause

GEOFFREY BROWN, residing at 46 Barbican Way, Aberdeen

PURSUER

against

TARMACADAM (ROADS) LIMITED, a company with its registered office at Aintree Road, Liverpool

DEFENDERS

The pursuer moves the court to grant summary decree sustaining the first plea-in-law for the pursuer, repelling the first, second and third pleas-in-law for the defenders and allowing a proof restricted to *quantum* only.

4 March 1994   IN RESPECT WHEREOF

Enrolled solicitor
14 Bank Drive
Aberdeen
Solicitor for the pursuer

c. Motion for pursuer to be ordained to submit himself to medical examination

SHERIFFDOM OF GRAMPIAN, HIGHLAND AND ISLANDS AT PETERHEAD

Court ref no A45/1994

MOTION FOR THE DEFENDERS

in the cause

GEOFFREY BROWN, residing at 46 Barbican Way, Aberdeen

PURSUER

against

TARMACADAM (ROADS) LIMITED, a company with its registered office at Aintree Road, Liverpool

DEFENDERS

The defenders move the court to ordain the pursuer to submit himself for medical examination by Mr Robert Jenkins, Department of Neurosurgery, Aberdeen Royal Infirmary, within 28 days.

4 July 1994   IN RESPECT WHEREOF

Enrolled solicitor
4 Manse Road
Aberdeen
Solicitor for the defenders

d. Motion for interim payment of damages (OCR 36.9)

SHERIFFDOM OF GRAMPIAN, HIGHLAND AND ISLANDS AT PETERHEAD

Court ref no A45/1994

MOTION FOR THE PURSUER

in the cause

GEOFFREY BROWN, residing at 46 Barbican Way, Aberdeen

PURSUER

against

TARMACADAM (ROADS) LIMITED, a company with its registered office at Aintree Road, Liverpool

DEFENDERS

The pursuer moves the court to ordain the defenders to make an interim payment of damages to the pursuer of the sum of THIRTY THOUSAND POUNDS (£30,000) or such other sum as the court thinks fit.

Documents lodged with the motion:

Medical report dated 4 June 1994
Statement of earnings dated 19 May 1994

14 September 1994   IN RESPECT WHEREOF

Enrolled solicitor
14 Bank Drive
Aberdeen
Solicitor for the pursuer

e. Joint minute of settlement (extra-judicial) (including certification of skilled witnesses and sanction for employment of counsel)

SHERIFFDOM OF GRAMPIAN, HIGHLAND AND ISLANDS AT PETERHEAD

JOINT MINUTE OF SETTLEMENT

for the parties

in the cause

GEOFFREY BROWN, residing at 46 Barbican Way, Aberdeen

PURSUER

against

TARMACADAM (ROADS) LIMITED, a company with its registered office at Aintree Road, Liverpool

DEFENDERS

BLACK for the pursuer and HARRIS for the defenders stated to the court that this action has been settled extra-judicially; and they therefore craved and hereby crave the court (1) to assoilzie the defenders from the first crave of the initial writ; (2) to find the defenders liable to the pursuer in the expenses of the action as taxed; (3) to certify Mr Alexander Nelson, Consultant Neurosurgeon, Glasgow General Hospital, and Dr Peter Mason, Consultant Psychiatrist, Dundee Royal Hospital, for additional remuneration as skilled witnesses for the pursuer; and (4) to sanction the employment of counsel in the action.

IN RESPECT WHEREOF

Enrolled solicitor
14 Bank Drive
Aberdeen
Solicitor for the pursuer

Enrolled solicitor
4 Manse Road
Aberdeen
Solicitor for the defenders

f. Joint motion for decree in terms of joint minute of settlement

SHERIFFDOM OF GRAMPIAN, HIGHLAND AND ISLANDS AT PETERHEAD

Court ref no A45/1994

JOINT MOTION OF THE PARTIES

in the cause

GEOFFREY BROWN, residing at 46 Barbican Way, Aberdeen

PURSUER

against

TARMACADAM (ROADS) LIMITED, a company with its registered office at Aintree Road, Liverpool

DEFENDERS

The parties jointly move the court to interpone authority to the joint minute of settlement, no. 25 of process, and to grant decree in terms thereof.

Part of process lodged with the motion:
Joint minute of settlement

4 December, 1994   IN RESPECT WHEREOF

Enrolled solicitor
14 Bank Drive
Aberdeen
Solicitor for the pursuer

Enrolled solicitor
4 Manse Road
Aberdeen
Solicitor for the defenders

8. BLACK v INVERCLYDE METALS LTD

Payment—Damages—Personal injuries—Accident at work—Negligence—Safe system of work—Breach of statutory duty—Manual handling operation—Necessary services to injured person

a. Initial writ

SHERIFFDOM OF NORTH STRATHCLYDE AT GREENOCK

INITIAL WRIT

in the cause

JAMES BLACK, residing at 61 Glasgow Road, Greenock

PURSUER

against

INVERCLYDE METALS LIMITED, a company with a place of business at South Shore Street, Greenock

DEFENDERS

The pursuer craves the court:

1. To grant decree against the defenders for payment to the pursuer of the sum of NINETY THOUSAND POUNDS (£90,000), with interest thereon at the rate of eight *per centum per annum* from the date of decree to follow hereon until payment.

2. To find the defenders liable for the expenses of the action.

CONDESCENDENCE

1. The pursuer resides at 61 Glasgow Road, Greenock. The defenders are a company incorporated under the Companies Acts with a place of business at South Shore Street, Greenock. They are domiciled there. In any event, the pursuer seeks reparation for loss, injury and damage sustained by him through the defenders' negligence. The harmful event in consequence of which the pursuer suffered the said loss, injury and damage occurred in Greenock. This court accordingly has jurisdiction. To the knowledge of the pursuer, no proceedings are pending before any other court involving the present cause of action and between the parties

hereto. To the knowledge of the pursuer, no agreement exists between the parties prorogating jurisdiction over the subject-matter of the present cause to another court.

2. On or about 4 April 1993, the pursuer was working in the course of his employment with the defenders as a machine operator at their said premises. His duties *inter alia* involved placing stainless steel sheets upon the top surface of a guillotine machine for them to be cut. The sheets were stacked on a pallet on the floor in front of the machine to a height of about two feet. The surface of the machine was about 4½ feet from floor level. The pursuer required to bend down and lift each sheet in turn, turn 180 degrees and place the sheet on the top surface of the machine aforesaid. He was required so to process 150 sheets per hour. Such placed considerable strain on his back. The risk of back injury in such circumstances was well known in industry at the time. The process of cutting the said sheets could have been fully automated. The operation itself could have been mechanised by use of electric or hydraulic hoist or powered vacuum lifter or rotating lift-table and roller conveyors or conveyor belt. The machine could have been repositioned and adjacent thereto sited a plinth of suitable height upon which the sheets could be stacked. On the said date, at or about 11 am, in the course of the said manoeuvre the pursuer felt severe pain at the base of his spine, having sustained the injury hereinafter condescended upon.

3. The said accident was caused by the fault of the defenders. It was their duty to take reasonable care for the safety of the pursuer and to avoid exposing him to unnecessary risk of injury. It was their duty to take reasonable care to institute and maintain a safe system of work. It was their duty to take reasonable care to adopt measures to avoid or at least reduce the risk of injury, such as the measures set forth in the preceding article of condescendence. In these duties the defenders failed and by their failures so caused the said accident. But for their failures in duty, the accident would not have happened.

4. Further and in any event, the said accident was caused by the defenders' breach of statutory duty. It was their duty to comply with regulation 4(a) of the Manual Handling Operations Regulations 1992, which *inter alia* provides: 'Each employer shall . . . avoid the need for his employees to undertake any manual handling operations at work which involve a risk of their being injured . . .'. The operation upon which the pursuer was engaged aforesaid was a manual handling operation which involved a risk of his being injured, as he in fact was. The need for the pursuer to undertake that operation could have been avoided. The process could have been automated or the operation mechanised as averred in article 3 hereof. *Esto* the said need could not have been avoided (which is denied), it was the defenders' duty to comply with regulation 4(b) of the said regulations which *inter alia* required them to: '. . . (i) make a suitable and sufficient assessment of all such manual handling operations to be undertaken . . . [having regard to the factors and questions specified in Schedule 1 to the regulations] [and] (ii) take appropriate steps to reduce the risk of injury to . . . employees arising out of their undertaking any such manual handling operations . . .'. No assessment of the said operation was made. No steps were taken to reduce the risk of injury to the pursuer, such as in the manner averred in article 3 hereof. In the foregoing circumstances, the defenders were in breach of the said duties and by their

failures so caused the said accident. But for their said failures in duty, the accident would not have happened.

5. As a result of the said accident, the pursuer has suffered loss, injury and damage. He sustained a lumbar disc lesion. He was treated by Dr Johnston, the Health Centre, Greenock and subsequently referred to Greenock Royal Infirmary. He suffered back pain and stiffness. He was and continues to be treated by physiotherapy and traction. He is now obliged to wear a lumbo-sacral support. He experienced and will continue to experience pain in his back and both legs. His back movements are and will continue to be restricted. He is now unable to walk long distances. His enjoyment of life has been impaired. He can no longer engage in his pre-accident pursuits of swimming and skating. On 1 November 1993 the pursuer's employment with the defenders was terminated as a result of his said injury. He remains unfit for work. He has lost and will continue to lose wages at the rates applicable from time to time to machine operators employed by the defenders, which rates have increased annually. In any event, he is disadvantaged on the labour market. Further, he will sustain loss in relation to his occupational pension. By virtue of the said termination in employment, he will suffer a diminution in benefits received at the age of 65 years, the normal date of retirement. The pursuer also seeks damages in respect of necessary services. He has frequently required and will continue to require assistance *inter alia* in dressing and bathing. Such services have been and will continue to be rendered to him by his cohabitant, with whom he has been and continues to be living as man and wife. In the circumstances, the sum sued for constitutes a reasonable estimate of the pursuer's said loss, injury and damage and reasonable remuneration for the said services.

6. The defenders have been called upon to make reasonable reparation to the pursuer for his said loss, injury and damage but they refuse or delay to do so. This action is accordingly necessary.

PLEAS-IN-LAW

1. The pursuer having suffered loss, injury and damage through the defenders' fault and breach of statutory duty, is entitled to reparation from them therefor.

2. The sum sued for being a reasonable estimate of the pursuer's said loss, injury and damage and reasonable remuneration for the said services, decree therefor should be pronounced as craved.

IN RESPECT WHEREOF

Enrolled solicitor
5 Charles Street
Greenock
Solicitor for the pursuer

b. Note of adjustments

SHERIFFDOM OF NORTH STRATHCLYDE AT GREENOCK

NOTE OF ADJUSTMENTS

for the pursuer

in the cause

JAMES BLACK, residing at 61 Glasgow Road, Greenock

PURSUER

against

INVERCLYDE METALS LIMITED, a company with a place of business at South Shore Street, Greenock

DEFENDERS

1. Add at the end of article 5 of the condescendence the following:

'The averment in answer is denied.'

2. Add a new plea-in-law as follows:

'3. The defences being irrelevant *et separatim* being lacking in specification, proof should be restricted to *quantum* only.'

c. Minute of admission of liability

SHERIFFDOM OF NORTH STRATHCLYDE AT GREENOCK

MINUTE OF ADMISSION OF LIABILITY

for the defenders

in the cause

JAMES BLACK, residing at 61 Glasgow Road, Greenock

PURSUER

against

INVERCLYDE METALS LIMITED, a company with a place of business at South Shore Street, Greenock

DEFENDERS

EVANS for the defenders stated to the court that for the purposes of the present action only the defenders admit liability to make reparation to the pursuer for any loss, injury and damage sustained by him as a result of his accident on 4 April 1993 at South Shore Street, Greenock.

IN RESPECT WHEREOF

Enrolled solicitor
191 Clyde Drive
Greenock
Solicitor for the defenders

d. Specification of documents (OCR 28.2(2))

SHERIFFDOM OF NORTH STRATHCLYDE AT GREENOCK

SPECIFICATION OF DOCUMENTS

for the recovery of which a commission and diligence is sought by the pursuer

in the cause

JAMES BLACK, residing at 61 Glasgow Road, Greenock

PURSUER

against

INVERCLYDE METALS LIMITED, a company with a place of business at South Shore Street, Greenock

DEFENDERS

1. All medical records relating to the pursuer, including case notes, letters, reports, cards, charts, illustrations and all other documents, and x-ray and all other photographs kept by or for Greenock Royal Infirmary, in order that excerpts may be taken therefrom at the sight of the commissioner of all entries therein showing or tending to show the nature and extent of the injuries from which the pursuer was suffering when he was referred thereto during April 1993 and the nature and extent of the treatment he received therefor.

2. All medical records relating to the pursuer, including case notes, letters, reports, cards, charts, illustrations and all other documents, and x-ray and all other photographs kept by or for Dr Johnston, the Health Centre, Greenock, in order that excerpts may be taken therefrom at the sight of the commissioner of all entries therein showing or tending to show the nature and extent of the injuries from which the pursuer was

suffering when he consulted the said doctor or a colleague during April 1993 and subsequently, and the nature and extent of the treatment he received therefor.

3. All wages records kept by or for the defenders for the period from 4 October 1992 to date, in order that excerpts may be taken therefrom at the sight of the commissioner of all entries therein showing or tending to show (i) the gross and net earnings of the pursuer including statutory sick pay and all other payments received by him in his employment with them during the said period; (ii) the basic and overtime rates of pay for machine operators employed by the defenders during the said period; and (iii) the date or dates on which any increase in such rates came into effect.

4. All documents relating to the pension scheme of which the pursuer was a member kept by or for the defenders in order that excerpts may be taken therefrom of all entries therein showing or tending to show (i) the terms and conditions governing the scheme; (ii) the amount of the contributions made to the scheme; (iii) the benefits which the pursuer will receive at the age of 65 years; and (iv) the benefits which the pursuer would have received at the age of 65 years had he continued in employment with the defenders until then.

5. Failing principals, drafts, copies or duplicates of the above or any of them.

e. Motion for commission and diligence to recover documents

SHERIFFDOM OF NORTH STRATHCLYDE AT GREENOCK

Court ref no A43/1994

MOTION FOR THE PURSUER

in the cause

JAMES BLACK, residing at 61 Glasgow Road, Greenock

PURSUER

against

INVERCLYDE METALS LIMITED, a company with a place of business at South Shore Street, Greenock

DEFENDERS

The pursuer moves the court to grant a commission and diligence for the recovery of the documents specified in the specification of documents, no 12 of process.

Part of process lodged with the motion:

Specification of documents.

14 May 1995　　　　　　　　　　IN RESPECT WHEREOF

Enrolled solicitor
5 Charles Street
Greenock
Solicitor for the pursuer

f. Joint minute of admissions

SHERIFFDOM OF NORTH STRATHCLYDE AT GREENOCK

JOINT MINUTE OF ADMISSIONS

for the parties

in the cause

JAMES BLACK, residing at 61 Glasgow Road, Greenock

PURSUER

against

INVERCLYDE METALS LIMITED, a company with a place of business at South Shore Street, Greenock

DEFENDERS

McKENZIE for the pursuer and REID for the defenders stated to the court that for the purposes of this action, the parties have agreed as follows:

1. That numbers 21/1 and 21/2 of process are, respectively, the records relating to the pursuer of Greenock Royal Infirmary and the Health Centre, Greenock, and accurately record the extent of and treatment for the injury sustained by him.

2. That numbers 24/1, 24/2 and 24/3 of process are, respectively, reports prepared by the persons by whom they bear to have been prepared; and insofar as their contents relate to injuries suffered by the pursuer as a result of the accident referred to on Record and their sequelae are true and accurate reports.

3. That had the pursuer remained in the employment of the defenders, his average net weekly earnings throughout the following periods would have been as follows:

(a) from 1 November 1993 to 10 January 1994—£145.17;

(b) from 11 January 1994 to 13 August 1994—£147.01; and
(c) from 14 August 1994 to 31 October 1994—£155.00.

IN RESPECT WHEREOF

Enrolled solicitor
5 Charles Street
Greenock
Solicitor for the pursuer

Enrolled solicitor
14 Green Street
Greenock
Solicitor for the defenders

9. ANDERSON v PRESS (UK) LTD

Payment—Damages—Personal injuries—Accident at work—Negligence—Safe place of work—Breach of statutory duty—Workplace safety—Plea of contributory negligence—Plea of time bar

a. Initial writ

SHERIFFDOM OF TAYSIDE, CENTRAL AND FIFE
AT DUNDEE

INITIAL WRIT

in the cause

JAMES ANDERSON, residing at 44 Whitehouse Grove, Dundee

PURSUER

against

PRESS (UK) LIMITED, a company with a place of business at Anstruther Park, Dundee

DEFENDERS

The pursuer craves the court:

1. To grant decree against the defenders for payment to the pursuer of the sum of FIFTEEN THOUSAND POUNDS (£15,000), with interest thereon at the rate of eight *per centum per annum* from the date of decree to follow hereon until payment.
2. To find the defenders liable in the expenses of the action.

CONDESCENDENCE

1. The pursuer resides at 44 Whitehouse Grove, Dundee. The defenders are a company incorporated under the Companies Acts and have a place of business at Anstruther Park, Dundee. They are domiciled there. This court has jurisdiction. To the knowledge of the pursuer, no proceedings are pending before any other court involving the present cause of action and between the parties hereto. To the knowledge of the pursuer, no agreement exists between the parties prorogating jurisdiction over the subject-matter of the present cause to another court.

2. On or about 8 July 1991, the pursuer was engaged in the course of his employment with the defenders as a machine operator of a metal press, Dorst Press No K1222, at their said place of business. In order to operate the machine, the pursuer required to stand on a wooden platform at a height of about five feet to which access required to be gained by wooden steps. The steps were not secured to the platform and were capable of independent movement. At or about 2.30 am on the said date, as the pursuer was descending the said steps, his left heel caught in a gap between the steps and the platform. The gap had opened up because the steps had moved during the course of their use. As a result of so catching his heel, the pursuer lost his balance and fell approximately four feet to the ground. He thereby sustained the serious loss, injury and damage hereinafter condescended upon.

3. The said accident was caused by the fault of the defenders. It was their duty to take reasonable care for the safety of their employees, including the pursuer. It was their duty to take reasonable care to provide and maintain for him a safe workplace. It was their duty to take reasonable care to have the steps secured in such a way that no gap would open up. In these duties, the defenders failed and by their failures so caused the said accident. Had they fulfilled the said duties incumbent upon them, the accident would not have occurred.

4. Further and in any event, the said accident was caused by the defenders' breach of statutory duty. The said steps were a traffic route in a workplace within the meaning of the Workplace (Health, Safety and Welfare) Regulations 1992. Regulation 17(2) thereof provides: 'Traffic routes in a workplace shall be suitable for the persons . . . using them . . .'. The said steps were not suitable for the pursuer who used them. They were not secured to the platform and were capable of independent movement with the result that a gap opened up in which the pursuer's heel could be caught. The defenders were in breach of the said regulation and by such breach so caused the said accident. Had they fulfilled the statutory duty incumbent upon them, the said accident would not have occurred.

5. As a result of the said accident, the pursuer has sustained loss, injury and damage. He bruised his back and left knee. He attended his doctor, Dr A George of the City Health Centre, Dundee. He was referred to the orthopaedic out-patient department of Dundee Royal Infirmary where he underwent a course of physiotherapy. He was unfit to return to work until about late September 1991. He has suffered and continues to suffer pain and inconvenience. As a result of the accident, the pursuer was off work and lost wages. In the circumstances, the sum sued for is a reasonable estimate of the loss, injury and damage suffered by the pursuer.

6. The defenders have been called upon to make reparation to the pursuer for his said loss, injury and damage but they refuse or at least delay to do so. This action is accordingly necessary.

PLEAS-IN-LAW

1. The pursuer having suffered loss, injury and damage through the defenders' fault and breach of statutory duty, the pursuer is entitled to reparation from them therefor.

2. The sum sued for being a reasonable estimate of the pursuer's said loss, injury and damage, decree should be pronounced as craved.

IN RESPECT WHEREOF

Enrolled solicitor
1 Bank Street
Dundee
Solicitor for the pursuer

b. Defences

SHERIFFDOM OF TAYSIDE, CENTRAL AND FIFE AT DUNDEE

DEFENCES

in the cause

JAMES ANDERSON, residing at 44 Whitehouse Grove, Dundee

PURSUER

against

PRESS (UK) LIMITED, a company with a place of business at Anstruther Park, Dundee

DEFENDERS

ANSWERS TO CONDESCENDENCE

1. The averments relating to the defenders and the existence of jurisdiction are admitted. *Quoad ultra* not known and not admitted.

2. Admitted that on the said date the pursuer was engaged in the course of his employment with the defenders as a machine operator of said metal press at their said place of business. Admitted that in order to operate the machine, the pursuer required to stand on a wooden platform at a height of about five feet to which access required to be gained by wooden steps. Not known and not admitted that the pursuer sustained injury, or if he did, in what circumstances he did so. *Quoad ultra* denied. Explained and averred that an incident similar to that averred was reported to the defenders as having occurred on 2 July 1991. No such incident occurred on 8 July 1991.

3. Denied. Explained and averred that the defenders duly fulfilled all duties incumbent upon them. Explained further and averred that *esto* the pursuer sustained an accident on the said date as averred by him, such was materially contributed to by his own fault. It was his duty to take reasonable care for his own safety. It was his duty to watch where he was placing his feet. It was his duty to take reasonable care to avoid losing his

footing on the said steps. In these duties he failed and so materially contributed to the said accident. But for his said failures in duty the accident would not have occurred.

4. The said statutory provision is referred to for its terms. *Quoad ultra* denied under reference to the preceding answer.

5. The nature, extent and consequences of any loss, injury and damage suffered by the pursuer are not known and not admitted. *Quoad ultra* denied. Explained and averred that the pursuer did not stop work until 12 July 1991. He resumed work on 31 July 1991. Explained further and averred that in any event the sum sued for is excessive.

6. Denied that the action is necessary. Explained and averred that *esto* the pursuer sustained an accident as averred by him, such occurred on 2 July 1991. The initial writ in the present action was served upon the defenders on 4 July 1994. The action is time-barred.

PLEAS-IN-LAW

1. The action being time-barred, should be dismissed.
2. The pursuer's averments being irrelevant *et separatim* being lacking in specification, the action should be dismissed.
3. The pursuer's averments so far as material being unfounded in fact, the defenders should be assoilzied.
4. The pursuer not having suffered loss, injury or damage through fault or breach of statutory duty on the part of the defenders, decree of absolvitor should be pronounced.
5. *Separatim, esto* the pursuer has suffered loss, injury and damage through fault or breach of statutory duty on the part of the defenders (which is denied), such having been materially contributed to by his own fault, any damages awarded should be reduced in terms of the Law Reform (Contributory Negligence) Act 1945, s 1.
6. In any event, the sum sued for being excessive, decree should not be pronounced as craved.

IN RESPECT WHEREOF

Enrolled solicitor
26 Main Street
Dundee
Solicitor for the defenders

c. Specification of property (OCR 28.2(2))

SHERIFFDOM OF TAYSIDE, CENTRAL AND FIFE
AT DUNDEE

SPECIFICATION OF
PROPERTY

for the inspection and photographing of which an order is sought by the pursuer

in the cause

JAMES ANDERSON, residing at 44 Whitehouse Grove, Dundee

PURSUER

against

PRESS (UK) LIMITED, a company with a place of business at Anstruther Park, Dundee

DEFENDERS

The Dorst Press No K1222, situated within the defenders' place of business at Anstruther Park, Dundee.

d. Motion for order for inspection and photographing of property

SHERIFFDOM OF TAYSIDE, CENTRAL AND FIFE
AT DUNDEE

Court ref no A29/1994

MOTION FOR THE
PURSUER

in the cause

JAMES ANDERSON, residing at 44 Whitehouse Grove, Dundee

PURSUER

against

PRESS (UK) LIMITED, a company with a place of business at Anstruther Park, Dundee

DEFENDERS

The pursuer moves the court to authorise and appoint James Blackburn, Glasgow Institute of Technology, to inspect and photograph the property specified in the specification of property no 16 of process.

Part of process lodged with the motion:
Specification of property

14 October 1994   IN RESPECT WHEREOF

Enrolled solicitor
1 Bank Street
Dundee
Solicitor for the pursuer

e. **List of witnesses (OCR 9.14(1))**

SHERIFFDOM OF TAYSIDE, CENTRAL AND FIFE AT DUNDEE

LIST OF WITNESSES

for the pursuer

in the cause

JAMES ANDERSON, residing at 44 Whitehouse Grove, Dundee

PURSUER

against

PRESS (UK) LIMITED, a company with a place of business at Anstruther Park, Dundee

DEFENDERS

1. James Anderson, machine operator, 44 Whitehouse Grove, Dundee.
2. Gordon Affleck, machine operator, 29 St Mary's Street, Dundee.
3. James Blackburn, lecturer, Glasgow Institute of Technology.
4. Dr Alan George, general practitioner, City Health Centre, Dundee.
5. Phyllis Fleming, physiotherapist, Dundee Royal Infirmary.
6. Marion Park, wages supervisor, c/o Press (UK) Limited, Anstruther Park, Dundee.

f. Motion for document to be admitted as evidence without calling maker as witness (OCR 29.3(2))

SHERIFFDOM OF TAYSIDE, CENTRAL AND FIFE
AT DUNDEE

Court ref no A29/1994

MOTION FOR THE
PURSUER

in the cause

JAMES ANDERSON, residing at 44 Whitehouse Grove, Dundee

PURSUER

against

PRESS (UK) LIMITED, a company with a place of business at Anstruther Park, Dundee

DEFENDERS

The pursuer moves the court to admit the letter from Press (UK) Limited dated 4 November 1993 as evidence without calling as a witness the maker thereof.

Document lodged with the motion:
Letter from Press (UK) Limited dated 4 November 1993

14 December 1994   IN RESPECT WHEREOF

Enrolled solicitor
1 Bank Street
Dundee
Solicitor for the pursuer

g. Motion for commission to examine a witness (OCR 28.10)

SHERIFFDOM OF TAYSIDE, CENTRAL AND FIFE
AT DUNDEE

Court ref no A29/1994

MOTION FOR THE
PURSUER

in the cause

JAMES ANDERSON, residing at 44 Whitehouse Grove, Dundee

PURSUER

against

PRESS (UK) LIMITED, a company with a place of business at Anstruther Park, Dundee

DEFENDERS

The pursuer moves the court to grant a commission to John Grayson, Solicitor, 4 Briers Road, Dundee to examine Gordon Affleck, 29 St Mary's Street, Dundee, a necessary witness for the pursuer.

Document lodged with the motion:
Medical certificate dated 19 November 1994

4 December 1994   IN RESPECT WHEREOF

Enrolled solicitor
1 Bank Street
Dundee
Solicitor for the pursuer

h. Motion for discharge of diet of proof

SHERIFFDOM OF TAYSIDE, CENTRAL AND FIFE
AT DUNDEE

Court ref no A29/1994

MOTION FOR THE
PURSUER

in the cause

JAMES ANDERSON, residing at 44 Whitehouse Grove, Dundee

PURSUER

against

PRESS (UK) LIMITED, a company with a place of business at Anstruther Park, Dundee

DEFENDERS

The pursuer moves the court to discharge the diet of proof fixed for 10 January 1995.

14 December 1994   IN RESPECT WHEREOF

Enrolled solicitor
1 Bank Street
Dundee
Solicitor for the pursuer

10. HUGHES v AMEX ENGINEERING LTD (IN LIQUIDATION)

Payment—Damages—Personal injuries—Occupational disease—Asbestosis—Negligence—Plea of apportionment—Plea of indemnity

a. Initial writ

SHERIFFDOM OF GLASGOW AND STRATHKELVIN
AT GLASGOW

INITIAL WRIT

in the cause

JOHN HUGHES, residing at 259a Marsh Grove, Glasgow

PURSUER

against

AMEX ENGINEERING LIMITED (IN LIQUIDATION), a company with its registered office at 361 East Nile Street, Glasgow and HAROLD RANDALL, Chartered Accountant, 361 East Nile Street, Glasgow, the official liquidator thereof

FIRST DEFENDERS

and

JOHN SMITH AND COMPANY LIMITED, a company with its registered office at 25 Clyde Avenue, Glasgow

SECOND DEFENDERS

The pursuer craves the court:

1. To grant decree against the defenders jointly and severally for payment to the pursuer of the sum of FIFTY THOUSAND POUNDS

(£50,000), with interest thereon at the rate of eight *per centum per annum* from the date of decree until payment.

2. To find the defenders liable in the expenses of the action.

CONDESCENDENCE

1. The pursuer resides at 259a Marsh Grove, Glasgow. The first defenders are a company incorporated under the Companies Acts, in liquidation, with its registered office at 361 East Nile Street, Glasgow, where they are domiciled, and the liquidator thereof. This court has jurisdiction. Leave to commence this action against the company (which is hereinafter referred to alone as 'the first defenders') was granted by the Sheriff of Glasgow and Strathkelvin at Glasgow on 19 March 1994. The second defenders are a company incorporated under the Companies Acts with its registered office at 25 Clyde Avenue, Glasgow. They took over the whole assets and liabilities of Albion Engineering Limited, a company incorporated under the Companies Acts with its registered office at 3 Fenner Place, Glasgow (and hereinafter referred to as 'the second defenders' predecessors'). To the knowledge of the pursuer, no proceedings are pending before any other court involving the present cause of action and between the parties hereto. To the knowledge of the pursuer, no agreement exists between the parties prorogating jurisdiction over the present subject-matter to another court.

2. Between about 1960 and about 1965 the pursuer worked for the first defenders as a labourer engaged in heating engineer work. The pursuer assisted with the repair and maintenance of boilers and heating systems in hospitals, schools, mills and factories in and around the Glasgow area. He was required to strip off old insulation lagging from boilers and pipes. Said lagging was asbestos based and generally consisted of an asbestos based cloth known as 'monkey dung' and asbestos cement underneath. To strip it off, the pursuer would hack at it with a knife or spade. The pursuer would be required to sweep up the old lagging. Thereafter, new lagging of the same type was applied to the boilers and pipes by contractors. The pursuer was required to work alongside and nearby while said contractors would mix up the monkey dung and apply it. His said work involved him in working in confined spaces underneath pipes and behind boilers. The working conditions were dusty and dirty.

3. Between about 1965 and about 1971 the pursuer worked for the second defenders' predecessors as a labourer engaged in heating engineer work. The pursuer assisted with the repair and maintenance of boilers and heating systems in hospitals, schools, mills and factories in and around the Glasgow area. He was required to strip off old insulation lagging from boilers and pipes. Said lagging was asbestos based and generally consisted of an asbestos based cloth known as 'monkey dung' and asbestos cement underneath. To strip it off, the pursuer would hack it off with a knife or spade. The pursuer would be required to sweep up the old lagging. Thereafter, new lagging of the same type was applied to the boilers and pipes by contractors. The pursuer was required to work alongside and nearby while said contractors would mix up the monkey dung and apply

it. His said work involved him in working in confined spaces underneath pipes and behind boilers. The working conditions were dusty and dirty.

4. Throughout his periods of employment with the first defenders and the second defenders' predecessors, the pursuer was frequently exposed to particles of asbestos. Said particles were in the air and gathered on the plant and equipment the pursuer used. Said particles gathered in the premises in which the pursuer worked, on the floors, walls, ceilings and other internal surfaces. Asbestos dust and particles landed on the pursuer and his clothing. No proper efficient ventilation and ventilating apparatus nor any efficient exhaust appliances for removing said dust and particles from the air were provided. No efficient masks or respirators were provided. No damping down was carried out to keep the dust and particles down. No suitable protective clothing was provided. No accommodation for or cleaning of his working and non-working clothes was provided. No bathing or shower facilities were provided nor was the pursuer advised to wash after work. No warnings were given to the pursuer of the dangers to him of exposure to asbestos. In consequence of the conditions and nature of the work during the pursuer's employment with the first defenders and the second defenders' predecessors, the pursuer was exposed to breathing in an atmosphere impregnated by asbestos dust and particles. The pursuer breathed in large quantities of asbestos which lodged in and around his lungs as a result of which he sustained the loss, injury and damage hereinafter condescended upon.

5. Said loss, injury and damage was caused by the fault of the first defenders and the second defenders' predecessors. It was their duty during the period when the pursuer was employed by them to take reasonable care for the safety of their employees such as the pursuer and not to expose them unnecessarily to the risk of injury. It was their duty to take reasonable care to protect the pursuer against the risks of suffering injury and damage and contracting disease caused by the inhalation of dust containing injurious particles such as asbestos. It was their duty to provide and maintain a proper, adequate and efficient system of ventilation which would provide and maintain an adequate supply of fresh air in the pursuer's workplaces. It was their duty to take all reasonable steps to remove the dust produced by the said work in said workplaces. It was their duty to provide efficient exhaust appliances for drawing off the said dust. It was their duty to provide and maintain suitable and sufficient masks or respirators to protect the pursuer against the inhalation of asbestos dust-impregnated air. It was their duty to keep floors, walls, ceilings and internal surfaces of premises and of the plant and equipment therein effectively damped to prevent dust rising. It was their duty to provide the pursuer with suitable protective clothing, with adequate accommodation for such working clothes and for his non-working clothes, to instruct him to wear such clothing, and to institute and maintain a system for cleaning such clothing so as to avoid or minimise the risk of inhaling or having contact with asbestos from such clothing. It was their duty to provide bathing or shower facilities and to advise the pursuer to wash after each shift. It was their duty to warn the pursuer of the risk to his health of contact with and inhalation of asbestos dust or particles. The said precautions were obviously necessary in the circumstances, it being well known in industry generally from at least prior to the period of

employment of the pursuer by the first defenders that dust containing said materials was extremely dangerous and inhalation thereof was likely to lead to damage of the respiratory system. In these duties the first defenders and the second defenders' predecessors failed and by their failures caused the pursuer to sustain said loss, injury and damage. Had they during the periods when the pursuer was employed by them fulfilled the duties incumbent on them, the pursuer would not have sustained said loss, injury and damage.

6. As a result of being exposed to and inhaling air impregnated with asbestos dust and particles, the pursuer has suffered loss, injury and damage. In about early 1990 he began to have chest problems. He developed a sharp intermittent pain in his chest. Climbing ladders caused him to have dizzy turns. He developed shortness of breath. He attended his general practitioner, Dr Jason, Health Centre, Govan who referred him to the Chest Clinic, Kings Hospital, Glasgow. Following tests in October 1990, he was diagnosed as suffering from asbestosis. He has finger clubbing. He is now only able to walk on the level at slow speeds. He has difficulty with the stairs in his house. He develops shortness of breath while at rest. He has pain in his right arm, leg and abdomen. He has required to give up work and has lost earnings, details whereof will be provided. The sum sued for is a reasonable estimate of the pursuer's said loss, injury and damage.

7. The defenders have been called upon to make reparation to the pursuer for his said loss, injury and damage. They refuse or at least delay to do so. This action is accordingly necessary.

PLEAS-IN-LAW

1. The pursuer having suffered loss, injury and damage through the fault and breach of statutory duty of the first defenders and the second defenders' predecessors, is entitled to reparation from the defenders therefor.

2. The sum sued for being a reasonable estimate of the pursuer's said loss, injury and damage, decree should be pronounced as craved.

IN RESPECT WHEREOF

Enrolled solicitor
41 Carlton Drive
Glasgow
Solicitor for the pursuer

b. Defences

SHERIFFDOM OF GLASGOW AND STRATHKELVIN
AT GLASGOW

DEFENCES FOR THE
SECOND DEFENDERS

in the cause

JOHN HUGHES, residing at 259A Marsh Grove, Glasgow

PURSUER

against

AMEX ENGINEERING LIMITED (IN LIQUIDATION), a company with its registered office at 361 East Nile Street, Glasgow and HAROLD RANDALL, Chartered Accountant, 361 East Nile Street, Glasgow, the liquidator thereof

FIRST DEFENDERS

and

JOHN SMITH AND COMPANY LIMITED, a company with its registered office at 25 Clyde Avenue, Glasgow

SECOND DEFENDERS

ANSWERS TO CONDESCENDENCE

1. The averments relating to the second defenders and the existence of jurisdiction against them are admitted. *Quoad ultra* not known and not admitted.
2. Not known and not admitted.
3. Admitted that between about 1965 and about 1971 the pursuer worked for the second defenders' predecessors as a labourer engaged in heating engineer work. *Quoad ultra* denied.

4. Not known and not admitted *quoad* the pursuer's employment with the first defenders. *Quoad ultra* denied.

5. On the hypothesis of fact upon which they proceed, the pursuer's averments of fault, so far as directed against the first defenders, are admitted and adopted. *Quoad ultra* denied.

6. The nature, extent and consequences of any loss, injury and damage sustained by the pursuer are not known and not admitted. *Quoad ultra* denied. Explained and averred that the sum sued for is in any event excessive.

7. Denied that the action is necessary. Explained and averred that *esto* the second defenders are liable to make reparation to the pursuer as a result of the fault of their predecessors, the said Albion Engineering Limited, they are entitled to be indemnified therefor by the said company in terms of the Sale Agreement between them, dated 4 July 1972, clause Twenty Fifth of which provides: 'The vendors [viz. the said Albion Engineering Limited] accept full responsibility for payment of all sums which are or may become due by the purchasers [viz. the defenders] to all the employees thereof by reason of their employment with the vendors . . .'

PLEAS-IN-LAW

1. The pursuer's averments so far as directed against the second defenders, being irrelevant *et separatim* being lacking in specification, the action against them should be dismissed.

2. The pursuer's averments so far as directed against the second defenders being unfounded in fact, they should be assoilzied.

3. The pursuer not having suffered loss, injury and damage through fault on the part of the second defenders' predecessors, the second defenders should be assoilzied.

4. *Separatim esto* the pursuer has suffered loss, injury and damage through fault on the part of the second defenders' predecessor (which is denied), such also having been caused through the first defenders' fault, any liability to the pursuer in damages and expenses should be apportioned between the first and second defenders in terms of the Law Reform (Miscellaneous Provisions) (Scotland) Act 1940, s 3(1).

5. *Separatim, esto* the pursuer has suffered loss, injury and damage through fault on the part of the second defenders' predecessors (which is denied), the second defenders are entitled to be indemnified by their predecessors, the said Albion Engineering Limited, in terms of the said contract.

6. In any event, the sum sued for is excessive.

IN RESPECT WHEREOF

Enrolled solicitor
1 Jacklin Avenue
Glasgow
Solicitor for the second
defenders

c. Third party notice

SHERIFFDOM OF GLASGOW AND STRATHKELVIN AT GLASGOW

THIRD PARTY NOTICE

in the cause

JOHN HUGHES, residing at 259A Marsh Grove, Glasgow

PURSUER

against

AMEX ENGINEERING LIMITED (IN LIQUIDATION), a company with its registered office at 361 East Nile Street, Glasgow and HAROLD RANDALL, Chartered Accountant, 361 East Nile Street, Glasgow, the liquidator thereof

FIRST DEFENDERS

and

JOHN SMITH AND COMPANY LIMITED, a company with its registered office at 25 Clyde Avenue, Glasgow

SECOND DEFENDERS

To Albion Engineering Limited, 3 Fenner Place, Glasgow
You are hereby given notice by John Smith and Company Limited of an order granted by Sheriff P Benson in this action in which John Hughes is the pursuer, Amex Engineering Limited (in liquidation) and the liquidator thereof are the first defenders and John Smith and Company Limited are the second defenders. In the action the pursuer claims against

the defenders the sum of £50,000 as damages in respect of his contraction of asbestosis as a result of alleged exposure to asbestos dust during the course of his employment with the defenders, as more fully appears in the pleadings enclosed.

The second defenders deny liability to the pursuer but claim that if they are liable to the pursuer, you are liable to relieve them wholly of their liability by virtue of the indemnity set forth in the contract between the second defenders and you dated 4 July 1972, as more fully appears from the defences lodged by them in the action.

IF YOU WISH to resist either the claim of the pursuer against the second defenders, or the claim of the second defenders against you, you must lodge answers with the sheriff clerk at the above address within 28 days of 19 May 1994. You must also pay the court fee of £42.

18 May 1994   Enrolled solicitor
                           1 Jacklin Avenue
                           Glasgow
                           Solicitor for the second defenders

Glasgow 10 June 1994
I, Thomas Paterson, hereby certify that on 18 May 1994 I duly cited Albion Engineering Limited, third party, to answer the foregoing notice. This I did by recorded delivery post.

'T. Paterson' (Solicitor for the second defenders)

d. Notice to admit (document) (OCR 29.14(1)(b))

SHERIFFDOM OF GLASGOW AND STRATHKELVIN
AT GLASGOW

NOTICE TO ADMIT

for the second defenders

in the cause

JOHN HUGHES, residing at 259a Marsh Grove, Glasgow

PURSUER

against

AMEX ENGINEERING LIMITED (IN LIQUIDATION), a company with its registered office at 361 East Nile Street, Glasgow and HAROLD RANDALL, Chartered Accountant, 361 East Nile Street, Glasgow, the liquidator thereof

FIRST DEFENDERS

and

JOHN SMITH AND COMPANY LIMITED, a company with its registered office at 25 Clyde Avenue, Glasgow

SECOND DEFENDERS

and

ALBION ENGINEERING LIMITED, a company with its registered office at 3 Fenner Place, Glasgow

THIRD PARTY

To: Albion Engineering Limited, Third Party
The second defenders call upon you to admit for the purposes of this action only that the document entitled 'Sale Agreement' dated 4 July 1972, no 23/1 of process, is a true copy of an original and properly authenticated document.

4 August 1994　　　　　　　　IN RESPECT WHEREOF

　　　　　　　　　　　　　　　Enrolled solicitor
　　　　　　　　　　　　　　　1 Jacklin Avenue
　　　　　　　　　　　　　　　Glasgow
　　　　　　　　　　　　　　　Solicitor for the second defenders

e. **Specification of matters (OCR 28.2(2))**

SHERIFFDOM OF GLASGOW AND STRATHKELVIN AT GLASGOW

SPECIFICATION OF MATTERS

in respect of which information is sought as to the identity of a person who might be a witness by the pursuer

in the cause

JOHN HUGHES, residing at 259A Marsh Grove, Glasgow

PURSUER

against

AMEX ENGINEERING LIMITED (IN LIQUIDATION), a company with its registered office at 361 East Nile Street, Glasgow and HAROLD RANDALL, Chartered Accountant, 361 East Nile Street, Glasgow, the liquidator thereof

FIRST DEFENDERS

and

JOHN SMITH AND COMPANY LIMITED, a company with its registered office at 25 Clyde Avenue, Glasgow

SECOND DEFENDERS

and

ALBION ENGINEERING LIMITED, a company with its registered office at 3 Fenner Place, Glasgow

THIRD PARTY

1. (a) The engagement of the pursuer as a labourer in heating engineer work on the first defenders' behalf between about 1960 and about 1965; and (b) the provision of assistance to the first defenders by him during that period with the repair and maintenance of boilers and heating systems in hospitals, schools, mills and factories in and around the Glasgow area.

2. The provision of assistance to the second defenders' predecessors by the pursuer during the period between about 1965 and about 1971 with the repair and maintenance of boilers and heating systems in hospitals, schools, mills and factories in and around the Glasgow area.

f. Motion for defenders to be ordained to disclose information anent identity of potential witness

SHERIFFDOM OF GLASGOW AND STRATHKELVIN
AT GLASGOW

Court ref no A21/1994

MOTION FOR THE PURSUER

in the cause

JOHN HUGHES, residing at 259A Marsh Grove, Glasgow

PURSUER

against

AMEX ENGINEERING LIMITED (IN LIQUIDATION), a company with its registered office at 361 East Nile Street, Glasgow and HAROLD RANDALL, Chartered Accountant, 361 East Nile Street, Glasgow, the liquidator thereof

FIRST DEFENDERS

and

JOHN SMITH AND COMPANY LIMITED, a company with its registered office at 25 Clyde Avenue, Glasgow

SECOND DEFENDERS

and

ALBION ENGINEERING LIMITED, a company with its registered office at 3 Fenner Place, Glasgow

THIRD PARTY

The pursuer moves the court to ordain the first defenders to disclose to the pursuer such information as they have as to the identity of any person who might be a witness in respect of the matters specified in paragraph 1 of the specification of matters, no 15 of process; and to ordain the second defenders to disclose to the pursuer such information as they have as to the identity of any person who might be a witness in respect of the matter specified in paragraph 2 of the said specification of matters.

Part of process lodged with the motion:
Specification of matters

4 November 1994   IN RESPECT WHEREOF

Enrolled solicitor
1 Carlton Drive
Glasgow
Solicitor for the pursuer

g. Minute of tender (Houston tender)

SHERIFFDOM OF GLASGOW AND STRATHKELVIN AT GLASGOW

MINUTE OF TENDER

for the first defenders

in the cause

JOHN HUGHES, residing at 259A Marsh Grove, Glasgow

PURSUER

against

AMEX ENGINEERING LIMITED (IN LIQUIDATION), a company with its registered office at 361 East Nile Street, Glasgow and HAROLD RANDALL, Chartered Accountant, 361 East Nile Street, Glasgow, the liquidator thereof

FIRST DEFENDERS

and

JOHN SMITH AND COMPANY LIMITED, a company with its registered office at 25 Clyde Avenue, Glasgow

SECOND DEFENDERS

and

ALBION ENGINEERING LIMITED, a company with its registered office at 3 Fenner Place, Glasgow

THIRD PARTY

WILKINS for the first defenders stated to the court that under reservation of their whole rights and pleas and without admission of liability, the first defenders tendered and hereby tender to the pursuer and the second defenders to settle this action on the basis (i) that the first defenders and the second defenders shall contribute to the amount of any award of damages and expenses to which the pursuer may be found entitled in the proportions of 45 *per centum* to the first defenders and 55 *per centum* to the second defenders; and (ii) that the pursuer shall be entitled to decree against the defenders jointly and severally in the sum of THIRTY THOUSAND POUNDS (£30,000), together with the taxed expenses of process of date, in full of the craves of the initial writ.

IN RESPECT WHEREOF

Enrolled solicitor
14 Derby Street
Glasgow
Solicitor for the first defenders

h. Minute of withdrawal of tender

SHERIFFDOM OF GLASGOW AND STRATHKELVIN
AT GLASGOW

MINUTE OF WITHDRAWAL
OF TENDER

for the first defenders

in the cause

JOHN HUGHES, residing at 259A Marsh Grove, Glasgow

PURSUER

against

AMEX ENGINEERING LIMITED (IN LIQUIDATION), a company with its registered office at 361 East Nile Street, Glasgow and HAROLD RANDALL, Chartered Accountant, 361 East Nile Street, Glasgow, the liquidator thereof

FIRST DEFENDERS

and

JOHN SMITH AND COMPANY LIMITED, a company with its registered office at 25 Clyde Avenue, Glasgow

SECOND DEFENDERS

and

ALBION ENGINEERING LIMITED, a company with its registered office at 3 Fenner Place, Glasgow

THIRD PARTY

WILKINS for the first defenders stated to the court that the first defenders withdrew and hereby withdraw the tender contained in the minute of tender, no 25 of process.

IN RESPECT WHEREOF

Enrolled solicitor
14 Derby Street
Glasgow
Solicitor for the first defenders

11. SMITH v LANARKSHIRE REGIONAL COUNCIL

Payment—Damages—Personal injuries—Occupational disease—Dermatitis—Negligence—Safe plant and equipment—Breach of statutory duty—Control of substances hazardous to health

a. Initial writ

SHERIFFDOM OF SOUTH STRATHCLYDE, DUMFRIES AND GALLOWAY AT LANARK

INITIAL WRIT

in the cause

LAURA JANE SMITH, residing at 51 Hope Street, Lanark

PURSUER

against

LANARKSHIRE REGIONAL COUNCIL, 4 Town Square, Lanark

DEFENDERS

The pursuer craves the court:

1. To grant decree against the defenders for payment to the pursuer of the sum of FIFTEEN THOUSAND POUNDS (£15,000), with interest thereon at the rate of eight *per centum per annum* from the date of decree until payment.

2. To find the defenders liable in the expenses of the action.

CONDESCENDENCE

1. The pursuer resides at 51 Hope Street, Lanark. The defenders are a local authority with its headquarters at 4 Town Square, Lanark. They are domiciled there. This court has jurisdiction. To the knowledge of the pursuer, no proceedings are pending before any other court involving the present cause of action and between the parties hereto. To the knowledge of the pursuer, no agreement exists between the parties prorogating jurisdiction over the subject-matter of the present cause to another court.

2. For several years prior to about mid-July 1993, the pursuer was employed by the defenders as a cleaner at their premises at Forgan Road, Lanark. Her duties included cleaning toilets there. She was supplied by the defenders with a product known as 'Supa Concentrate' for the purpose of cleaning urinals and toilet pans. The said product contains benzalkonium chloride, which is a substance listed in Part 1A of the Approved List as harmful and corrosive for the purposes of the Control of Substances Hazardous to Health Regulations 1988. The manufacturers' product data sheet supplied with the product included the foregoing information. The defenders did not carry out any suitable and sufficient assessment of the risks created by the work which they required the pursuer to carry out aforesaid or of the steps that needed to be taken to meet the requirements of the said regulations. They did not provide the pursuer with such information, instruction or training as was sufficient for her to know the risks to her health created by exposure to the said substance and the precautions which should be taken. While undertaking the said tasks, the pursuer wore the items supplied to her by the defenders. Such comprised a tabard with short sleeves and rubber gloves without cotton liners. In carrying out her duties aforesaid, fine particles of the said product would form a mist in the air and come into contact with her bare arms and, running down into her gloves, with her wrists and hands. As a result, in about mid-July 1993, the pursuer developed contact irritant dermatitis, thereby sustaining the loss, injury and damage hereinafter condescended upon.

3. The said loss, injury and damage was caused by the defenders' fault. It was their duty to take reasonable care for the safety of their employees, such as the pursuer and not to expose them unnecessarily to the risk of injury. It was their duty to provide the pursuer with suitable protective clothing, such as overalls and gloves with cotton liners. It was their duty to provide her with such information, instruction and training as was suitable for her to know the risks to her health created by exposure to the said product and the precautions which should be taken. Alternatively, it was their duty to supply another product not containing the said substance. In these duties the defenders failed and by their failures so caused the pursuer to sustain loss, injury and damage. But for their said failures in duty, the pursuer would not have sustained such loss, injury and damage.

4. Further and in any event, the pursuer's loss, injury and damage was caused by the defenders' breach of statutory duty. It was their duty to comply with the Control of Substances Hazardous to Health Regulations 1988. Regulation 6(1) thereof requires *inter alia* that 'an employer shall not carry on any work which is liable to expose any employees to any substance hazardous to health unless he has made a suitable and sufficient assessment of the risks created by that work to the health of those employees and of the steps that need to be taken to meet the requirements of these regulations'. The defenders made no such assessment. Regulation 7(1) thereof requires that 'every employer shall ensure that the exposure of his employees to substances hazardous to health is either prevented or, where this is not reasonably practicable, adequately controlled'. The defenders failed to ensure that such exposure was prevented

or adequately controlled. Regulation 12(1) thereof requires that 'an employer who undertakes work which may expose any of his employees to substances hazardous to health shall provide that employee with such information, instruction and training as is suitable and sufficient for him to know—(a) the risks to health created by such exposure; and (b) the precautions which should be taken'. The defenders provided no such information, instruction or training to the pursuer. In each and all of the said statutory duties, the defenders failed and by their failures so caused the pursuer to sustain loss, injury and damage. But for their said failures in statutory duty, the pursuer would not have sustained the said loss, injury and damage.

5. As a result of the defenders' fault and breach of statutory duty, the pursuer has suffered loss, injury and damage. As hereinbefore averred, she developed a contact irritant dermatitis. She required to consult her general practitioner, Dr Davies, The Health Centre, Lanark. She has suffered and continues to suffer rashes on her arms, wrists and hands. The outbreaks were and are unsightly, itchy and sore. She requires to wear rubber gloves when washing dishes or her hair at home. Her skin nips upon bathing. She has required to be absent from work for lengthy periods and has lost earnings, as will be vouched. In the circumstances, the sum sued for is a reasonable estimate of the pursuer's loss, injury and damage.

6. The defenders have been called upon to make reparation to the pursuer for her said loss, injury and damage. They refuse or at least delay to do so. This action is accordingly necessary.

PLEAS-IN-LAW

1. The pursuer having suffered loss, injury and damage through the defenders' fault and breach of statutory duty, is entitled to reparation from them therefor.

2. The sum sued for being a reasonable estimate of the pursuer's loss, injury and damage, decree should be pronounced as craved.

IN RESPECT WHEREOF

Enrolled solicitor
1 Brandon Street
Lanark
Solicitor for the pursuer

b. Motion for evidence of witness to be received by way of affidavit (OCR 29.3(1))

SHERIFFDOM OF SOUTH STRATHCLYDE, DUMFRIES AND GALLOWAY AT LANARK

Court ref no C29/1994

MOTION FOR THE PURSUER

in the cause

LAURA JANE SMITH, residing at 51 Hope Street, Lanark

PURSUER

against

LANARKSHIRE REGIONAL COUNCIL, 4 Town Square, Lanark

DEFENDERS

The pursuer moves the court to allow the evidence of Margaret Jensen, 12 Telfer Street, Lanark, to be received by way of affidavit.

Part of process lodged with the motion:

Affidavit of Margaret Jensen

4 August 1994   IN RESPECT WHEREOF

Enrolled solicitor
1 Brandon Street
Lanark
Solicitor for the pursuer

c. Affidavit

SHERIFFDOM OF SOUTH STRATHCLYDE, DUMFRIES AND GALLOWAY AT LANARK

AFFIDAVIT

of Margaret Jensen, residing at 12 Telfer Street, Lanark

in the cause

LAURA JANE SMITH, residing at 51 Hope Street, Lanark

PURSUER

against

LANARKSHIRE REGIONAL COUNCIL, 4 Town Square, Lanark

DEFENDERS

At Lanark the Twenty Seventh day of July Nineteen Hundred and Ninety Four in the presence of CHRISTOPHER BROWN, Solicitor and Notary Public, 1 Brandon Street, Lanark compeared MARGARET JENSEN, residing at 12 Telfer Street, Lanark, who being solemnly sworn depones as follows:

1. I am Margaret Jensen. I am 27 years of age and live at 12 Telfer Street, Lanark. I am employed by Office Cleaning Service Limited as a cleaner. I used to work for Lanarkshire Regional Council.

2. I know Laura Jane Smith, the pursuer in this action. I used to work beside her cleaning toilets at the Forgan Road premises. We worked together for about a year preceding mid-July 1993. We were both supplied by our employers with a product known as 'Supa Concentrate' for the purpose of cleaning urinals and toilet pans. We both wore a tabard with short sleeves and rubber gloves without cotton liners. That was all we were ever given by the Council to wear. As we worked away with the 'Supa Concentrate', there would be a mist of the stuff in the air which

would settle on our bare arms and run into our gloves and come into contact with our hands and wrists. Nothing was ever said about the stuff by our employers and I never thought anything of it. I know, though, that Laura Jane went off work in about the middle of July 1993 with some kind of skin problem. I have not seen her since.

All of which is truth as the deponent shall answer to God.

.... DEPONENT

.... NOTARY PUBLIC

d. Minute of amendment

SHERIFFDOM OF SOUTH STRATHCLYDE, DUMFRIES AND GALLOWAY AT LANARK

MINUTE OF AMENDMENT

for the pursuer

in the cause

LAURA JANE SMITH, residing at 51 Hope Street, Lanark

PURSUER

against

LANARKSHIRE REGIONAL COUNCIL, 4 Town Square, Lanark

DEFENDERS

BROWN for the pursuer craved and hereby craves the court to allow the closed record to be opened up and amended as follows:

1. By deleting in the first crave 'FIFTEEN THOUSAND POUNDS (£15,000)' and substituting therefor 'FIFTY THOUSAND POUNDS (£50,000)'; and

2. By deleting in article 5 of the condescendence the sentence commencing 'She has required . . .' and substituting therefor the following:

> 'The pursuer has lost earnings. She required to be absent from work for lengthy periods. As a result, her employment was terminated on or about 24 July 1994. She is now unemployed. She will continue to lose earnings and increases in earnings. Details will be provided.'

And of new to close the record.

IN RESPECT WHEREOF

Enrolled solicitor
1 Brandon Street
Lanark
Solicitor for the pursuer

e. Motion for minute of amendment to be received and answered

SHERIFFDOM OF SOUTH STRATHCLYDE, DUMFRIES AND GALLOWAY AT LANARK

Court ref no A29/1994

MOTION FOR THE PURSUER

in the cause

LAURA JANE SMITH, residing at 51 Hope Street, Lanark

PURSUER

against

LANARKSHIRE REGIONAL COUNCIL, 4 Town Square, Lanark

DEFENDERS

The pursuer moves the court to allow the minute of amendment, no 18 of process, to be received and answered within 21 days.

Part of process lodged with the motion:

Minute of amendment

10 August 1994   IN RESPECT WHEREOF

Enrolled solicitor
1 Brandon Street
Lanark
Solicitor for the pursuer

f. Motion for prorogation of time to lodge answers

SHERIFFDOM OF SOUTH STRATHCLYDE, DUMFRIES AND GALLOWAY AT LANARK

Court ref no A29/1994

MOTION FOR THE DEFENDERS

in the cause

LAURA JANE SMITH, residing at 51 Hope Street, Lanark

PURSUER

against

LANARKSHIRE REGIONAL COUNCIL, 4 Town Square, Lanark

DEFENDERS

The defenders move the court to prorogate the time for lodging answers to the pursuer's minute of amendment, no 19 of process, by a further 14 days.

31 August 1994 IN RESPECT WHEREOF

Enrolled solicitor
4 Town Square
Lanark
Solicitor for the defenders

g. Answers

SHERIFFDOM OF SOUTH STRATHCLYDE, DUMFRIES AND GALLOWAY AT LANARK

ANSWERS

for the defenders

in the cause

LAURA JANE SMITH, residing at 51 Hope Street, Lanark

PURSUER

against

LANARKSHIRE REGIONAL COUNCIL, 4 Town Square, Lanark

DEFENDERS

HENDERSON for the defenders craved and hereby craves the court to allow the minute of amendment for the pursuer, no 18 of process, to be answered as follows:

By adding at the end of answer 5 the following:
'Further explained and averred that the pursuer was made redundant on 24 July 1994. Her redundancy was unrelated to her previous absences from work.'

IN RESPECT WHEREOF

Enrolled solicitor
4 Town Square
Lanark
Solicitor for the defenders

h. Motion for amendment in terms of minute of amendment and answers

SHERIFFDOM OF SOUTH STRATHCLYDE, DUMFRIES AND GALLOWAY AT LANARK

Court ref no A29/1994

MOTION FOR THE PURSUER

in the cause

LAURA JANE SMITH, residing at 51 Hope Street, Lanark

PURSUER

against

LANARKSHIRE REGIONAL COUNCIL, 4 Town Square, Lanark

DEFENDERS

The pursuer moves the court to allow the closed record to be opened up and amended in terms of the minute of amendment, no 18 of process, and the answers thereto, no 21 of process.

4 October 1994   IN RESPECT WHEREOF

Enrolled solicitor
1 Brandon Street
Lanark
Solicitor for the pursuer

12. HOGG v MAXWELL & CO

Payment—Damages—Breach of contract—Negligence—Professional negligence—Interest from prior to citation at different rates

a. Initial writ

SHERIFFDOM OF SOUTH STRATHCLYDE, DUMFRIES AND GALLOWAY AT AYR

INITIAL WRIT

in the cause

SUSAN MARY MARGARET HOGG, residing at 195 Irvine Road, Ayr

PURSUER

against

MAXWELL & CO, 16 Doune Street, Ayr

DEFENDERS

The pursuer craves the court:

1. To grant decree against the defenders for payment to the pursuer of the sum of SEVEN THOUSAND FIVE HUNDRED POUNDS (£7,500), with interest thereon at the rate of fifteen *per centum per annum* from 14 July 1991 until 1 April 1993 thereafter and at the rate of eight *per centum per annum* until payment.
2. To find the defenders liable in the expenses of the action.

CONDESCENDENCE

1. The pursuer resides at 195 Irvine Road, Ayr. The defenders are a firm of chartered surveyors. They are a partnership formed under the law of Scotland. Their central management and control is exercised in Scotland. They have a place of business at 16 Doune Street, Ayr. They are domiciled there. This court has jurisdiction. To the knowledge of the pursuer, no proceedings are pending before any other court involving the

present cause of action and between the parties hereto. To the knowledge of the pursuer, no agreement exists between the parties prorogating jurisdiction over the subject-matter of the present cause to another court.

2. On or about 14 May 1991, the defenders accepted instructions from solicitors acting on behalf of the pursuer to carry out a survey on a heritable property at 195 Irvine Road, Ayr. The defenders were advised that the pursuer was interested in purchasing the property. On or about 18 May 1991, the defenders duly carried out such survey and submitted to the said solicitors a report, dated 21 May 1991, a copy of which is produced. Therein they stated: 'There is no visible evidence of dampness or timber defect or infestation . . . We are of the opinion that the property under report has a present fair open market value of £35,000'. As a result of and in reliance upon the report, the pursuer submitted an offer to purchase the property at a price of £35,000, which offer was accepted. She obtained title and entry to the property on 14 July 1991, when she paid the price. Shortly thereafter, she discovered defects in the property. In particular there was timber defect in the form of rotted wood affecting window frames and doors throughout the property. The porch was in danger of collapse because of rotted wood. The frames of the garage door were similarly affected. These defects were apparent upon visual inspection at the date of the said survey. They had a material bearing on the value of the property, whereby the pursuer has sustained loss and damage, as hereinafter condescended on.

3. The pursuer's loss and damage were caused by breach of contract on the part of the defenders. It was an implied term of the parties' contract that the defenders, having accepted instructions from the pursuer, would exercise the degree of care and skill to be expected of reasonably competent members of their profession. In so doing it was the defenders' duty to carry out a proper visual inspection of the property. It was their duty to have regard to defects apparent upon such an inspection. It was their duty to report thereon to the pursuer. It was their duty to reflect the same in their assessment of the open market value of the property. Any surveyor of ordinary skill would have so acted. In all these duties, the defenders failed and accordingly were in breach of contract.

4. *Separatim*, the pursuer's loss and damage were caused by the defenders' fault. It was their duty, having accepted instructions from the pursuer, to exercise the degree of care and skill to be expected of reasonably competent members of their profession. Reference is made to the averments of duty in the preceding article of condescendence, which are held as repeated *brevitatis causa*. In these duties the defenders failed and thereby caused the pursuer to sustain the said loss and damage. But for their said failures in duty, the pursuer's loss and damage would not have occurred.

5. As a result of the defenders' said breach of contract *et separatim* fault, the pursuer has suffered loss and damage. The said property at the date of her purchase thereof (taking into account the said defects) was worth about £27,500. Reference is made to valuation and estimate of the cost at date of purchase of eliminating the said defects, each produced herewith. As hereinbefore averred, she in fact paid the sum of £35,000 therefor. The sum sued for is a reasonable estimate of the pursuer's loss and damage.

6. The defenders have been called upon to make reparation to the pursuer for her said loss and damage. They refuse or at least delay to do so. This action is accordingly necessary.

PLEAS-IN-LAW

1. The pursuer having suffered loss and damage through the defenders' breach of contract *et separatim* fault, is entitled to reparation therefor.

2. The sum sued for being a reasonable estimate of the pursuer's said loss and damage, decree should be pronounced as craved.

IN RESPECT WHEREOF

Enrolled solicitor
49 Frederick Street
Ayr
Solicitor for the pursuer

b. Motion for sist for negotiation

SHERIFFDOM OF SOUTH STRATHCLYDE, DUMFRIES AND GALLOWAY AT AYR

Court ref no A22/1994

MOTION FOR THE
DEFENDERS

in the cause

SUSAN MARY MARGARET HOGG, residing at 195 Irvine Road, Ayr

PURSUER

against

MAXWELL & CO, 16 Doune Street, Ayr

DEFENDERS

The defenders move the court to sist the cause for negotiation.

10 July 1994   IN RESPECT WHEREOF

Enrolled solicitor
29 Jarvis Road
Ayr
Solicitor for the defenders

c. Motion for recall of sist

SHERIFFDOM OF SOUTH STRATHCLYDE, DUMFRIES AND GALLOWAY AT AYR

Court ref no A22/1994

MOTION FOR THE PURSUER

in the cause

SUSAN MARY MARGARET HOGG, residing at 195 Irvine Road, Ayr

PURSUER

against

MAXWELL & CO, 16 Doune Street, Ayr

DEFENDERS

The pursuer moves the court to recall the sist and re-enrol the cause for further procedure.

5 December 1994   IN RESPECT WHEREOF

Enrolled solicitor
49 Frederick Street
Ayr
Solicitor for the pursuer

13. JONES v MIDLOTHIAN HEALTH BOARD

Payment—Damages—Negligence—Professional negligence—Vicarious liability

a. Initial writ

SHERIFFDOM OF LOTHIAN AND BORDERS
AT EDINBURGH

INITIAL WRIT

in the cause

MRS JENNIFER JONES, residing at 3 Melton Avenue, Edinburgh, suing as guardian of Alison Jones, residing with her

PURSUER

against

MIDLOTHIAN HEALTH BOARD, 1 George Place, Edinburgh

DEFENDERS

The pursuer craves the court:

1. To grant decree against the defenders for payment to the pursuer as guardian of Alison Jones of the sum of TWENTY THOUSAND POUNDS (£20,000), with interest thereon at the rate of eight *per centum per annum* from the date of decree until payment.

2. To find the defenders liable in the expenses of the action.

CONDESCENDENCE

1. The pursuer resides at 3 Melton Avenue, Edinburgh. She sues as guardian of her daughter, Alison Jones (hereinafter 'the child'), who was born on 3 June 1984 and who resides with her. The defenders are a health authority with its headquarters at 1 George Place, Edinburgh. They are domiciled there. This court has jurisdiction. To the knowledge of the pursuer, no proceedings are pending before any other court involving the present cause of action and between the parties hereto. To the knowledge

of the pursuer, no agreement exists between the parties prorogating jurisdiction over the subject-matter of the present cause to another court.

2. On or about 1 November 1990 the child fractured her right arm in a fall. She was taken by the pursuer to the Casualty Department at Edinburgh District Hospital. She was there examined by a doctor whose identity is to the pursuer unknown (hereinafter 'the doctor') employed by the defenders and for whose acts and omissions in the course of his employment the defenders are responsible. The doctor was fully informed as to the circumstances of the accident. The pursuer told him that she thought the child's arm had been fractured. The doctor examined the arm. He moved it, whereupon the child complained of pain. The doctor thereupon explained to the pursuer that the child's arm could not be broken for otherwise he would not have been able to move it. He diagnosed a sprain or strain. The pursuer took the child home. On or about the following day the pursuer telephoned the said Department anent the child and conversed with the doctor. She explained that she was not happy with the child's condition and that she felt the child's arm should have been x-rayed. The pursuer further explained that the child had been and was still in a great deal of pain, that the arm had swollen to about four times its size, that the child was white with pain and had been unable to sleep, and that paracetamol had failed to relieve the child's pain. The doctor advised the pursuer that he remembered the child well. He insisted that the arm was not broken. He said that it was possible that a muscle in the arm had been affected. He advised that the child should be encouraged to use the arm after a period for otherwise it would stiffen up. He did not suggest that the child should be brought back to the said Department. He did not offer to arrange an x-ray of the child's arm. During the following weeks, the said swelling subsided and the arm became very stiff. The child was most reluctant to use it. In about February 1991, the child's father took her to the fracture clinic at the said hospital. An x-ray was taken and the existence of a supra-condylar fracture of the arm revealed. As a result of the doctor's said actings, the child has suffered loss, injury and damage as hereinafter condescended upon.

3. The child's aftermentioned loss, injury and damage was caused by the fault of the doctor for whose acts and omissions in the course of his employment the defenders are responsible. It was his duty to act in the manner to be expected of a doctor of ordinary skill exercising reasonable care. It was his duty in so acting to diagnose a fracture of the child's arm, or at any rate to arrange for an x-ray thereof, in the light of the information given him by the pursuer in the said telephone conversation. No doctor of ordinary skill exercising reasonable care would have failed to do so. The doctor failed in the said duties and by his failures so caused the child to suffer loss, injury and damage. But for his said failures in duty, the loss, injury and damage hereinafter referred to would not have happened.

4. As a result of the doctor's fault the child has suffered loss, injury and damage. Had a fracture been diagnosed at the material time, suitable treatment resulting in the minimisation of pain and the period during which pain was experienced and in the avoidance of lasting disabilities

could and would have been effected. In the event, the child suffered very much more considerable pain and that for a significantly lengthier period than would otherwise have been the case had such treatment been effected. The child has also in direct consequence of the absence of such suitable treatment been left with lasting disabilities. Her lower right arm hangs at an abnormal angle, there being some 16 degrees difference from that of her lower left arm. The child cannot touch her right shoulder with her right hand. She cannot put her right arm behind her back. Her right arm lacks much strength. She now favours her non-dominant left hand and arm. She has had to give up gymnastics. She has not been able to participate to the full in activities with other children. Her right shoulder blade now sticks out, giving an appearance of poor posture, such being compensatory for her said reduced arm mobility. Cosmetic surgery, which could only be carried out once the child has attained the age of sixteen years, might improve the appearance of the arm to an extent. Such would not however improve the function of the arm aforesaid. In the event of such surgery, the child would be left with scarring. In the circumstances, the sum sued for is a reasonable estimate of the child's loss, injury and damage.

5. The defenders have been called upon to make reparation for the child's loss, injury and damage. They refuse or at least delay to do so. This action is therefore necessary.

PLEAS-IN-LAW

1. The child having suffered loss, injury and damage through fault for which the defenders are liable, is entitled to reparation therefor.

2. The sum sued for being a reasonable estimate of the said loss, injury and damage, decree should be pronounced as craved.

IN RESPECT WHEREOF

Enrolled solicitor
3 Doune Place
Edinburgh
Solicitor for the pursuer

b. Minute of tender

SHERIFFDOM OF LOTHIAN AND BORDERS AT EDINBURGH

MINUTE OF TENDER

for the defenders

in the cause

MRS JENNIFER JONES, residing at 3 Melton Avenue, Edinburgh, suing as guardian of Alison Jones, residing with her

PURSUER

against

MIDLOTHIAN HEALTH BOARD, 1 George Place, Edinburgh

DEFENDERS

JACKSON for the defenders stated to the court that without prejudice to and under reservation of their whole rights and pleas, the defenders tendered and hereby tender to the pursuer the sum of EIGHT THOUSAND POUNDS (£8,000), with the taxed expenses of process to the date hereof, in full of the craves of the initial writ.

IN RESPECT WHEREOF

Enrolled solicitor
1 Abercromby Street
Edinburgh
Solicitor for the defenders

c. Minute of acceptance of tender

SHERIFFDOM OF LOTHIAN AND BORDERS AT EDINBURGH

MINUTE OF ACCEPTANCE OF TENDER

for the pursuer

in the cause

MRS JENNIFER JONES, residing at 3 Melton Avenue, Edinburgh, suing as guardian of Alison Jones, residing with her

PURSUER

against

MIDLOTHIAN HEALTH BOARD, 1 George Place, Edinburgh

DEFENDERS

JOHNS for the pursuer stated to the court that the pursuer accepted and hereby accepts the tender contained in the minute of tender, no 17 of process, in full of the craves of the initial writ.

IN RESPECT WHEREOF

Enrolled solicitor
3 Doune Place
Edinburgh
Solicitor for the pursuer

d. Motion for decree in terms of minutes of tender and acceptance of tender

SHERIFFDOM OF LOTHIAN AND BORDERS
AT EDINBURGH

Court ref no A25/1994

MOTION FOR THE
PURSUER

in the cause

MRS JENNIFER JONES, residing at 3 Melton Avenue, Edinburgh, suing as guardian of Alison Jones, residing with her

PURSUER

against

MIDLOTHIAN HEALTH BOARD, 1 George Place, Edinburgh

DEFENDERS

The pursuer moves the court to grant decree in terms of the minute of tender, no 17 of process, and the minute of acceptance of tender no 18 of process.

14 July 1994   IN RESPECT WHEREOF

Enrolled solicitor
3 Doune Place
Edinburgh
Solicitor for the pursuer

e. Note of objections to Auditor's report (OCR 32.4)

SHERIFFDOM OF LOTHIAN AND BORDERS
AT EDINBURGH

NOTE OF OBJECTIONS

for the defenders

to report by the Auditor of Court on the pursuer's account of expenses

in the cause

MRS JENNIFER JONES, residing at 3 Melton Avenue, Edinburgh, suing as guardian of Alison Jones, residing with her

PURSUER

against

MIDLOTHIAN HEALTH BOARD, 1 George Place, Edinburgh

DEFENDERS

The defenders object to the report by the Auditor of Court dated 4 December 1994 upon the pursuer's account of expenses as regards the following items:

1, Mr AB Collins, for examination and report
   (page 2)

	fee paid	£800
	taxed off	£400
	allowed	£400

The defenders submit that the fee allowed was excessive and out of line with recent practice; that in so taxing the item, the Auditor exercised his discretion unreasonably; and that the fee allowed should not exceed £250.

2. Mr AB Collins, for preparation of evidence and attendance at court as certified skilled witness (page 3)

fee paid £1,000
taxed off £ 300
allowed £ 700

The defenders submit that the fee allowed was excessive and out of line with recent practice; that in so taxing the item, the Auditor exercised his discretion unreasonably; and that the fee allowed should not exceed £450.

IN RESPECT WHEREOF

Enrolled solicitor
1 Abercromby Street
Edinburgh
Solicitor for the defenders

14. ANDREWS v THOMPSON

Payment—Count reckoning and payment (partnership)

a. Initial writ

SHERIFFDOM OF GRAMPIAN, HIGHLAND AND ISLANDS
AT ABERDEEN

INITIAL WRIT

in the cause

MICHAEL ANDREWS, residing at 4 Glebe Street, Cowdenbeath

PURSUER

against

THOMAS THOMPSON, residing at 4 Jeffrey Place, Aberdeen

DEFENDER

The pursuer craves the court:

1. To ordain the defender to produce the whole books and accounts of the dissolved firm of Thompson, Andrews & Co, together with a full account of his intromissions with the assets of the said dissolved firm, that the true balance due to the pursuer may be ascertained; and to pay to the pursuer the sum of ONE HUNDRED THOUSAND POUNDS (£100,000) or such other sum as may appear to be the true balance due to him, with interest thereon at the rate of eight *per centum per annum* from the date of citation until payment; and, in the event of the defender failing to enter appearance or failing to produce such account, to ordain the defender to pay to the pursuer the sum of ONE HUNDRED THOUSAND POUNDS (£100,000), with interest as aforesaid.
2. To grant warrant to arrest on the dependence of the action.
3. To find the defender liable in the expenses of the action.

CONDESCENDENCE

1. The pursuer resides at 4 Glebe Street, Cowdenbeath. The defender resides at 4 Jeffrey Place, Aberdeen. He has been so resident for at least three months immediately preceding the raising of this action. He is domiciled there. This court has jurisdiction. To the knowledge of the

pursuer, no proceedings are pending before any other court involving the present cause of action and between the parties hereto. To the knowledge of the pursuer, no agreement exists between the parties prorogating jurisdiction over the subject-matter of the present cause to another court.

2. Between about 20 July 1989 and about 13 June 1993, the parties were partners in the firm of Thompson, Andrews & Co. The said firm was dissolved by agreement as at the latter date. It was agreed at that time that the defender would wind up the affairs of the dissolved partnership and arrange for the final settlement of accounts between the parties. He retained the whole books and accounts of the firm for that purpose.

3. The pursuer has called upon the defender to produce an account of his intromissions with the assets of the firm and to make payment of the balance due to him. The defender refuses or at least delays to do so. This action is therefore necessary.

PLEAS-IN-LAW

1. The defender being bound to account to the pursuer for his intromissions, should be ordained to produce an account as craved.

2. Failing production of an account, decree should be granted against the defender in terms of the alternative crave for payment.

IN RESPECT WHEREOF

Enrolled solicitor
4 Howe Place
Cowdenbeath
Solicitor for the pursuer

b. Motion for pursuer to be ordained to find caution (OCR 27.2)

SHERIFFDOM OF GRAMPIAN, HIGHLAND AND ISLANDS AT ABERDEEN

Court ref no A69/1994

MOTION FOR THE DEFENDER

in the cause

MICHAEL ANDREWS, residing at 4 Glebe Street, Cowdenbeath

PURSUER

against

THOMAS THOMPSON, residing at 4 Jeffrey Place, Aberdeen

DEFENDER

The defender moves the court to ordain the pursuer to find caution in the sum of £7,500 or such other sum as the court thinks fit within 28 days, under certification that if he fails to do so decree of absolvitor will be granted; all on the ground that the pursuer is an undischarged bankrupt.

Document lodged with the motion:

Copy order of the court awarding sequestration of the pursuer.

4 August 1994   IN RESPECT WHEREOF

Enrolled solicitor
21 Flodden Place
Aberdeen
Solicitor for the defender

15. CARGILL v CARGILL'S EXECUTOR

Payment—Count reckoning and payment (executry)

a. Initial writ

SHERIFFDOM OF SOUTH STRATHCLYDE, DUMFRIES AND GALLOWAY AT AIRDRIE

INITIAL WRIT

in the cause

LOUISE CARGILL, residing at 42 Maxwell Street, London

PURSUER

against

GEORGE ALFRED STOCKTON, residing at 22 Hill Place, Airdrie, executor-nominate of the late Ronald Joseph Cargill by will and confirmation

DEFENDER

The pursuer craves the court:

1. To ordain the defender to produce a full account of his intromissions as executor-nominate aforesaid with the estate of the said late Ronald Joseph Cargill and to pay to the pursuer the sum of THIRTY THOUSAND POUNDS (£30,000), or such other sum as may appear to be the true balance due by him, with interest thereon at the rate of eight *per centum per annum* from the date of citation until payment; and, in the event of the defender failing to enter appearance or failing to produce such account, to ordain the defender to pay to the pursuer the sum of THIRTY THOUSAND POUNDS (£30,000), with interest as aforesaid.
2. To grant warrant to arrest on the dependence of the action.
3. To find the defender liable in the expenses of the action.

CONDESCENDENCE

1. The pursuer resides at 42 Maxwell Street, London. The defender resides at 22 Hill Place, Airdrie. He has been so resident for at least three months immediately preceding the raising of this action. He is domiciled

there. This court accordingly has jurisdiction. To the knowledge of the pursuer, no proceedings are pending before any other court involving the present cause of action and between the parties hereto. To the knowledge of the pursuer, no agreement exists between the parties prorogating jurisdiction over the subject-matter of the present cause to another court.

2. The pursuer is the only child of the late Ronald Joseph Cargill (hereinafter 'the deceased') who resided latterly at 153 Calderwood Drive, Airdrie and who died on 1 January 1990. By holograph will dated 20 March 1985, the deceased appointed the defender as his executor-nominate. The defender was confirmed as executor conform to confirmation in his favour granted by the Sheriff of South Strathclyde, Dumfries and Galloway at Airdrie on 18 July 1990. In respect that the pursuer is the daughter of the deceased, and as such is in right of legitim, she is entitled to an accounting from the defender. The defender has been called upon to produce an account of his intromissions with the said estate. He delays to do so. This action is accordingly necessary.

PLEAS-IN-LAW

1. The defender being bound to account to the pursuer for his intromissions, should be ordained to produce an account as craved.

2. Failing production of an account, decree should be granted against the defender in terms of the alternative crave for payment.

IN RESPECT WHEREOF

Enrolled solicitor
1 High Street
Airdrie
Solicitor for the pursuer

b. Defences

SHERIFFDOM OF SOUTH STRATHCLYDE, DUMFRIES AND GALLOWAY AT AIRDRIE

DEFENCES

in the cause

LOUISE CARGILL, residing at 42 Maxwell Street, London

PURSUER

against

GEORGE ALFRED STOCKTON, residing at 22 Hill Place, Airdrie, executor-nominate of the late Ronald Joseph Cargill by will and confirmation

DEFENDER

ANSWERS TO CONDESCENDENCE

1. Admitted.
2. Admitted. Accounts will be produced.

IN RESPECT WHEREOF

Enrolled solicitor
46 Main Street
Airdrie
Solicitor for the defender

c. Note of objections to accounts

SHERIFFDOM OF SOUTH STRATHCLYDE, DUMFRIES AND GALLOWAY AT AIRDRIE

NOTE OF OBJECTIONS

for the pursuer

to accounts produced by the defender

in the cause

LOUISE CARGILL, residing at 42 Maxwell Street, London

PURSUER

against

GEORGE ALFRED STOCKTON, residing at 22 Hill Place, Airdrie, executor-nominate of the late Ronald Joseph Cargill by will and confirmation

DEFENDER

The pursuer objects to the accounts produced by the defender, with respect to the following items:

1. *25 October 1990.* The sum of £200 is credited as the sale price of the deceased's motor car. That car was worth several thousand pounds at the date of death.

2. *16 December 1990.* The sum of £500 is debited for travelling expenses. No such expenses required to be incurred. *Separatim* the sum debited is grossly excessive.

3. *10 March 1991.* The sum of £600 is debited for payment of creditors of the deceased. No specification is given as to the identity of said creditors or the nature of the debt.

IN RESPECT WHEREOF

Enrolled solicitor
1 High Street
Airdrie
Solicitor for the pursuer

16. JOHNSON'S TRUSTEES v DUNS BUILDING SOCIETY

Payment—Furthcoming—Arrested funds—Defender's whereabouts not known

a. Initial writ

SHERIFFDOM OF LOTHIAN AND BORDERS AT DUNS

INITIAL WRIT

in the cause

JAMES ALBERT BLACK WS, 1 Charlotte Street, Edinburgh and PETER JACOBS, 3 Ferry Street, Edinburgh trustees acting under the trust disposition and settlement of the late John Johnson dated 5 July 1986 and registered in the Books of Council and Session on 19 September 1991

PURSUERS

against

(FIRST) DUNS BUILDING SOCIETY 40 Main Square, Duns, Arrestees and (SECOND) PETER ARTHUR JOHNSON, whose whereabouts are not known, Common Debtor

DEFENDERS

The pursuers crave the court:

1. To grant decree against the first defenders for payment to the pursuers of the sum of ONE THOUSAND FIVE HUNDRED AND TWENTY POUNDS (£1,520) or such other sum as may be owing by them to the second defender and arrested in their hands at the instance of the pursuers on 12 January 1994 by virtue of a decree for the sum of £1,400 and expenses in favour of the pursuers against the second defender granted by the Sheriff of Tayside, Central and Fife at Dundee on 11 November 1993.

2. To grant warrant to cite the second defender by displaying on the walls of court a copy of the instance and crave of the initial writ, the warrant of citation and a notice in Form G4.

3. To find the second named defender liable in the expenses of the action.

4. To find the first defenders liable in the expenses of the action only in the event of their offering opposition thereto.

CONDESCENDENCE

1. The pursuers are the trustees acting under the trust, disposition and settlement of the late John Johnson dated 5 July 1986 and registered in the Books of Council and Session on 19 September 1991. They are designed in the instance. The first defenders are a building society with a branch at 40 Main Square, Duns. They are domiciled there. The whereabouts of the second defender are not known and cannot reasonably be ascertained. His last known residence was at 41 Main Street, Duns, which he vacated in early 1994 leaving no forwarding address. Attempts by sheriff officers instructed by the pursuers to locate him have met with no success. The present action is brought to assert the pursuers' rights in and to moveable property situated at the first defenders' said branch, namely monies arrested there. This court has jurisdiction. To the knowledge of the pursuers, no proceedings are pending before any other court involving the present cause of action and between the parties hereto. To the knowledge of the pursuers, no agreement exists between the parties prorogating jurisdiction over the subject-matter of the present cause to another court.

2. On 11 November 1993 the Sheriff of Tayside, Central and Fife at Dundee granted decree in favour of the pursuers against the second defender in the sum of £1,400, with interest and expenses. Extract decree is produced herewith. The second defender has made no payments to the pursuers in respect thereof. The total sum due by him to them, including the cost of the arrestment in execution hereinafter mentioned, is £1,520.

3. On 12 January 1994 the pursuers executed an arrestment by virtue of the said decree in the hands of the first defenders for the sum of £1,520, less or more. Execution of arrestment is produced herewith. The pursuers believe and aver that there has been attached by virtue of the said arrestment a sum of £2,000, or at any rate a sum sufficient to extinguish the second defender's liability to the pursuers. The second defender has signed no mandate in the pursuers' favour to enable them to uplift such sum as would extinguish liability aforesaid. This action is accordingly necessary.

PLEA-IN-LAW

The pursuers having used arrestments in the hands of the arrestees of the sums owing by them to the common debtor, are entitled to have same made furthcoming, so far as necessary, in satisfaction of his debt.

IN RESPECT WHEREOF

Enrolled solicitor
1 Charlotte Street
Edinburgh
Solicitor for the pursuers

17. PETE'S GARAGE LTD v HARRISON

Payment—Multiplepoinding (raised by party holding fund in medio)

a. Initial writ

> SHERIFFDOM OF LOTHIAN AND BORDERS
> AT EDINBURGH
>
> INITIAL WRIT
>
> *in the cause*
>
> PETE'S GARAGE LIMITED, a company with a place of business at Brougham Avenue, Edinburgh
>
> PURSUERS
>
> against
>
> ALVIN HARRISON, residing at 3 Brown Road, Edinburgh
>
> FIRST DEFENDER
>
> and
>
> MICHAEL ALAN JACKS, residing at 43 Maltby Drive, Edinburgh
>
> SECOND DEFENDER

The pursuers crave the court:

1. To grant decree for the delivery of a BMW motor car, registration number G65 FGP, or the distribution of the sale proceeds thereof, in favour of the party or parties found entitled thereto, and for the exoneration of the pursuers.
2. To find the defenders liable in the expenses of the action.

CONDESCENDENCE

1. The pursuers are a company incorporated under the Companies Acts with a place of business at Brougham Avenue, Edinburgh. The first

defender resides at 3 Brown Road, Edinburgh. The second defender resides at 43 Maltby Drive, Edinburgh. The present action is brought to obtain authority for the pursuers to dispose of moveable property (hereinafter referred to as 'the fund *in medio*') situated at Brougham Avenue, Edinburgh. This court accordingly has jurisdiction. To the knowledge of the pursuers, no proceedings are pending before any other court involving the present cause of action and between the parties hereto. To the knowledge of the pursuers, no agreement exists between the parties prorogating jurisdiction over the subject-matter of the present cause to another court.

2. The fund *in medio* is a BMW motor car registration number G65 FGP. The defenders are the only persons so far as known to the pursuers having an interest therein.

3. The pursuers have been in possession of the car since about 12 July 1994. It was delivered to them by the second defender for the purpose of carrying out repairs thereto. The first defender has claimed the car on the ground that it belongs to him. Both defenders have threatened to litigate against the pursuers. This action is accordingly necessary.

PLEA-IN-LAW

The pursuers being liable only in once and single delivery of the fund *in medio*, and questions having arisen as to the party now in right thereof, decree should be pronounced as craved.

IN RESPECT WHEREOF

Enrolled solicitor
41 Bank Square
Edinburgh
Solicitor for the pursuers

b. **Condescendence and claim (OCR 35.11(1))**

SHERIFFDOM OF LOTHIAN AND BORDERS
AT EDINBURGH

CONDESCENDENCE AND CLAIM

for the second defender

in the cause

PETE'S GARAGE LIMITED, a company with a place of business at Brougham Avenue, Edinburgh

PURSUERS

against

ALVIN HARRISON, residing at 3 Brown Road, Edinburgh

FIRST DEFENDER

and

MICHAEL ALAN JACKS, residing at 43 Maltby Drive, Edinburgh

SECOND DEFENDER

CONDESCENDENCE

The second defender is the owner of the car. He purchased it in good faith and for value from a Mr John Smith in about March 1994. Smith purchased it from the first defender. The first defender maintains that Smith stole it from him by virtue of having tendered a forged cheque therefor. The second defender contends that title to the car has passed. In these circumstances, the second defender

CLAIMS

to be ranked and preferred to the fund *in medio*.

PLEA-IN-LAW

The second defender being the owner of the said motor car, is entitled to be ranked and preferred thereto.

IN RESPECT WHEREOF

Enrolled solicitor
612 Charlotte Street
Edinburgh
Solicitor for the second defender

c. Minute of transference (OCR 25.2)

SHERIFFDOM OF LOTHIAN AND BORDERS
AT EDINBURGH

MINUTE OF
TRANSFERENCE

for the pursuers

in the cause

PETE'S GARAGE LIMITED, a company with a place of business at Brougham Avenue, Edinburgh

PURSUERS

against

ALVIN HARRISON, residing at 3 Brown Road, Edinburgh

FIRST DEFENDER

and

MICHAEL ALAN JACKS, residing at 43 Maltby Drive, Edinburgh

SECOND DEFENDER

The pursuers crave the court:

To grant leave for the cause, so far as directed against the first defender, to be transferred against Mrs Eleanor Harrison, residing at 3 Brown Road, Edinburgh, as representative of the estate of the first defender, now deceased.

STATEMENT OF FACTS

The first defender died on 14 August 1994. The representative of his estate is his widow, Mrs Eleanor Harrison, designed in the crave. The pursuers seek transference of the cause against her, as craved.

PLEA-IN-LAW

The said Eleanor Harrison being the representative of the estate of the first defender, now deceased, the cause should be transferred against her as craved.

IN RESPECT WHEREOF

Enrolled solicitor
41 Bank Square
Edinburgh
Solicitor for the pursuers

d. Motion for transference of cause against representative of defender's estate

SHERIFFDOM OF LOTHIAN AND BORDERS AT EDINBURGH

Court ref no A291/1994

MOTION FOR THE PURSUERS

in the cause

PETE'S GARAGE LIMITED, a company with a place of business at Brougham Avenue, Edinburgh

PURSUERS

against

ALVIN HARRISON, residing at 3 Brown Road, Edinburgh

FIRST DEFENDER

and

MICHAEL ALAN JACKS, residing at 43 Maltby Drive, Edinburgh

SECOND DEFENDER

The pursuers move the court to grant the crave of the minute.

Part of process lodged with the motion:

Minute of transference.

IN RESPECT WHEREOF

Enrolled solicitor
41 Bank Square
Edinburgh
Solicitor for the pursuers

18. KUMAR v RASHID

Payment—Multiplepoinding (raised by party not holding fund in medio)

a. Initial writ

SHERIFFDOM OF TAYSIDE, CENTRAL AND FIFE AT PERTH

INITIAL WRIT

in the cause

ASHRAF KUMAR, residing at 41 Alton View, Dundee

PURSUER

against

HANNAN RASHID, residing at 2 Abbey Park, Perth

FIRST DEFENDER

and

LATIF ASHTAR MAJEER, residing at 4 Black Place, Dundee

SECOND DEFENDER

The pursuer craves the court:

1. To grant decree for the distribution of the estate of the late Azzar Danif among the claimants found entitled thereto and for the exoneration of the first defender.
2. To find the second defender liable in the expenses of the action.

CONDESCENDENCE

1. The pursuer resides at 41 Alton View, Dundee. The first defender resides at 2 Abbey Park, Perth and is believed to be domiciled there. The second defender resides at 4 Black Place, Dundee and is believed to be domiciled there. The present action is brought to assert the pursuer's

proprietary rights in moveable property (hereinafter referred to as 'the fund *in medio*') situated in Perth. This court has jurisdiction. To the knowledge of the pursuer, no proceedings are pending before any other court involving the present cause of action and between the parties hereto. To the knowledge of the pursuer, no agreement exists between the parties prorogating jurisdiction over the subject-matter of the present cause to another court.

2. The fund *in medio* is the moveable estate of the late Azzar Danif (hereinafter referred to as 'the deceased') who died at Perth on 16 July 1991. The first defender is the representative of the deceased and holder of the fund *in medio*. The second defender is the son of the deceased and the only other person so far as known to the pursuer having an interest therein.

3. The pursuer is entitled to a share in the fund *in medio* by virtue of a testamentary writing of the deceased dated 5 November 1991, which is produced. The second defender contends that the writing has no legal validity *separatim* that on a proper interpretation it does not bestow such entitlement upon the pursuer. The pursuer is therefore under necessity of bringing the present action.

PLEA-IN-LAW

The pursuer being entitled to a share in the fund *in medio* and questions having arisen in respect thereof, is entitled to decree as craved.

IN RESPECT WHEREOF

        Enrolled solicitor
        1 Newtown Drive
        Dundee
        Solicitor for the pursuer

b. Condescendence and list (OCR 35.4(2))

SHERIFFDOM OF TAYSIDE, CENTRAL AND FIFE AT PERTH

CONDESCENDENCE AND LIST

for the first defender

in the cause

ASHRAF KUMAR, residing at 41 Alton View, Dundee

PURSUER

against

HANNAN RASHID, residing at 2 Abbey Park, Perth

FIRST DEFENDER

and

LATIF ASHTAR MAJEER, residing at 4 Black Place, Dundee

SECOND DEFENDER

CONDESCENDENCE

1. The fund *in medio* is as follows:
(a) £21,297 in Irish Bank plc deposit account number 4261587;
(b) 250 British Telecom shares;
(c) £621 premium bonds; and
(d) Ford Escort motor car, registration number J29 APQ.

2. The first defender states no claim or lien on the fund *in medio*.

LIST

The only persons known to the first defender to have an interest in the fund *in medio* are the pursuer and the second defender.

IN RESPECT WHEREOF

Enrolled solicitor
1 Exeter View
Perth
Solicitor for the first defender

c. Motion for approval of condescendence of fund (OCR 35.13(2))

SHERIFFDOM OF TAYSIDE, CENTRAL AND FIFE AT PERTH

Court ref no A25/1994

MOTION FOR THE FIRST DEFENDER

in the cause

ASHRAF KUMAR, residing at 41 Alton View, Dundee

PURSUER

against

HANNAN RASHID, residing at 2 Abbey Park, Perth

FIRST DEFENDER

and

LATIF ASHTAR MAJEER, residing at 4 Black Place, Dundee

SECOND DEFENDER

The first defender moves the court to approve the condescendence of the fund and find the first defender liable only in one single payment.

14 November 1994   IN RESPECT WHEREOF

Enrolled solicitor
1 Exeter View
Perth
Solicitor for the first defender

19. JENKINS v YOUNG

Ad factum praestandum—Implement—Missives for sale of heritage (seller pursuing action)—Plea to competency—Plea of exception

a. Initial writ

SHERIFFDOM OF NORTH STRATHCLYDE AT DUNOON

INITIAL WRIT

in the cause

GEORGE JENKINS and MRS MARGARET JENKINS, residing at 59 Lime Drive, Dunoon

PURSUERS

against

ALASTAIR GORDON YOUNG and MRS MARIA YOUNG, residing at 44 Ashton Terrace, Birmingham

DEFENDERS

The pursuers crave the court:

1. To ordain the defenders to implement their part of the missives of sale entered into between the parties dated 5, 9, 13 and 14 July 1993, whereby the pursuers agreed to sell and the defenders agreed to purchase at the price of £40,000 the subjects at 59 Lime Drive, Dunoon, and that by making payment to the pursuers, in exchange for delivery of a valid disposition of the said subjects executed by the pursuers in favour of the defenders, of the said sum of £40,000 with interest thereon at the rate of two *per centum per annum* above Eastern Bank plc's rate from time to time from 15 October 1993 until payment, and that within 14 days or such other period as to the court seems proper of the date of decree to follow hereon.

2. Alternatively, failing implement as aforesaid, to grant decree against the defenders jointly and severally for payment to the pursuers of the sum of SIX THOUSAND POUNDS (£6,000), with interest thereon at the rate of eight *per centum per annum* from the date of decree until payment.

3. To grant warrant for arrestment on the dependence of the action.

4. To find the defenders liable in the expenses of the action.

CONDESCENDENCE

1. The pursuers reside at 59 Lime Drive, Dunoon (hereinafter referred to as 'the subjects'). The defenders reside at 44 Ashton Terrace, Birmingham, They are believed to be domiciled there. The pursuers in the present action claim payment of the sum due to them by the defenders under and in terms of the contract hereinafter condescended on. This sum ought to have been paid by the defenders to the pursuers in Dunoon. This court accordingly has jurisdiction. To the knowledge of the pursuers, no proceedings are pending before any other court involving the present cause of action and between the parties hereto. To the knowledge of the pursuers, no agreement exists between the parties prorogating jurisdiction over the subject-matter of the present cause to another court.

2. By missives dated 5, 9, 13 and 14 July 1993, the pursuers agreed to sell and the defenders agreed to purchase the subjects at a price of £40,000, payable on 15 October 1993 with interest thereon at the rate of two *per centum per annum* above Eastern Bank plc's base rate from time to time until payment. The defenders failed to make payment of the said price on the said date. The pursuers have been and continue to be willing and able to execute a valid disposition of the subjects. Despite repeated requests for payment, the defenders refuse or at least delay to implement their part of the bargain. The pursuers accordingly seek decree for implement as first craved.

3. Alternatively, failing implement aforesaid, the pursuers will suffer loss and damage as a result of the defenders' breach of the said contract. They will require to re-advertise the subjects. They will incur further legal expenses in connection with re-sale of the subjects. The subjects are unlikely to command a price of more than about £35,000 upon re-sale. In these circumstances, the sum second craved is a reasonable estimate of the pursuers' loss and damage.

PLEAS-IN-LAW

1. The defenders being bound to implement the contract concluded between the parties in terms of the missives for the sale of the subjects, decree should be pronounced as first craved.

2. In the event of the defenders' failure to implement the said contract, they are liable in damages to the pursuers for the breach thereof, and the sum second craved being a reasonable estimate of the pursuers' loss and damage, decree therefor should be pronounced.

IN RESPECT WHEREOF

Enrolled solicitor
15 Doune Street
Dunoon
Solicitor for the pursuer

b. Defences

SHERIFFDOM OF NORTH STRATHCLYDE AT DUNOON

DEFENCES

in the cause

GEORGE JENKINS and MRS MARGARET JENKINS, residing at 59 Lime Drive, Dunoon

PURSUERS

against

ALASTAIR GORDON YOUNG and MRS MARIA YOUNG, residing at 44 Ashton Terrace, Birmingham

DEFENDERS

ANSWERS TO CONDESCENDENCE

1. Admitted.

2. Not known and not admitted that the pursuers have been and are willing to execute such disposition. *Quoad ultra* admitted. Explained and averred that the defenders entered into the said bargain in reliance upon certain representations on material matters made by the pursuers. In particular, on or about 6 May 1993, at a meeting at the subjects, the pursuers represented to the defenders that the roof of the subject had recently been renovated and was in good condition. They further represented that the subjects had not during the period of their ownership been afflicted with dry rot. These representations were false. No works had been executed to the roof for many years. It requires renovation works. The subjects had been infested with dry rot during said period, namely between about 1986 and about 1989. The defenders were induced to contract by these false representations. In these circumstances, the defenders are entitled to repudiate the bargain and are not bound to perform their obligations thereunder.

3. The nature and extent of any loss and damage sustained by the

pursuers are not known and not admitted. *Quoad ultra* denied. Explained and averred that the sum sued for is in any event excessive.

PLEAS-IN-LAW

1. A crave for payment of a lump sum in favour of separate pursuers being incompetent, the second crave should be dismissed.

2. The defenders having been induced to enter into the said bargain by false representations on material matters made by the pursuers, are entitled to have the same set aside by way of exception.

3. In any event, the sum sued for as reparation for the pursuers' alleged loss and damage being excessive, decree should not be granted as second craved.

IN RESPECT WHEREOF

Enrolled solicitor
45 Harkness Street
Dunoon
Solicitor for the defenders

c. Minute of amendment (crave)

SHERIFFDOM OF NORTH STRATHCLYDE AT DUNOON

MINUTE OF AMENDMENT

for the pursuers

in the cause

GEORGE JENKINS and MRS MARGARET JENKINS, residing at 49 Lime Drive, Dunoon

PURSUERS

against

ALASTAIR GORDON YOUNG and MRS MARIA YOUNG, residing at 44 Ashton Terrace, Birmingham

DEFENDERS

SMITH for the pursuers craved and hereby craves the court to allow the initial writ to be amended by deleting in the second crave 'the pursuers of the sum of £6,000' and substituting therefor 'each of the pursuers of the sum of £3,000'.

IN RESPECT WHEREOF

Enrolled solicitor
15 Doune Street
Dunoon
Solicitor for the pursuers

d. Motion for minute of amendment to be received and for amendment

SHERIFFDOM OF NORTH STRATHCLYDE AT DUNOON

Court ref no A21/1994

MOTION FOR THE PURSUERS

in the cause

GEORGE JENKINS and MRS MARGARET JENKINS, residing at 49 Lime Drive, Dunoon

PURSUERS

against

ALASTAIR GORDON YOUNG and MRS MARIA YOUNG, residing at 44 Ashton Terrace, Birmingham

DEFENDERS

The pursuers move the court to allow the minute of amendment, no 9 of process, to be received and to allow amendment in terms thereof.

Part of process lodged with the motion:

Minute of amendment

4 December 1994　　　　　　　　IN RESPECT WHEREOF

Enrolled solicitor
15 Doune Street
Dunoon
Solicitor for the pursuers

20. BLACKWOOD PROPERTIES LTD (IN RECEIVERSHIP) v DUNN

Ad factum praestandum—Implement—Missives for sale of heritage (buyer pursuing action)

a. Initial writ

SHERIFFDOM OF GRAMPIAN, HIGHLAND AND ISLANDS AT ABERDEEN

INITIAL WRIT

in the cause

BLACKWOOD PROPERTIES LIMITED, (IN RECEIVERSHIP), a company with a place of business at 3 The Glebe, Aberdeen

PURSUERS

against

RICHARD LEWIS DUNN, residing at 14 Regent Street, Aberdeen

DEFENDER

The pursuers crave the court:

1. To ordain the defender to implement his part of the missives of sale entered into between the parties dated 6 and 26 November 1993, whereby the pursuers agreed to buy and the defender agreed to sell at the price of £90,000 the subjects at 91 Hanover Street, Aberdeen, and that by executing and delivering to the pursuers, in terms of the said missives and upon payment by the pursuers of the said sum of £90,000, a valid disposition in the pursuers' favour of the said subjects at 91 Hanover Street, Aberdeen, and such other deeds as may be necessary to give the pursuers a valid title to the said subjects, and that within one month or such other period as to the court seems proper of the date of decree to follow hereon; and, failing implement as aforesaid, to dispense with such execution and delivery by the defender and to direct the sheriff clerk to execute such disposition and other deeds, if any, as adjusted at his sight, in the pursuers' favour.

2. Alternatively, to grant decree against the defender for payment to the pursuers of the sum of TEN THOUSAND POUNDS (£10,000),

with interest thereon at the rate of eight *per centum per annum* from the date of decree to follow hereon until payment.

3. To grant warrant to arrest on the dependence of the action.

4. To find the defender liable in the expenses of the action.

CONDESCENDENCE

1. The pursuers are a company incorporated under the Companies Acts, in receivership, with a place of business at 3 The Glebe, Aberdeen. The defender resides at 14 Regent Street, Aberdeen. He has been so resident for more than three months immediately preceding the raising of this action. He is domiciled there. This court accordingly has jurisdiction. To the knowledge of the pursuers, no proceedings are pending before any other court involving the present cause of action and between the parties hereto. To the knowledge of the pursuers, no agreement exists between the parties prorogating jurisdiction over the subject-matter of the present cause to another court.

2. By missives dated 6 and 26 November 1993 the pursuers agreed to buy and the defender agreed to sell the subjects at 91 Hanover Street, Aberdeen at a price of £90,000, with entry at 14 March 1993. The defender failed to give entry at the said date, or subsequently. He has failed to execute and deliver a valid disposition of the subjects. The pursuers have all along been and remain willing and able to pay the said price. Despite repeated requests, the defender refuses or at least delays to implement his part of the bargain. The pursuers accordingly seek decree for implement as first craved.

3. Alternatively, the pursuers seek damages as second craved. The subjects now have a market value of at least £100,000. In the event of non-implement of the contract, the pursuers will suffer loss and damage in the amount second craved.

PLEAS-IN-LAW

1. The defender being bound to implement the contract concluded between the parties in terms of the missives for the sale of the subjects, decree should be pronounced as first craved.

2. Failing implement aforesaid, the pursuers will suffer loss and damage and are entitled to reparation therefor in the sum second craved.

IN RESPECT WHEREOF

Enrolled solicitor
1 Hunter's Quay
Aberdeen
Solicitor for the pursuers

21. EAZEE CREDIT LTD v KHAN

Ad factum praestandum—Delivery—Payment—Damages—Debt—Hire-purchase—Interest from prior to citation

a. Initial writ

SHERIFFDOM OF GLASGOW AND STRATHKELVIN AT GLASGOW

INITIAL WRIT

in the cause

EAZEE CREDIT LIMITED, a company with its head office at Bath House, Faber Street, London

PURSUERS

against

ABDUL AZIZ KHAN, residing at 41 East Street, Glasgow

DEFENDER

The pursuers crave the court:

1. To ordain the defender to deliver to the pursuers a Ford Fiesta motor car, registration number C469 LSC, within 14 days of the date of decree to follow hereon or within such other period as the court thinks fit; and, failing delivery aforesaid, to grant warrant to officers of court to search for and take possession of the said motor car and deliver the same to the pursuers, and to that end to open shut and lockfast places; and, failing recovery of the said motor car, to grant decree against the defender for payment to the pursuers of the sum of THREE THOUSAND FIVE HUNDRED POUNDS (£3,500) with interest thereon at the rate of eight *per centum per annum* from the date of decree until payment.

2. To grant decree against the defender for payment to the pursuers of the sum of ONE THOUSAND SIX HUNDRED POUNDS (£1,600), with interest thereon at the rate of two *per centum per* month from 16 November 1993 until payment.

3. To grant warrant for arrestment on the dependence of the action.

4. To find the defender liable in the expenses of the action.

CONDESCENDENCE

1. The pursuers are a company incorporated under the Companies Acts with their head office at Bath House, Faber Street, London. The defender resides at 41 East Street, Glasgow. He has been so resident for more than three months immediately preceding the raising of this action. He is domiciled there. In any event, the pursuers in the present action claim payment of sums due to them by the defender under and in terms of the contract hereinafter condescended upon. These sums ought to have been paid by the defender at the pursuers' branch in Glasgow. This court accordingly has jurisdiction. To the knowledge of the pursuers, no proceedings are pending before any other court involving the present cause of action and between the parties hereto. To the knowledge of the pursuers no agreement exists between the parties prorogating jurisdiction over the subject-matter of the present cause to another court.

2. On or about 15 July 1992 the defender entered into a hire-purchase agreement with the pursuers (hereinafter 'the agreement') whereby he hired from them a Ford Fiesta motor car, registration number C469 LSC (hereinafter 'the vehicle') at a cost of £200 per month for a period of 24 months. Condition 2 of the agreement provides that overdue payments shall bear interest at the rate of 2 *per centum per* month from the due date until the date of payment. Condition 4(b) of the agreement provides that in the event of breach of contract on the part of the defender, the pursuers are entitled to terminate the agreement and recover possession of the vehicle.

3. The defender made payments under and in terms of the agreement until about 15 March 1993. Since then he has failed to make any payments. He is accordingly in breach of contract. By notice dated 16 November 1993 the pursuers terminated the agreement. They are therefore entitled to recover possession of the vehicle. Decree of delivery should be pronounced as craved. Failing such recovery, the pursuers seek reparation therefor in the sum sued for in the first crave. The said sum represents the pursuers' reasonable estimate of the value of the vehicle as at the date hereof.

4. As at 16 November 1993, the sum due by the defender under and in terms of the agreement was £1,600, which is the sum second craved.

5. The pursuers have repeatedly called upon the defender to return the vehicle and make payment of the said arrears. He refuses or at least delays to do so. This action is accordingly necessary.

PLEAS-IN-LAW

1. The pursuers having hired the said motor car to the defender, and the defender having failed to pay the hire therefor, the pursuers are entitled to decree for delivery thereof as first craved.

2. Failing delivery, the pursuers are entitled to reparation therefor, and the sum alternatively sued for in the first crave being reasonable, decree should be granted accordingly.

3. The sum second sued for being due and resting owing under and in

terms of the parties' contract as condescended on, decree should be granted in terms of the second crave.

IN RESPECT WHEREOF

Enrolled solicitor
1 Grant Street
Glasgow
Solicitor for the pursuers

22. ENGINEERING ACCESSORIES LTD v ROSS

Interdict—Breach of contract—Restrictive covenant

a. Initial writ

SHERIFFDOM OF GLASGOW AND STRATHKELVIN
AT GLASGOW

INITIAL WRIT

in the cause

ENGINEERING ACCESSORIES LIMITED, a company with its registered office at Mansion House, Old Road, Liverpool

PURSUERS

against

WILLIAM ROSS, residing at 56 Peach Drive, Glasgow

DEFENDER

The pursuers crave the court:

1. To interdict the defender either solely or jointly with or as manager or agent or officer or employee for any person, firm or company from directly or indirectly carrying on or being engaged or interested in any business supplying engineering accessories to industry within a radius of five miles from Unit 2, Avonhouse Industrial Estate, Glasgow until 28 March 1995; and to grant interdict *ad interim*.

2. To find the defender liable in the expenses of the action.

CONDESCENDENCE

1. The pursuers are a company incorporated under the Companies Acts with its registered office at Mansion House, Old Road, Liverpool. The defender resides at 56 Peach Drive, Glasgow. He has been so resident for at least three months immediately preceding the raising of this action. He is domiciled there. In any event, the pursuers seek interdict against the defender prohibiting him from committing a breach of his contract with them by carrying out certain activities, as detailed in the first crave, within the Sheriffdom of Glasgow and Strathkelvin. This

court accordingly has jurisdiction. To the knowledge of the pursuers, no proceedings are pending before any other court involving the present cause of action and between the parties hereto. To the knowledge of the pursuers no agreement exists between the parties prorogating jurisdiction over the subject-matter of the present cause to another court.

2. The pursuers have a depot at Unit 2, Avonhouse Industrial Estate, Glasgow. They carry on business as suppliers of engineering accessories to industry. They sell *inter alia* bearings, power transmission equipment, oil seals, O ring seals and industrial adhesives. Prior to 28 October 1994 they employed the defender as manager of their said depot. At the commencement of the said employment, the pursuers and the defender signed a contract of employment which *inter alia* provided as follows:

> '17. The Employee hereby undertakes to the Company that . . . (b) . . . he will not for a period of six months after the termination of his employment hereunder either solely or jointly with or as Manager or Agent or Officer or Employee for any person, firm or company directly or indirectly carry on or be engaged or interested in any business selling goods or services of the kind supplied by the Company within a radius of five miles of any depot or branch at which the Employee has been employed during the last twelve months of his employment with the Company.'

3. The defender's employment with the pursuers terminated, after notice, on 28 October 1994. Thereafter the defender commenced employment with Glasgow Engineering Services Ltd, Leith Street, Glasgow (hereinafter referred to as 'the company'). The company carries on business which is similar to the business of the pursuers. In particular, the company is engaged in the distribution of bearings, oil seals, and industrial adhesives to industry. The defender is employed by the company to carry out similar duties to those which he carried out on behalf of the pursuers. These duties are being carried out by the defender within a radius of five miles from the said depot at which he was employed during the last 12 months of his employment with the pursuers. The defender has been asked to cease his employment with the company but he refuses to do so. In these circumstances, the defender is in breach of clause 17(b) of the parties' contract and it is likely that he will continue to act in breach thereof. The defender had daily personal contact with the pursuers' customers. He is well placed to solicit business from them for his own purposes. In November 1994 he sought an order for engineering products from Amex Spares Ltd, customers of the pursuers, whose premises are within five miles of the pursuers' said depot. In these circumstances, the pursuers are under necessity of seeking an interdict in order to protect their business connections. In the meantime they seek interdict *ad interim*, which the balance of convenience favours. If the defender is not so restrained, the pursuers are liable to suffer serious loss of custom and thereby sustain substantial loss and damage.

PLEAS-IN-LAW

1. The defender being in breach of clause 17(b) of the contract as above set forth, and the pursuers being reasonably apprehensive that he will continue to act in breach thereof, interdict should be granted as craved.

2. Having regard to the balance of convenience, *interim* interdict should be granted as craved.

IN RESPECT WHEREOF

Enrolled solicitor
1 Shaw Road
Glasgow
Solicitor for the pursuers

23. BARTON v LONGSTONE GOLF CLUB

Interdict—Nuisance—Plea of prescription

a. Initial Writ

SHERIFFDOM OF TAYSIDE, CENTRAL AND FIFE AT DUNDEE

INITIAL WRIT

in the cause

ANDREW BARTON, residing at 14 Clark Road, Longstone, Dundee

PURSUER

against

LONGSTONE GOLF CLUB, Golf Course Road, Longstone, Dundee, and JOHN ARTHUR, residing at 14 Park Street, Dundee, Captain; ALASTAIR DOBBIE, residing at 44 Ashby Avenue, Dundee, Vice Captain; PETER JOHN JENNINGS, residing at 4 Dunning Grove, Dundee, Secretary; and EVAN PEARSON, residing at 41 Ivy Place, Dundee, Treasurer, office-bearers of the said club, as representatives of the club and as individuals

DEFENDERS

The pursuer craves the court:

1. To interdict the defenders from using the golf course at Golf Course Road, Longstone, Dundee, in a manner liable to interfere with the pursuer's use and enjoyment of his heritable property at 14 Clark Road, Longstone, Dundee and that by driving off or permitting others to drive off golf balls from a tee within the area hatched in blue in the Ordnance Survey plan annexed hereto in any direction between north and east,

inclusive, or otherwise so as to be likely to result in golf balls landing in the pursuer's said heritable property; and to grant interdict *ad interim*.

2. To find the defenders liable in the expenses of the action.

CONDESCENDENCE

1. The pursuer resides at 14 Clark Road, Longstone, Dundee. The first named defenders are a voluntary association, namely a club. They were formed under the law of Scotland. Their central management and control is exercised in Scotland. They have a place of business at Golf Course Road, Longstone, Dundee. They are domiciled there. This court accordingly has jurisdiction. The second to fifth defenders are the office-bearers of the club and reside, respectively, at the addresses set forth in the instance. To the knowledge of the pursuer, no proceedings are pending in any other court involving the present cause of action and between the parties hereto. To the knowledge of the pursuer no agreement exists between the parties prorogating jurisdiction over the subject-matter of the present cause to another court.

2. The pursuer is the heritable proprietor of the dwelling house and garden at the address at which he resides aforesaid. His property is immediately adjacent to the said golf course occupied by the defenders at Golf Course Road, Longstone, Dundee, conform to Ordnance Survey plan annexed hereto. The defenders organise and maintain the course for the purpose of golf play. The arrangement of the course, including the siting of the tees and holes, is within the control of the defenders. The fifth tee is sited within the area hatched in blue in the said plan about 120 yards west-south-west of the pursuer's property. The fifth hole on the said course lies about 250 yards north of that tee.

3. A significant proportion of golfers sometimes slice the ball to the right on driving off from a tee. Accordingly, many balls driven from within the said area have tended to veer to the east, landing in the pursuer's property. Each year in excess of 20 have done so. Consequently, the pursuer and his family residing with him have regularly been exposed to danger. In particular, on or about 15 March 1994, a golf ball narrowly missed the pursuer and struck the front door of his property. On or about 14 July 1994, a ball smashed a front window of the property, causing shards of glass to be scattered about the interior of the pursuer's living room.

4. The pursuer has requested the defenders to desist from driving off or permitting others to drive off from within the said area in any direction between north and east, inclusive. They refuse to comply with this request. In the circumstances, such use of the said golf course by the defenders constitutes a nuisance in respect that it interferes with the pursuer's use and enjoyment of his said heritable property. The pursuer seeks interdict as craved. Meantime, the balance of convenience favours the granting of interdict *ad interim*. The defenders could relocate the fifth tee elsewhere on the course, such as in a valley at present being infilled. The risk of injury to the pursuer and his family and of damage to his property is in the present circumstances substantial.

Interdict—Nuisance 185

PLEAS-IN-LAW

1. The use by the defenders of the said golf course constituting a nuisance, interdict should be granted as craved.
2. Having regard to the balance of convenience, interdict *ad interim* should be granted.

IN RESPECT WHEREOF

Enrolled solicitor
14 Bell Street
Dundee
Solicitor for the pursuer

b. Motion to allow defences to be received late

SHERIFFDOM OF TAYSIDE, CENTRAL AND FIFE AT DUNDEE

Court ref no A161/1994

MOTION FOR THE FIRST TO FIFTH DEFENDERS

in the cause

ANDREW BARTON, residing at 14 Clark Road, Longstone, Dundee

PURSUER

against

LONGSTONE GOLF CLUB, Golf Course Road, Longstone, Dundee, and JOHN ARTHUR, residing at 14 Park Street, Dundee, Captain; ALASTAIR DOBBIE, residing at 44 Ashby Avenue, Dundee, Vice Captain; PETER JOHN JENNINGS, residing at 4 Dunning Grove, Dundee, Secretary; and EVAN PEARSON, residing at 41 Ivy Place, Dundee, Treasurer, office-bearers of the said club, as representatives of the club and as individuals

DEFENDERS

The first to fifth defenders move the court to allow defences to be received late.

Part of process lodged with the motion:

Defences

14 September 1994   IN RESPECT WHEREOF

                           Enrolled solicitor
                           49 Stafford Road
                           Dundee
                           Solicitor for the first to fifth
                           defenders

c. Defences

SHERIFFDOM OF TAYSIDE, CENTRAL AND FIFE
AT DUNDEE

DEFENCES FOR THE FIRST
TO FIFTH DEFENDERS

in the cause

ANDREW BARTON, residing at 14 Clark Road, Longstone, Dundee

PURSUER

against

LONGSTONE GOLF CLUB, Golf Course Road, Longstone, Dundee, and JOHN ARTHUR, residing at 14 Park Street, Dundee, Captain; ALASTAIR DOBBIE, residing at 44 Ashby Avenue, Dundee, Vice Captain; PETER JOHN JENNINGS, residing at 4 Dunning Grove, Dundee, Secretary; and EVAN PEARSON, residing at 41 Ivy Place, Dundee, Treasurer, office-bearers of the said club, as representatives of the club and as individuals

DEFENDERS

ANSWERS TO CONDESCENDENCE

1. The designation of the defenders and the existence of jurisdiction are admitted. *Quoad ultra* not known and not admitted.
2. Admitted under reference to the plan for its terms.
3. Not known and not admitted that a significant proportion of golfers sometimes slice the ball to the right on driving off from a tee. Not known

and not admitted that incidents occurred on the said dates. *Quoad ultra* denied. Explained and averred that the course has been used in substantially the same manner for golf play since about 1968. In particular, the said fifth tee and hole have been sited in or about their present positions since then. None of the pursuer's predecessors in title complained about golf balls to the defenders during all that time. In these circumstances, *esto* golf balls have landed in the pursuer's property to such an extent as to constitute a nuisance (which is denied), such nuisance has existed for a continuous period of twenty years preceding the raising of this action.

4. Admitted that the pursuer has so requested the defenders. Admitted that they refuse to comply with this request. Admitted that the pursuer seeks interdict as craved. *Quoad ultra* denied. Explained and averred that *esto* the use of the said golf course by the defenders constitutes a nuisance (which is denied), the right to challenge such nuisance has subsisted for a continuous period of twenty years unexercised and unenforced and without any claim in relation to it having been made. Accordingly, such right has been extinguished by operation of prescription. Further explained and averred that the balance of convenience does not favour the granting of interdict *ad interim*. The said fifth tee could only be repositioned upon substantial redesign of the whole course. The granting of interdict *ad interim* would result in distress and substantial loss of enjoyment for the defenders and others using the course. The *status quo* should be maintained pending conclusion of these proceedings.

PLEAS-IN-LAW

1. The pursuer's averments being irrelevant *et separatim* being lacking in specification, the action should be dismissed.
2. The pursuer's right to challenge said alleged nuisance having prescribed, the defenders should be assoilzied.
3. The pursuer's averments so far as material being unfounded in fact, decree of absolvitor should be pronounced.
4. The use by the defenders of the said golf course not constituting a nuisance, interdict should not be granted as craved.
5. The balance of convenience not favouring interdict *ad interim*, such order should not be granted.

IN RESPECT WHEREOF

Enrolled solicitor
49 Stafford Road
Dundee
Solicitor for the first to fifth defenders

d. Motion for pursuer whose solicitor has withdrawn from acting to be ordained to appear or be represented at specified diet (OCR 24.2)

SHERIFFDOM OF TAYSIDE, CENTRAL AND FIFE
AT DUNDEE

Court ref no A161/1994

MOTION FOR THE FIRST TO
FIFTH DEFENDERS

in the cause

ANDREW BARTON, residing at 14 Clark Road, Longstone, Dundee

PURSUER

against

LONGSTONE GOLF CLUB, Golf Course Road, Longstone, Dundee, and JOHN ARTHUR, residing at 14 Park Street, Dundee, Captain; ALASTAIR DOBBIE, residing at 44 Ashby Avenue, Dundee, Vice Captain; PETER JOHN JENNINGS, residing at 4 Dunning Grove, Dundee, Secretary; and EVAN PEARSON, residing at 41 Ivy Place, Dundee, Treasurer, office-bearers of the said club, as representatives of the club and as individuals

DEFENDERS

The first to fifth defenders move the court to ordain the pursuer to appear or be represented at a specified diet fixed by the court to state whether or not he intends to proceed, under certification that if he fails to do so the court may grant decree of absolvitor or dismissal or make such other order or finding as it thinks fit.

1 November 1994　　　　　　　IN RESPECT WHEREOF

　　　　　　　　　　　　　　　Enrolled solicitor
　　　　　　　　　　　　　　　49 Stafford Road
　　　　　　　　　　　　　　　Dundee
　　　　　　　　　　　　　　　Solicitor for the first to fifth defenders

e. Note of adjustments

SHERIFFDOM OF TAYSIDE, CENTRAL AND FIFE
AT DUNDEE

NOTE OF ADJUSTMENTS

for the pursuer

in the cause

ANDREW BARTON, residing at 14 Clark Road, Longstone, Dundee

PURSUER

against

LONGSTONE GOLF CLUB, Golf Course Road, Longstone, Dundee, and JOHN ARTHUR, residing at 14 Park Street, Dundee, Captain; ALASTAIR DOBBIE, residing at 44 Ashby Avenue, Dundee, Vice Captain; PETER JOHN JENNINGS, residing at 4 Dunning Grove, Dundee, Secretary; and EVAN PEARSON, residing at 41 Ivy Place, Dundee, Treasurer, office-bearers of the said club, as representatives of the club and as individuals

DEFENDERS

1. Add at the end of article 3 of the condescendence the following:

'On or about 3 November 1994, the pursuer's car was hit by a golf ball in the driveway of his property. With reference to the averments in answer, not known and not admitted that the said fifth tee and hole have been sited in or about their present positions since about 1968.

Not known and not admitted that none of the pursuer's predecessors in title complained about golf balls to the defenders during all that time. *Quoad ultra* denied except insofar as coinciding herewith. Explained and averred that there has been a substantial increase in club membership since about 1991. The number of golfers playing the course has risen significantly. Before that date, only a handful of balls landed each year in the pursuer's property. In these circumstances, the nuisance complained of has not existed for a continuous period of twenty years preceding the raising of this action.'

2. Add at the end of article 4 of the condescendence the following:

'The averments in answer are denied.'

f. Record (OCR 9.11)

SHERIFFDOM OF TAYSIDE, CENTRAL AND FIFE
AT DUNDEE

RECORD

in the cause

ANDREW BARTON, residing at 14 Clark Road, Longstone, Dundee

PURSUER

against

LONGSTONE GOLF CLUB, Golf Course Road, Longstone, Dundee, and JOHN ARTHUR, residing at 14 Park Street, Dundee, Captain; ALASTAIR DOBBIE, residing at 44 Ashby Avenue, Dundee, Vice Captain; PETER JOHN JENNINGS, residing at 4 Dunning Grove, Dundee, Secretary; and EVAN PEARSON, residing at 41 Ivy Place, Dundee, Treasurer, office-bearers of the said club, as representatives of the club and as individuals

DEFENDERS

The pursuer craves the court:

1. To interdict the defenders from using the golf course at Golf Course Road, Longstone, Dundee, in a manner liable to interfere with the pursuer's use and enjoyment of his heritable property at 14 Clark Road, Longstone, Dundee and that by driving off or permitting others to drive off golf balls from a tee within the area hatched in blue in the Ordnance Survey plan annexed hereto in any direction between north and east,

inclusive, or otherwise so as to be likely to result in golf balls landing in the pursuer's said heritable property; and to grant interdict *ad interim*.

2. To find the defenders liable in the expenses of the action.

CONDESCENDENCE FOR PURSUER AND ANSWERS THERETO FOR DEFENDERS

COND. 1 The pursuer resides at 14 Clark Road, Longstone, Dundee. The first named defenders are a voluntary association, namely a club. They were formed under the law of Scotland. Their central management and control is exercised in Scotland. They have a place of business at Golf Course Road, Longstone, Dundee. They are domiciled there. This court accordingly has jurisdiction. The second to fifth defenders are the office-bearers of the club and reside, respectively, at the addresses set forth in the instance. To the knowledge of the pursuer, no proceedings are pending in any other court involving the present cause of action and between the parties hereto. To the knowledge of the pursuer no agreement exists between the parties prorogating jurisdiction over the subject-matter of the present cause to another court.

ANS. 1 for DEFENDERS. The designation of the defenders and the existence of jurisdiction are admitted. *Quoad ultra* not known and not admitted.

COND. 2 The pursuer is the heritable proprietor of the dwelling house and garden at the address at which he resides aforesaid. His property is immediately adjacent to the golf course occupied by the defenders at Golf Course Road, Longstone, Dundee, conform to Ordnance Survey plan annexed hereto. The defenders organise and maintain the course for the purpose of golf play. The arrangement of the course, including the siting of the tees and holes, is within the control of the defenders. The fifth tee is sited within the area hatched in blue in the said plan about 120 yards west-south-west of the pursuer's property. The fifth hole on the said course lies about 250 yards north of that tee.

ANS. 2 for DEFENDERS. Admitted under reference to the plan for its terms.

COND. 3 A significant proportion of golfers sometimes slice the ball to the right on driving off from a tee. Accordingly, many balls driven from within the said area have tended to veer to the east, landing in the pursuer's property. Each year in excess of 20 have done so. Consequently, the pursuer and his family residing with him have regularly been exposed to danger. In particular, on or about 15 March 1994, a golf ball narrowly missed the pursuer and struck the front door of his property. On or about 14 July 1994, a ball smashed a front window of the property causing shards of glass to be scattered about the interior of the pursuer's living room. On or about 3 November 1994, the pursuer's car was hit by a golf ball in the driveway of his property. With reference to the averments in answer, not known and not admitted that the said fifth tee and hole have been sited in or about their present positions since about

1968. Not known and not admitted that none of the pursuer's predecessors in title complained about golf balls to the defenders during all that time. *Quoad ultra* denied except insofar as coinciding herewith. Explained and averred that there has been a substantial increase in club membership since about 1991. The number of golfers playing the course has risen significantly. Before that date, only a handful of balls landed each year in the pursuer's property. In these circumstances, the nuisance complained of has not existed for a continuous period of twenty years preceding the raising of this action.

> ANS. 3 for DEFENDERS. Not known and not admitted that a significant proportion of golfers sometimes slice the ball to the right on driving off from a tee. Not known and not admitted that incidents occurred on the said dates. *Quoad ultra* denied. Explained and averred that the course has been used in substantially the same manner for golf play since about 1968. In particular, the said fifth tee and hole have been sited in or about their present positions since then. None of the pursuer's predecessors in title complained about golf balls to the defenders during all that time. In these circumstances, *esto* golf balls have landed in the pursuer's property to such an extent as to constitute a nuisance (which is denied), such nuisance has existed for a continuous period of twenty years preceding the raising of this action.

COND. 4 The pursuer has requested the defenders to desist from driving off or permitting others to drive off from a tee within the said area in any direction between north and east, inclusive. They refuse to comply with this request. In the circumstances, such use of the said golf course by the defenders constitutes a nuisance in respect that it interferes with the pursuer's use and enjoyment of his said heritable property. The pursuer seeks interdict as craved. Meantime, the balance of convenience favours the granting of interdict *ad interim*. The defenders could relocate the fifth tee elsewhere on the course, such as in a valley at present being infilled. The risk of injury to the pursuer and his family and of damage to his property is in the present circumstances substantial. The averments in answer are denied.

> ANS. 4 for DEFENDERS. Admitted that the pursuer has so requested the defenders. Admitted that they refuse to comply with this request. Admitted that the pursuer seeks interdict as craved. *Quoad ultra* denied. Explained and averred that *esto* the use of the said golf course by the defenders constitutes a nuisance (which is denied), the right to challenge such nuisance has subsisted for a continuous period of twenty years unexercised and unenforced and without any claim in relation to it having been made. Accordingly, such right has been extinguished by operation of prescription. Further explained and averred that the balance of convenience does not favour the granting of interdict *ad interim*. The said fifth tee could only be repositioned upon substantial redesign of the whole course. The granting of interdict *ad interim* would result in distress and substantial loss of enjoyment for the defenders and others using the course. The *status quo* should be maintained pending conclusion of these proceedings.

PLEAS-IN-LAW FOR PURSUER

1. The use by the defenders of the said golf course constituting a nuisance, interdict should be granted as craved.
2. Having regard to the balance of convenience, interdict *ad interim* should be granted.

IN RESPECT WHEREOF

Enrolled solicitor
2 Royal Drive
Dundee
Solicitor for the pursuer

PLEAS-IN-LAW FOR DEFENDERS

1. The pursuer's averments being irrelevant *et separatim* being lacking in specification, the action should be dismissed.
2. The pursuer's right to challenge said alleged nuisance having prescribed, the defenders should be assoilzied.
3. The pursuer's averments so far as material being unfounded in fact, decree of absolvitor should be pronounced.
4. The use by the defenders of the said golf course not constituting a nuisance, interdict should not be granted as craved.
5. The balance of convenience not favouring interdict *ad interim*, such order should not be granted.

IN RESPECT WHEREOF

Enrolled solicitor
49 Stafford Road
Dundee
Solicitor for the defenders

24. THE BREAD-BASKET v BREAD-BASKET LIMITED

Interdict—Passing off

a. Initial writ

SHERIFFDOM OF NORTH STRATHCLYDE AT PAISLEY

INITIAL WRIT

in the cause

JOHN WALLACE, residing at 2 Albert Place, Paisley and carrying on business under the name of 'THE BREAD-BASKET' at 35 Grove Street, Paisley

PURSUER

against

BREAD-BASKET LIMITED, a company with its registered office at 29 Alva Place, Carlisle

DEFENDERS

The pursuer craves the court:

1. To interdict the defenders and all others acting under their authority or on their behalf from passing off as being bread or other baked goods produced by the pursuer under the name of 'The Bread-basket' any bread or other baked goods supplied by the defenders and that by trading under the name of 'Bread-basket Limited' or any other name colourably similar thereto in Paisley, and otherwise; and to grant interdict *ad interim*.
2. To find the defenders liable in the expenses of the action.

CONDESCENDENCE

1. The pursuer resides at 2 Albert Place, Paisley. He carries on business under the name of 'The Bread-basket' at 35 Grove Street, Paisley. The defenders are a company incorporated under the Companies Acts with its registered office at 29 Alva Place, Carlisle. The pursuer seeks interdict against the defenders prohibiting them from passing off as being bread or other baked goods produced by the pursuer under the name of 'The Bread-basket' any bread or other baked goods supplied by them and that

by trading under the name of 'Bread-basket Limited' or any other name colourably similar thereto in Paisley, and otherwise. This court accordingly has jurisdiction. The pursuer is unaware of any proceedings pending before any other court involving the present cause of action and between the parties hereto. The pursuer is unaware of any agreement between the parties prorogating jurisdiction over the subject-matter of the present cause to another court.

2. The pursuer has carried on his said business at his shop premises at 35 Grove Street, Paisley since about 10 November 1986. He has specialised in the production and supply of high quality wholemeal bakery products. In addition to several varieties of brown bread, he bakes quiches, pizzas and a variety of patisserie at his shop premises. He has enjoyed a substantial retail trade there in the supply of his goods to members of the public. He has a substantial turnover and sizeable profits from such trade. He has also engaged in a considerable wholesale trade in the locality. He has for many years supplied bread and other baked goods to a number of restaurants and hotels in Paisley, including 'The Blackstone Inn', 'The Blanefield Hotel' and 'The Almaree Hotel'. He has derived significant profits therefrom also. The pursuer has acquired a high reputation with the general public and within the catering trade in Paisley for the production and supply of freshly baked wholemeal bread and other baked goods. The name of 'The Bread-basket' is well known to the public and the catering trade in Paisley. The name is associated in the minds of the public and the catering trade in Paisley with the pursuer's products. The pursuer has acquired substantial goodwill and business reputation in the said name.

3. On or about 4 July 1994, the defenders placed an advertisement for bakery staff in a publication named 'The British Baker'. Therein they stated *inter alia*: 'Due to our expansion, we are opening a shop in Paisley shortly . . .'. By letters dated 8 and 15 July and 3 August 1994, the pursuer's solicitors have sought to ascertain from the defenders the name under which they propose to trade at the said shop. No reply has been received to these letters.

4. In these circumstances, the pursuer is reasonably apprehensive that the defenders propose to engage in the bakery trade under the name 'Bread-basket Limited' in Paisley. Any such trade by the defenders would be likely to deceive the general public and others supplied by the pursuer as to the origin of the bread and other baked goods supplied by them. The general public and the catering trade in Paisley would be misled by the use of the name 'Bread-basket Limited' by the defenders in the course of trade into believing that they were being supplied with the pursuer's products. In these circumstances, the use by the defenders of the name 'Bread-basket Limited' or a colourably similar name in the course of trade would amount to a passing off by the defenders of goods supplied by them as those of the pursuer. The pursuer therefore seeks interdict as craved. In the meantime, he seeks interdict *ad interim*, which the balance of convenience favours. If the defenders are not so restrained, the pursuer's trade will be affected. His business reputation is liable to suffer in respect that the defenders' goods are unlikely to be of such high quality as his own. It is open to them to use another trading name.

PLEAS-IN-LAW

1. The pursuer being reasonably apprehensive that the defenders are about to pass off their goods as his, interdict should be granted as craved.

2. Having regard to the balance of convenience, interdict *ad interim* should be granted.

IN RESPECT WHEREOF

Enrolled solicitor
1 High Street
Paisley
Solicitor for the pursuer

III FAMILY PROCEEDINGS

1. PETERSON v PETERSON

Divorce—Adultery—Orders for financial provision—Capital sum—Incidental order

a. Initial writ
b. Defences
c. Note of adjustments
d. Record (OCR 9.11)
e. Motion for incidental order *pendente lite* (OCR 33.49(1))
f. Notice to admit (fact) (OCR 29.14(2))
g. Notice of non-admission (OCR 29.14(2)(a))
h. Motion for defender to be ordained to lead at diet of proof

2. TOMKINSON v TOMKINSON

Divorce—Unreasonable behaviour—Protective measure—Exclusion order—Property order—Transfer of tenancy—Custody order—Child accepted as one of the family

a. Initial writ
b. Affidavit of pursuer (OCR 33.27)
c. Affidavit of witness (OCR 33.27)
d. Motion for interim order suspending occupancy rights (OCR 33.69(1)(b))
e. Motion for interim custody (OCR 33.43(a)(ii))
f. Supplementary affidavit of pursuer
g. Supplementary affidavit of witness

3. BELL v BELL

Divorce—Desertion—Defender's whereabouts not known

a. Initial writ (including minute for decree)
b. Affidavit of pursuer
c. Affidavit of witness

4. WHITE v WHITE

Divorce—Two years non-cohabitation and defender's consent—Child in care

a. Initial writ

5. WILKES v WILKES

Divorce—Five years non-cohabitation—Orders for financial provision—Transfer of property—Capital sum—Periodical allowance—Incidental orders

a. Initial writ
b. Defences
c. Motion for order for provision of details of resources
d. Specification of documents (OCR 28.2(2))
e. Joint minute of agreement (OCR 33.26)

6. BARTON v BARTON

Separation—Unreasonable behaviour—Protective measures—Matrimonial interdict—Power of arrest

a. Initial writ
b. Minute of abandonment (OCR 23.1(1)(b))
c. Motion for defender to be ordained to lodge an account of expenses
d. Motion for decree of dismissal

7. JOHNSON v JOHNSON

Aliment (husband and wife)

a. Initial writ
b. Motion for interim aliment (OCR 33.58(1))
c. Motion for sist for legal aid

8. JONES v JONES

Aliment (husband and wife)—Variation of agreement on aliment

a. Initial writ (OCR 33.59(1))

9. JACKSON v POLLOCK

Children—Parentage—Declarator of parentage

a. Initial writ (including minute of decree)
b. Affidavit of pursuer
c. Affidavit of witness

10. HEPWORTH v HEPWORTH

Children—Custody order—Access

a. Initial writ
b. Defences

c. Motion for warrant for intimation (OCR 33.15(2))
d. Motion for interim access (OCR 33.43(a))
e. Motion for leave to appeal
f. Motion for defender to be ordained to appear at the bar
g. Minute of variation (OCR 33.44(1)(a))

11. BLANE v BLANE

Children—Custody order—Custody and delivery—Interdict against removal of child—Order to disclose child's whereabouts—Defender's whereabouts not known—Child's whereabouts not known

a. Initial writ
b. Motion for order to disclose child's whereabouts (OCR 33.23(1))
c. Motion for interim interdict prohibiting removal of child from jurisdiction (OCR 33.24(1)(a))
d. Motion for warrant for intimation or to dispense with intimation (OCR 33.7(6))

12. BLACK v BLACK

Matrimonial home—Dispensation with spouse's consent to dealing

a. Initial writ (OCR 33.67(2))

1. PETERSON v PETERSON

Divorce—Adultery—Orders for financial provision—Capital sum—Incidental order

a. Initial writ

SHERIFFDOM OF SOUTH STRATHCLYDE, DUMFRIES AND GALLOWAY AT AIRDRIE

INITIAL WRIT

in the cause

NORMAN PETERSON (Assisted Person), residing at 51 Hawthorne Place, Airdrie

PURSUER

against

MRS OLIVIA HARVEY or PETERSON, residing at 161 Knightley Park, Hamilton

DEFENDER

The pursuer craves the court:

1. To divorce the defender from the pursuer on the ground that the marriage has broken down irretrievably as established by the defender's adultery.

2. To grant warrant to intimate this initial writ to John Lowe Prescott, residing at 161 Knightley Park, Hamilton as a person with whom the defender is alleged to have committed adultery.

3. To find the defender liable in the expenses of the action.

CONDESCENDENCE

1. The parties were married at Kilmarnock on 14 July 1981. They have no children. Extract certificate of marriage is produced.

2. The pursuer was born in Scotland of Scottish parents. He intends to live permanently in Scotland. He is domiciled in Scotland. He has been resident within the Sheriffdom of South Strathclyde, Dumfries and Galloway for a period exceeding 40 days immediately preceding the raising

of this action. He is unaware of any proceedings continuing in Scotland or elsewhere which are in respect of the marriage or are capable of affecting its validity or subsistence.

3. After their marriage the parties lived together until about 21 July 1993. Since then they have not lived together nor had marital relations.

4. The marriage has broken down irretrievably as established by the defender's adultery. The defender has formed an adulterous relationship with John Lowe Prescott, designed in the second crave. Since about September 1993, they have cohabited at 161 Knightley Park, Hamilton. In particular, they stayed alone overnight at the said address on or about 16 October 1993. They associate together in public as man and wife. In the circumstances, the pursuer seeks decree of divorce.

PLEA-IN-LAW

The marriage having broken down irretrievably, the pursuer is entitled to decree of divorce as craved.

IN RESPECT WHEREOF

Enrolled solicitor
41 Leven Street
Airdrie
Solicitor for the pursuer

b. Defences

SHERIFFDOM OF SOUTH STRATHCLYDE, DUMFRIES AND GALLOWAY AT AIRDRIE

DEFENCES

in the cause

NORMAN PETERSON (Assisted Person), residing at 51 Hawthorne Place, Airdrie

PURSUER

against

MRS OLIVIA HARVEY or PETERSON (Assisted Person), residing at 161 Knightley Park, Hamilton

DEFENDER

The defender craves the court:

To grant decree against the pursuer for payment to the defender of a capital sum of TWO THOUSAND SEVEN HUNDRED AND FIFTY POUNDS (£2,750), payable at such date and by such method as the court thinks fit, with interest thereon at the rate of eight *per centum per annum* from such date as the court deems proper until payment.

ANSWERS TO CONDESCENDENCE

1. Admitted.
2. Believed to be true. The defender knows of no such proceedings.
3. Admitted.
4. No admission is made. Explained and averred that the defender seeks a capital sum as craved. As at the date of the parties' separation, they had matrimonial property as hereinafter condescended on. They owned jointly the matrimonial home at 51 Hawthorne Place, Airdrie, together with the furniture and furnishings therein. The said household contents

are reasonably valued as at the said date at about £3,000. The pursuer has retained the said items and the defender is content that he should keep them. At the said date, the pursuer had savings of about £1,000 and a life insurance policy. The defender is unaware of the precise value of the proportion of the pursuer's interest in the said policy referable to the period between the date of the marriage and the relevant date. She estimates the same at £1,500 or thereby. The defender seeks a fair sharing of the value of the said household contents, savings and policy. The defender has no resources other than her said interest in the matrimonial home. She is unaware of the pursuer's current resources. In the circumstances, decree should be granted as craved.

PLEA-IN-LAW

The order craved for payment of a capital sum representing a fair sharing of the net value of the matrimonial property, decree therefor should be granted.

IN RESPECT WHEREOF

Enrolled solicitor
192 High Street
Hamilton
Solicitor for the defender

c. Note of adjustments

SHERIFFDOM OF SOUTH STRATHCLYDE, DUMFRIES AND GALLOWAY AT AIRDRIE

NOTE OF ADJUSTMENTS

for the pursuer

in the cause

NORMAN PETERSON (Assisted Person), residing at 51 Hawthorne Place, Airdrie

PURSUER

against

MRS OLIVIA HARVEY or PETERSON (Assisted Person), residing at 161 Knightley Park, Hamilton

DEFENDER

1. Add at the end of article 4 of the condescendence:

'With reference to the defender's averments in answer, it is admitted that the defender seeks a capital sum. Admitted that at the date of separation the parties jointly owned the said matrimonial home. Admitted that at the said date the parties had furniture and furnishings therein, under explanation that the value thereof is not known and not admitted. Admitted that the pursuer has retained the said items. Admitted that at the said date the pursuer had savings, under explanation that the total thereof was £769. Admitted that the pursuer had a life insurance policy, under explanation that the value of the pursuer's interest attributable to the said period is not known and not admitted. Not known and not admitted what resources the defender currently has. *Quoad ultra* denied except insofar as coinciding herewith. Explained and averred that certain of the said household contents are subject to hire-purchase agreements in respect of which payments totalling about £500 were outstanding at the relevant date. At the said date the pursuer had an overdraft on his bank current account of about £500. The said policy has a present surrender value of about £600. The pursuer has now expended his savings *inter alia* to pay off his overdraft. In the whole circumstances, no capital sum should be awarded. *Esto* (which is denied) an award of a capital sum is justified and reasonable, the sum sued for is excessive.'

2. Add a new plea-in-law as follows:

'2. The order craved for payment of a capital sum not representing a fair sharing of the net value of the matrimonial property, decree therefor should be refused'.

d. Record (OCR 9.11)

SHERIFFDOM OF SOUTH STRATHCLYDE, DUMFRIES AND GALLOWAY AT AIRDRIE

RECORD

in the cause

NORMAN PETERSON (Assisted Person), residing at 51 Hawthorne Place, Airdrie

PURSUER

against

MRS OLIVIA HARVEY or PETERSON (Assisted Person), residing at 161 Knightley Park, Hamilton

DEFENDER

The pursuer craves the court:

1. To divorce the defender from the pursuer on the ground that the marriage has broken down irretrievably as established by the defender's adultery.
2. To grant warrant to intimate this initial writ to John Lowe Prescott, residing at 161 Knightley Park, Hamilton as a person with whom the defender is alleged to have committed adultery.
3. To find the defender liable in the expenses of the action.

The defender craves the court:

To grant decree against the pursuer for payment to the defender of a capital sum of TWO THOUSAND SEVEN HUNDRED AND FIFTY POUNDS (£2,750), payable at such date and by such method as the court thinks fit, with interest thereon at the rate of eight *per centum per annum* from such date as the court deems proper until payment.

CONDESCENDENCE FOR PURSUER AND ANSWERS THERETO FOR DEFENDER

COND. 1 The parties were married at Kilmarnock on 14 July 1981. They have no children. Extract certificate of marriage is produced.

ANS. 1 for DEFENDER. Agreed

COND. 2 The pursuer was born in Scotland of Scottish parents. He intends to live permanently in Scotland. He is domiciled in Scotland. He has been resident within the Sheriffdom of South Strathclyde, Dumfries and Galloway for a period exceeding 40 days immediately preceding the raising of this action. He is unaware of any proceedings continuing in Scotland or elsewhere which are in respect of the marriage or are capable of affecting the validity or subsistence.

ANS. 2 for DEFENDER. Believed to be true. The defender knows of no such proceedings.

COND. 3 After their marriage the parties lived together until about 21 July 1993. Since then they have not lived together nor had marital relations.

ANS. 3 for DEFENDER. Admitted.

COND. 4 The marriage has broken down irretrievably as established by the defender's adultery. The defender has formed an adulterous relationship with John Lowe Prescott, designed in the second crave. Since about September 1993, they have cohabited at 161 Knightley Park, Hamilton. In particular, they stayed alone overnight at the said address on or about 16 October 1993. They associate together in public as man and wife. In the circumstances, the pursuer seeks decree of divorce. With reference to the averments in answer, it is admitted that the defender seeks a capital sum. Admitted that at the date of separation the parties jointly owned the said matrimonial home. Admitted that at the said date the parties had furniture and furnishings therein, under explanation that the value thereof is not known and not admitted. Admitted that the pursuer has retained the said items. Admitted that at the said date the pursuer had savings, under explanation that the total thereof was £769. Admitted that the pursuer had a life insurance policy, under explanation that the value of the pursuer's interest attributable to the said period is not known and not admitted. Not known and not admitted what resources the defender currently has. *Quoad ultra* denied except insofar as coinciding herewith. Explained and averred that certain of the said household contents are subject to hire-purchase agreements in respect of which payments totalling about £500 were outstanding at the relevant date. At the said date the pursuer had an overdraft on his bank current account of about £500. The said policy has a present surrender value of about £600. The pursuer has now expended his savings *inter alia* to pay off his overdraft. In the whole circumstances, no capital sum should be awarded. *Esto* (which is denied) an award of a capital sum is justified and reasonable, the sum sued for is excessive.

ANS. 4 for DEFENDER. No admission is made anent the averments of adultery. The pursuer's averment anent expenditure is not known and not admitted. *Quoad ultra* denied except insofar as coinciding herewith. Explained and averred that the defender seeks a capital sum as craved. As at the date of the parties' separation aforesaid, the parties had matrimonial property as hereinafter condescended on. They owned jointly the matrimonial home at 51 Hawthorne Place, Airdrie, together with the furniture and furnishings therein. The said household contents are reasonably valued as at the said date at about £3,000. The pursuer has retained the said items and the defender is content that he should keep them. At the said date, the pursuer had savings of about £1,000 and a life insurance policy. The defender is unaware of the precise value of the proportion of the pursuer's interest in the said policy referable to the period between the date of the marriage and the relevant date. She estimates same at £1,500 or thereby. The defender seeks a fair sharing of the value of the said household contents, savings and policy. The defender has no resources other than her said interest in the matrimonial home. She is unaware of the pursuer's current resources. In the circumstances, decree should be granted as craved.

PLEAS-IN-LAW FOR PURSUER

1. The marriage having broken down irretrievably, the pursuer is entitled to decree of divorce as craved.
2. The order craved for payment of a capital sum not representing a fair sharing of the net value of the matrimonial property, decree therefor should be refused.

IN RESPECT WHEREOF

Enrolled solicitor
41 Leven Street
Airdrie
Solicitor for the pursuer

PLEA-IN-LAW FOR DEFENDER

The order craved for payment of a capital sum representing a fair sharing of the net value of the matrimonial property, decree therefor should be granted.

IN RESPECT WHEREOF

Enrolled solicitor
192 High Street
Hamilton
Solicitor for the defender

e. Motion for incidental order *pendente lite* (OCR 33.49(1))

SHERIFFDOM OF SOUTH STRATHCLYDE, DUMFRIES AND GALLOWAY AT AIRDRIE

Court ref no C29/1994

MOTION FOR THE DEFENDER

in the cause

NORMAN PETERSON (Assisted Person), residing at 51 Hawthorne Place, Airdrie

PURSUER

against

MRS OLIVIA HARVEY or PETERSON (Assisted Person), residing at 161 Knightley Park, Hamilton

DEFENDER

The defender moves the court to grant an incidental order for the sale of the heritable property at 51 Hawthorne Place, Airdrie; to that end, to grant warrant to Thomas Barton, Chartered Surveyor, 4 Main Square, Airdrie, or such other person as the court shall think fit, to dispose of the subjects in such manner and under such conditions as the court shall direct; and to ordain the parties to execute and deliver such disposition and other deeds as shall be necessary to give a valid title to the subjects to the purchaser or purchasers thereof, which failing to authorise the sheriff clerk to execute such disposition and deeds, as adjusted at his sight.

4 August 1994   IN RESPECT WHEREOF

Enrolled solicitor
192 High Street
Hamilton
Solicitor for the defender

f. Notice to admit (fact) (OCR 29.14(1)(a))

SHERIFFDOM OF SOUTH STRATHCLYDE, DUMFRIES AND GALLOWAY AT AIRDRIE

NOTICE TO ADMIT

for the defender

in the cause

NORMAN PETERSON (Assisted Person), residing at 51 Hawthorne Place, Airdrie

PURSUER

against

MRS OLIVIA HARVEY or PETERSON (Assisted Person), residing at 161 Knightley Park, Hamilton

DEFENDER

To: Norman Peterson, Pursuer.

The defender calls upon you to admit for the purposes of this action only the following facts:

(i) that as at the relevant date the contents of the matrimonial home had a value of £3,000; and

(ii) that the value of the proportion of the interest of the pursuer in his life insurance policy referable to the period between the date of the marriage and the relevant date is £1,500.

15 September 1994   IN RESPECT WHEREOF

Enrolled solicitor
192 High Street
Hamilton
Solicitor for the defender

g. Notice of non-admission (OCR 29.14(2)(a))

SHERIFFDOM OF SOUTH STRATHCLYDE, DUMFRIES AND GALLOWAY AT AIRDRIE

NOTICE OF NON-ADMISSION

for the pursuer

in the cause

NORMAN PETERSON (Assisted Person), residing at 51 Hawthorne Place, Airdrie

PURSUER

against

MRS OLIVIA HARVEY or PETERSON (Assisted Person), residing at 161 Knightley Park, Hamilton

DEFENDER

To: Mrs Olivia Harvey or Peterson, Defender

The pursuer hereby states that he does not admit the facts specified in the notice to admit dated 15 September 1994.

30 September 1994 IN RESPECT WHEREOF

Enrolled solicitor
41 Leven Street
Airdrie
Solicitor for the pursuer

h. Motion for defender to be ordained to lead at diet of proof

SHERIFFDOM OF SOUTH STRATHCLYDE, DUMFRIES AND GALLOWAY AT AIRDRIE

Court ref no C29/1994

MOTION FOR THE PURSUER

in the cause

NORMAN PETERSON (Assisted Person), residing at 51 Hawthorne Place, Airdrie

PURSUER

against

MRS OLIVIA HARVEY or PETERSON (Assisted Person), residing at 161 Knightley Park, Hamilton

DEFENDER

The pursuer moves the court to ordain the defender to lead at the diet of proof.

10 November 1994   IN RESPECT WHEREOF

Enrolled solicitor
41 Leven Street
Airdrie
Solicitor for the pursuer

2. TOMKINSON v TOMKINSON

Divorce—Unreasonable behaviour—Protective measure—Exclusion order—Property order—Transfer of tenancy—Custody order

a. Initial writ (including minute for decree)

SHERIFFDOM OF GLASGOW AND STRATHKELVIN
AT GLASGOW

INITIAL WRIT

in the cause

MRS JOYCE BROWN or TOMKINSON (Assisted Person), residing at 33 Horne Street, Glasgow

PURSUER

against

BRIAN TOMKINSON, residing at 33 Horne Street, Glasgow

DEFENDER

The pursuer craves the court:

1. To divorce the defender from the pursuer on the ground that the marriage has broken down irretrievably as established by the defender's behaviour.

2. (1) To grant an exclusion order suspending the defender's occupancy rights in the matrimonial home at 33 Horne Street, Glasgow; (2) to grant warrant for the summary ejection of the defender from the said matrimonial home; (3) to interdict the defender from entering the said matrimonial home without the express permission of the pursuer; and to grant interim interdict; and to attach a power of arrest to the said interdict and interim interdict; and (4) to interdict the defender from removing, except with the written consent of the pursuer or by a further order of the court, any furniture or plenishings in the said matrimonial home; and to grant interim interdict.

3. To grant decree for the transfer of the tenancy of the said matrimonial home from the defender to the pursuer.

4. To find the pursuer entitled to the custody of Alan Brown (known as Alan Tomkinson), child of the pursuer accepted as one of the family by the defender and under the age of 16 years.

5. To grant warrant to intimate this initial writ to (1) Colin Brown, residing at 14 The Grove, Paisley, father of the said Alan Brown (known as Alan Tomkinson); (2) Alva Housing Association, 15 Hope Street, Glasgow, landlords of the said matrimonial home; and (3) Alan Brown (known as Alan Tomkinson), aforesaid, residing at 33 Horne Street, Glasgow, as a child who is affected by this action.

6. To find the defender liable in the expenses of the action.

CONDESCENDENCE

1. The parties were married at Glasgow on 16 November 1992. There are no children of the marriage. The pursuer has a child accepted as one of the family by the defender: Alan Brown (known as Alan Tomkinson), born 29 July 1983. The natural father of the said child is Colin Brown, designed in the fifth crave. Extract certificates of marriage and birth are produced.

2. The pursuer has been habitually resident in Scotland for at least 12 months immediately preceding the raising of this action. She has been resident in the Sheriffdom of Glasgow and Strathkelvin for a period exceeding 40 days immediately preceding the raising of this action. She knows of no proceedings continuing or concluded in Scotland or elsewhere relating to the said child. She knows of no proceedings continuing in Scotland or elsewhere which are in respect of the marriage or capable of affecting its validity or subsistence.

3. The marriage has broken down irretrievably as established by the defender's behaviour. He has been drinking regularly to excess. He has frequently returned home drunk, particularly late at night. He has been abusive and aggressive towards the pursuer there, especially when he has been drinking. He has assaulted her in the matrimonial home on several occasions. In particular, on or about 15 November 1993, the defender punched the pursuer in the chest, causing her to sustain severe bruising. On or about 19 December 1993, he struck her on the head and shoulders. On or about 19 January 1994, he punched her in the face. In these circumstances, the pursuer cannot reasonably be expected to cohabit with the defender. She seeks decree of divorce.

4. The pursuer seeks an exclusion order and related remedies as second craved. The parties continue to reside together in the matrimonial home at 33 Horne Street, Glasgow. The defender has the tenancy thereof. The landlords are Alva Housing Association, designed in the fifth crave. An exclusion order is necessary for the protection of the health of the pursuer. She has good reason to fear a repetition of the aforementioned assaults upon her. The defender continues to drink to excess. In the circumstances, and under reference to the averments in the following article of condescendence, such an order and related remedies should be granted.

5. The pursuer seeks an order in terms of the third crave for the transfer of the said tenancy to her. Such would be just and reasonable in the

circumstances. The defender has offered no alternative accommodation to the pursuer. He could reside with his father or obtain accommodation elsewhere. The pursuer and the said child are accustomed to the matrimonial home as their residence. The said child attends the local school and is happy there. To remove elsewhere might involve a change of school for the said child. The pursuer receives state benefits. In the event of the pursuer acquiring the said tenancy, she would receive local authority assistance for payment of the rent, as the defender presently does. She is a suitable person to be the tenant of the matrimonial home. In the whole circumstances, decree should be granted as third craved.

6. The pursuer seeks custody of the said child. The pursuer has always looked after him. He is well cared for. It is in his best interests to be in the custody of the pursuer as fourth craved.

PLEAS-IN-LAW

1. The marriage of the parties having broken down irretrievably, decree of divorce should be pronounced.

2. An exclusion order being necessary for the protection of the health of the pursuer from conduct of the defender, an exclusion order suspending the defender's occupancy rights, and orders ancillary thereto, should be granted as craved.

3. It being just and reasonable that the said tenancy should be transferred from the defender to the pursuer, decree therefor should be granted as craved.

4. It being in the best interests of the said child to be in the custody of the pursuer, decree therefor should be granted.

IN RESPECT WHEREOF

Enrolled solicitor
15 Albany Street
Glasgow
Solicitor for the pursuer

BLOTT for the pursuer having considered the evidence contained in the affidavits and the other documents all as specified in the schedule hereto and being satisfied that upon the evidence a motion for decree in terms of the first, third, fourth and sixth craves of the initial writ may properly be made, moves the court accordingly.

IN RESPECT WHEREOF

Solicitor for the pursuer

SCHEDULE

1. Affidavit of the pursuer.
2. Supplementary affidavit of the pursuer.
3. Affidavit of Henrietta Blyth.
4. Supplementary affidavit of Henrietta Blyth.
5. Marriage certificate no. 7 of process.
6. Birth certificate no. 8 of process.
7. Medical report no. 11 of process.

b. Affidavit of pursuer

SHERIFFDOM OF GLASGOW AND STRATHKELVIN
AT GLASGOW

AFFIDAVIT

of the pursuer

in the cause

MRS JOYCE BROWN or TOMKINSON (Assisted Person), residing at 33 Horne Street, Glasgow

PURSUER

against

BRIAN TOMKINSON, residing at 33 Horne Street, Glasgow

DEFENDER

At Glasgow the Fourth day of February Nineteen Hundred and Ninety Four in the presence of IAN BLOTT, Solicitor and Notary Public, 15 Albany Street, Glasgow compeared MRS JOYCE BROWN or TOMKINSON, residing at 33 Horne Street, Glasgow, who being solemnly sworn depones as follows:

1. I am Joyce Brown or Tomkinson, I am 31 years of age and live at 33 Horne Street, Glasgow with my husband Brian Tomkinson, the defender in this action. He is the tenant of the matrimonial home.

2. I swear this affidavit in support of my application for an interim order suspending occupancy rights in the matrimonial home and related remedies against my husband. My husband has been drinking regularly to excess and beating me. He often comes home drunk. He gives me dog's abuse and is aggressive towards me. He has beaten me up several times. Once, on 15 November 1993, he punched me very hard in the chest. I was badly bruised, as the medical report from my general practitioner confirms. Just over a month later, on 19 December, after another

drinking session, he hit me on the head and shoulders. Exactly a month later, he punched me in the face. All these incidents took place at home. I know that he is going to attack me again some time soon when he has had a good drink and is in the mood to give me a beating. Nothing less than excluding him from the house can protect me, I am convinced.

3. I am unemployed and receive state benefits. My husband has not offered me alternative accommodation. He could go and live with his father or rent digs somewhere. I have to think about my son. Like me, he is used to the house. The local school is across the road. If we had to move, he might have to change school which would be a pity. I understand that if I were to take over the tenancy of the house, I would receive local authority assistance for payment of the rent, as my husband has done.

All of which is truth as the deponent shall answer to God.

.... DEPONENT

.... NOTARY PUBLIC

c. Affidavit of witness

SHERIFFDOM OF GLASGOW AND STRATHKELVIN
AT GLASGOW

AFFIDAVIT

of Henrietta Blyth

in the cause

MRS JOYCE BROWN or TOMKINSON (Assisted Person), residing at 33 Horne Street, Glasgow

PURSUER

against

BRIAN TOMKINSON, residing at 33 Horne Street, Glasgow

DEFENDER

At Glasgow the Fourth day of February Nineteen Hundred and Ninety Four in the presence of IAN BLOTT, Solicitor and Notary Public, 15 Albany Street, Glasgow compeared HENRIETTA BLYTH, residing at 31 Horne Street, Glasgow, who being solemnly sworn depones as follows:

1. I am Henrietta Blyth. I am 34 years of age and reside at 31 Horne Street, Glasgow.
2. I live next door to Brian, Joyce and Alan Tomkinson. I am very friendly with Joyce and see her virtually every day. We tend to have coffee together in the mornings in either my house or hers. I have come to know a great deal about her married life. I can confirm that she is under a great deal of strain at present. Her husband is a heavy drinker and a bully. I have often seen him abusing Joyce, calling her names, especially when he's drunk. He really is a foul man in every way. He has obviously been beating her as well. I recall seeing her in a state of distress in mid-November 1993 after he had punched her in the chest. I saw severe

bruising on Joyce's chest for weeks afterwards. She also told me of assaults in December and January just after they had happened. She was very distressed. I do not know how she can stand living with him. I know that Joyce is finding it all too much. I think her health is at risk. I support her in her application to have her husband excluded from the house.

All of which is truth as the deponent shall answer to God.

.... DEPONENT

.... NOTARY PUBLIC

d. Motion for interim order suspending occupancy rights (OCR 33.69(1)(b))

SHERIFFDOM OF GLASGOW AND STRATHKELVIN
AT GLASGOW

Court ref no C21/1994

MOTION FOR THE PURSUER

in the cause

MRS JOYCE BROWN or TOMKINSON (Assisted Person), residing at 33 Horne Street, Glasgow

PURSUER

against

BRIAN TOMKINSON, residing at 33 Horne Street, Glasgow

DEFENDER

The pursuer moves the court to grant an interim order suspending the defender's occupancy rights in the matrimonial home at 33 Horne Street, Glasgow; warrant for the summary ejection of the defender therefrom; interim interdict against the defender from entering the said matrimonial home without the express permission of the pursuer; and interim interdict against the defender from removing, except with the written consent of the pursuer or by a further order of the court, any furniture or plenishings in the said matrimonial home.

Documents lodged with the motion:

Affidavit of pursuer
Affidavit of Henrietta Blyth
Medical report

5 February 1994 IN RESPECT WHEREOF

Enrolled solicitor
15 Albany Street
Glasgow
Solicitor for the pursuer

e. Motion for interim custody (OCR 33.43(a)(ii))

SHERIFFDOM OF GLASGOW AND STRATHKELVIN
AT GLASGOW

Court ref no C21/1994

MOTION FOR THE
PURSUER

in the cause

MRS JOYCE BROWN or TOMKINSON (Assisted Person), residing at 33 Horne Street, Glasgow

PURSUER

against

BRIAN TOMKINSON, residing at 33 Horne Street, Glasgow

DEFENDER

The pursuer moves the court to grant an order in her favour for interim custody of Alan Brown (known as Alan Tomkinson), child of the pursuer accepted as one of the family by the defender and under the age of 16 years.

5 February 1994   IN RESPECT WHEREOF

Enrolled solicitor
15 Albany Street
Glasgow
Solicitor for the pursuer

f. Supplementary affidavit of pursuer

SHERIFFDOM OF GLASGOW AND STRATHKELVIN AT GLASGOW

SUPPLEMENTARY AFFIDAVIT

of the pursuer

in the cause

MRS JOYCE BROWN or TOMKINSON (Assisted Person), residing at 33 Horne Street, Glasgow

PURSUER

against

BRIAN TOMKINSON, residing c/o Tomkinson, 41 Marley Avenue, Glasgow

DEFENDER

At Glasgow the Sixteenth day of June Nineteen Hundred and Ninety Four in the presence of IAN BLOTT, Solicitor and Notary Public, 15 Albany Street, Glasgow compeared MRS JOYCE BROWN or TOMKINSON, residing at 33 Horne Street, Glasgow, who being solemnly sworn depones as follows:

1. I am Joyce Brown or Tomkinson. I am 31 years of age and live at 33 Horne Street, Glasgow.

2. I married Brian Tomkinson, now residing c/o Tomkinson, 41 Marley Avenue, Glasgow, at Glasgow on 16 May 1992. We have no children. I have a child, Alan Brown (known as Tomkinson) born 29 July 1983, who was accepted as one of the family by the defender. The natural father of Alan Brown is Colin Brown, 14 The Grove, Paisley. I produce extracts of the entries in the Registers of Marriages and Births, nos. 7 and 8 of process, which I have signed as relative hereto.

3. I was habitually resident in Scotland for at least 12 months

immediately preceding the raising of this action. I was resident in the Sheriffdom of Glasgow and Strathkelvin for at least 40 days prior to raising this action. I do not know of any proceedings concluded or continuing in Scotland or elsewhere concerning my child or relating to my marriage. I refer to my earlier affidavit, given in support of my application for an interim order suspending my husband's occupancy rights in the matrimonial home, which details my husband's behaviour during the period of our cohabitation, and the medical report, no. 11 of process, which I have signed as relative hereto. Following upon the granting of that order, my husband left the matrimonial home and I have not seen him since. I seek decree of divorce and transfer of the tenancy of the matrimonial home, under reference to my earlier affidavit.

5. My son Alan has always lived with me. Since I am unemployed, I can devote my whole time and attention to him. The matrimonial home is a four apartment; it has two bedrooms, so we have one bedroom each. He is a healthy and happy boy, particularly since my husband's departure. He attends Queensland Park School where he has lots of friends. He likes it there. I wish to be awarded custody of him.

All of which is truth as the deponent shall answer to God.

.... DEPONENT

.... NOTARY PUBLIC

g. Supplementary affidavit of witness

SHERIFFDOM OF GLASGOW AND STRATHKELVIN
AT GLASGOW

SUPPLEMENTARY
AFFIDAVIT

of Henrietta Blyth

in the cause

MRS JOYCE BROWN or TOMKINSON (Assisted Person), residing at 33 Horne Street, Glasgow

PURSUER

against

BRIAN TOMKINSON, residing c/o Tomkinson, 41 Marley Avenue, Glasgow

DEFENDER

At Glasgow the Sixteenth day of June Nineteen Hundred and Ninety Four in the presence of IAN BLOTT, Solicitor and Notary Public, 15 Albany Street, Glasgow compeared HENRIETTA BLYTH, residing at 31 Horne Street, Glasgow, who being solemnly sworn depones as follows:

1. I am Henrietta Blyth. I am 34 years of age and reside at 31 Horne Street, Glasgow. I am the next-door neighbour of the pursuer in this action.

2. I refer to my previous affidavit wherein I gave details of Brian Tomkinson's behaviour and its effect on his wife Joyce. I can confirm that following upon the recent court hearing, Mr Tomkinson left the house next door and has not been back. Joyce is visibly more relaxed and happy now.

3. I see the child Alan almost every day. He is a healthy lad, well looked after by his mother. She does not work and devotes all her time to

him. I have of course been in their house many times. It is always kept very clean and tidy. The boy has his own bedroom where he keeps his many toys. He goes to the school across the road. He seems to like it there. I see him with lots of different friends. I am in no doubt that it is in his best interests to stay with his mother.

All of which is truth as the deponent shall answer to God.

.... DEPONENT

.... NOTARY PUBLIC

3. BELL v BELL

Divorce—Desertion—Defender's whereabouts not known

a. Initial writ (including minute for decree)

SHERIFFDOM OF NORTH STRATHCLYDE AT OBAN

INITIAL WRIT

in the cause

MRS BELINDA SMYTHE or BELL (Assisted Person), residing at 41a Blyth Square, Oban

PURSUER

against

GEORGE WILLIAM BELL, whose whereabouts are not known

DEFENDER

The pursuer craves the court:

1. To divorce the defender from the pursuer on the ground that the marriage has broken down irretrievably as established by the defender's desertion of the pursuer for a continuous period of two years or more.

2. To grant warrant to cite the defender by the publication of an advertisement in Form G3 in the Glasgow Mail newspaper.

3. To grant warrant to intimate this initial writ to (1) Mrs Daphne Bell, residing at 3 Crooks Crescent, Oban, mother and one of the next-of-kin of the defender; (2) Alice Margaret Bell, residing at 41a Blyth Square, Oban, daughter of the defender over 16 years of age; and (3) George John Bell, residing at 601 Peach Grove, Birmingham, son of the defender over 16 years of age.

4. To find the defender liable in the expenses of the action.

CONDESCENDENCE

1. The parties were married at Glasgow on 21 February 1965. Extract certificate of marriage is produced. They have no children under the age of 16 years. The defender's whereabouts are not known and cannot

reasonably be ascertained. His last known address was 26/5 Forth View, Glasgow. He removed therefrom in about early 1993 and left no forwarding address. The pursuer has made enquiries with friends, family and neighbours without success. The pursuer seeks warrant to intimate this initial writ to Mrs Daphne Bell, mother and one of the next-of-kin of the defender and to Alice Margaret Bell and George John Bell, his children over 16 years of age, all designed in the third crave. The pursuer has been habitually resident in Scotland throughout the period of one year immediately preceding the raising of this action. She has been resident within the Sheriffdom of North Strathclyde for a period exceeding 40 days immediately preceding the raising of this action. She is unaware of any proceedings continuing in Scotland or elsewhere which are in respect of the marriage or are capable of affecting its validity or subsistence.

2. After their marriage the parties lived together until about 16 October 1991. Since then they have not lived together nor had marital relations.

3. On the said date, the defender deserted the pursuer. The pursuer was at that time willing to adhere. She gave the defender no cause so to act. She has not since refused any genuine and reasonable offer by the defender to resume cohabitation. The marriage has broken down irretrievably. There is no prospect of a reconciliation. The pursuer now seeks decree of divorce.

PLEA-IN-LAW

The marriage having broken down irretrievably, decree of divorce should be pronounced.

IN RESPECT WHEREOF

Enrolled solicitor
612 Queen Street
Oban
Solicitor for the pursuer

FLETCHER for the pursuer having considered the evidence contained in the affidavits and other document specified in the schedule hereto and being satisfied that upon the evidence a motion for decree in terms of the first crave of the initial writ may properly be made, moves the court accordingly.

IN RESPECT WHEREOF

Solicitor for the pursuer

SCHEDULE

1. Affidavit of pursuer.
2. Affidavit of Alice Margaret Bell.
3. Marriage certificate, no 7 of process.

b. Affidavit of pursuer

SHERIFFDOM OF NORTH STRATHCLYDE AT OBAN

AFFIDAVIT

of the pursuer

in the cause

MRS BELINDA SMYTHE or BELL, residing at 41a Blyth Square, Oban

PURSUER

against

GEORGE WILLIAM BELL, whose whereabouts are not known

DEFENDER

At Oban the Fifteenth day of May Nineteen Hundred and Ninety Four in the presence of PETER FLETCHER, Solicitor and Notary Public, 612 Queen Street, Oban compeared Mrs Belinda Smythe or Bell, residing at 41a Blyth Square, Oban, who being solemnly sworn depones as follows:

1. My full name is Belinda Smythe or Bell. I am 49 years of age, an office manageress and reside at 41a Blyth Square, Oban.

2. I married my husband, George William Bell, whose present whereabouts are to me unknown and whose last known address is 26/5 Forth View, Glasgow, at Glasgow on 21 February 1965. We have two children, both of whom are over 16 years of age. I produce an extract of the relevant entry in the Register of Marriages, no 7 of process, which I have signed as relative hereto.

3. I was habitually resident in Scotland throughout the period of one year immediately preceding the raising of this action. I was resident in the Sheriffdom of North Strathclyde for at least 40 days prior to raising this action. I know of no proceedings continuing in Scotland or elsewhere which are in respect of my marriage or are capable of affecting its validity or subsistence.

4. After our marriage I lived with my husband until 16 October 1991 when out of the blue he told me he was leaving me. I was absolutely shattered by this news and begged him to stay so that we could talk it through and sort out whatever was troubling him. To my dismay, he told me that it was not my fault but that he just did not love me any more. He said that he was planning to start a new life in Glasgow. He later wrote to me from 26/5 Forth View, Glasgow to say that he was all right and was thinking of going abroad. He did not then, or at any other time, suggest that we get together again. I later made enquiries with friends, family and neighbours of his in order to ascertain his whereabouts and learnt that he had moved away in about early 1993, leaving no forwarding address. There is no prospect of a reconciliation now. I seek decree of divorce.

All of which is truth as the deponent shall answer to God.

.... DEPONENT

.... NOTARY PUBLIC

c. Affidavit of witness

SHERIFFDOM OF NORTH STRATHCLYDE AT OBAN

AFFIDAVIT

of Alice Margaret Bell

in the cause

MRS BELINDA SMYTHE or BELL,
residing at 41a Blyth Square, Oban

PURSUER

against

GEORGE WILLIAM BELL,
whose whereabouts are not known

DEFENDER

At Oban the Fifteenth day of May Nineteen Hundred and Ninety Four in the presence of PETER FLETCHER, Solicitor and Notary Public, 612 Queen Street, Oban compeared Alice Margaret Bell, residing at 41a Blyth Square, Oban, who being solemnly sworn depones as follows:

1. My full name is Alice Margaret Bell, I am 18 years of age, undergoing youth training, and reside at 41a Blyth Square, Oban with my mother, who is the pursuer in this action.

2. I well remember the events of 16 October 1991. I returned home from school at about 4.30 pm. I overheard my father telling my mother that he did not love her any more and that he was off to start a new life for himself elsewhere. I know that my mother wanted him to stay but he would have none of it. He has not been back since and has not offered to get back together with my mother again. Had he done so, I would certainly have found out about it since my mother would not have kept news like that from me. I cannot understand why my father went off like that. My mother certainly didn't deserve that kind of treatment.

All of which is truth as the deponent shall answer to God.

.... DEPONENT

.... NOTARY PUBLIC

4. WHITE v WHITE

Divorce—Two years non-cohabitation and defender's consent—Child in care

a. Initial writ

SHERIFFDOM OF SOUTH STRATHCLYDE, DUMFRIES AND GALLOWAY AT STRANRAER

INITIAL WRIT

in the cause

ARTHUR WHITE (Assisted Person), residing at 4 Blackheath Drive, Stranraer

PURSUER

against

MRS LOUISE ANN WOOD or WHITE, residing at 14 Bankton Grove, Stranraer

DEFENDER

The pursuer craves the court:

1. To divorce the defender from the pursuer in respect that the marriage has broken down irretrievably as established by the parties' non-cohabitation for a continuous period of two years or more and the defender's consent to the granting of decree of divorce.

2. To grant warrant to intimate this initial writ to Wigtownshire Regional Council, Main Street, Wigtown as a local authority having care of Mark White, child of the parties' marriage under the age of 16 years; and to the said Mark White, c/o Wigtownshire Regional Council, Main Street, Wigtown, as a child who is affected by this action.

CONDESCENDENCE

1. The parties were married at Gosforth on 5 July 1984. They have one child, Mark White, born 10 August 1985. Extract certificates of marriage and birth are produced.

2. The pursuer has been habitually resident in Scotland throughout the period of one year immediately preceding the raising of this action. He has been resident within the Sheriffdom of South Strathclyde, Dumfries and Galloway for a period exceeding 40 days immediately preceding the raising of this action. He is unaware of any proceedings continuing in Scotland or elsewhere which are in respect of the marriage or are capable of affecting its validity or subsistence.

3. After their marriage the parties lived together until about 10 January 1991. Since then they have not lived together nor had marital relations. The defender is prepared to consent to the granting of decree of divorce. The marriage has broken down irretrievably. There is no prospect of a reconciliation. The pursuer seeks decree of divorce.

4. The said child is in the care of Wigtownshire Regional Council, designed in the second crave. It is believed that the present arrangements for his care and upbringing are satisfactory.

PLEA-IN-LAW

The marriage having broken down irretrievably, the pursuer is entitled to decree of divorce as craved.

IN RESPECT WHEREOF

Enrolled solicitor
5 Anderton Place
Stranraer
Solicitor for the pursuer

5. WILKES v WILKES

Divorce—Five years non-cohabitation—Orders for financial provision—Transfer of property—Capital sum—Periodical allowance—Incidental orders

a. Initial writ

SHERIFFDOM OF TAYSIDE, CENTRAL AND FIFE AT CUPAR

INITIAL WRIT

in the cause

MRS SUSAN APPLEBY or WILKES (Assisted Person), residing at 1 The Grange, Cupar

PURSUER

against

ALEXANDER PETER WILKES, residing at 46 Shannon Street, Dundee

DEFENDER

The pursuer craves the court:

1. To divorce the defender from the pursuer on the ground that the marriage has broken down irretrievably as established by the parties' non-cohabitation for a period exceeding five years.

2. To grant decree for the transfer of the defender's right, title and interest in the matrimonial home at 1 The Grange, Cupar, and the furniture and plenishings therein, to the pursuer and to ordain the defender within one month of the said decree or within such other period as the court may direct to execute and deliver to the pursuer a valid disposition of his said right, title and interest in the said matrimonial home and such other deeds as may be necessary to give the pursuer a valid title to the said matrimonial home, which failing, to make an order dispensing with such execution and delivery by the defender and directing the sheriff clerk to execute such disposition and other deeds, if any, in the pursuer's favour, all as adjusted at his sight.

3. Alternatively to the second crave, to grant an incidental order for such period as to the court seems proper (a) entitling the pursuer to reside

in the said matrimonial home and excluding the defender from occupation thereof; and (b) entitling the pursuer to the use of furniture and plenishings in the said matrimonial home.

4. In the event of decree being granted in terms of the second or third crave, to find the defender liable, as between the parties, for all sums due after the date of decree herein for such period as to the court seems proper to The Sheffield Permanent Building Society, designed in the seventh crave, under the standard security in its favour relative to the said matrimonial home.

5. To grant decree against the defender for payment to the pursuer of a capital sum of THIRTY THOUSAND POUNDS (£30,000), with interest thereon at the rate of eight *per centum per annum* from such date as the court thinks fit until payment.

6. To grant decree against the defender for payment to the pursuer of a periodical allowance of ONE HUNDRED POUNDS (£100) per week, payable weekly and in advance for a period of three years from the date of decree or less or until the remarriage or death of the pursuer, if sooner, with interest at the rate of eight *per centum per annum* on each weekly payment from the time the same falls due until payment.

7. To grant warrant to intimate this initial writ to The Sheffield Permanent Building Society, Shore Street, Sheffield, holders of a standard security over the said matrimonial home.

8. To grant such other order as the court thinks fit.

9. To find the defender liable in the expenses of the action.

CONDESCENDENCE

1. The parties were married at Dundee on 5 June 1959. They have no children under the age of 16 years. Extract certificate of marriage is produced.

2. The pursuer has been habitually resident in Scotland throughout the period of one year immediately preceding the raising of this action. She has been resident within the Sheriffdom of Tayside, Central and Fife for a period exceeding 40 days immediately preceding the raising of this action. She is unaware of any other proceedings continuing in Scotland or elsewhere which are in respect of the marriage or are capable of affecting its validity or subsistence.

3. After their marriage the parties lived together until about 5 January 1988. Since then they have not lived together nor had marital relations.

4. The pursuer seeks orders for financial provision as craved. She seeks a fair sharing of the net value of the matrimonial property. The pursuer's property at the relevant date comprised her interest in the matrimonial home at 1 The Grange, Cupar, which she owned jointly with the defender, certain shares, and savings of about £2,000. Valuations of the house and shares will be produced. The defender's property at that time included his controlling interest in an engineering company, APW Consultancy Services Limited, a share portfolio, life insurance policies and a pension, in addition to his said interest in the matrimonial home. The last-mentioned was (and remains) burdened with a loan from The Sheffield Permanent

Building Society, designed in the seventh crave. Valuations of the defender's property and a statement of mortgage will be produced. Further, the pursuer suffered economic disadvantage in the interests of the defender and their family. She gave up her career as a pharmacist, forgoing earnings and a substantial pension, in order to look after the parties' home and children. Further, she has been and continues to be dependent to a substantial degree upon the financial support of the defender. She has no job. Other than her interest in the matrimonial home, she has no resources. She receives maintenance from the defender in the sum of £300 per week. The defender earns a substantial income from the said company. He has ample resources with which to meet orders for financial provision as craved. Decree therefor should accordingly be pronounced.

PLEAS-IN-LAW

1. The marriage of the parties having broken down irretrievably, decree of divorce should be granted as craved.

2. The pursuer being entitled to a fair sharing of the net value of the matrimonial property *separatim* to fair account being taken of economic disadvantage suffered by her in the interests of the defender and their family *separatim* to reasonable provision to enable her to adjust to the loss upon divorce of the financial support of the defender upon which she has been dependent to a substantial degree, should be granted orders for financial provision.

IN RESPECT WHEREOF

Enrolled solicitor
16 West Street
Cupar
Solicitor for the pursuer

b. Defences

SHERIFFDOM OF TAYSIDE, CENTRAL AND FIFE AT CUPAR

DEFENCES

in the cause

MRS SUSAN APPLEBY or WILKES (Assisted Person), residing at 1 The Grange, Cupar

PURSUER

against

ALEXANDER PETER WILKES, residing at 46 Shannon Street, Dundee

DEFENDER

ANSWERS TO CONDESCENDENCE

1. Admitted.
2. Believed to be true. The defender knows of no such proceedings.
3. Admitted.
4. Admitted that the pursuer seeks orders for financial provision as craved. Admitted that at the relevant date the defender's property included the said property, under explanation that he also had savings, as will be vouched. Admitted that the matrimonial home was (and remains) so burdened. Admitted that the pursuer has no job. Admitted that she receives maintenance from the defender in the sum of £300 per week. Her property at the relevant date and her resources at the date hereof are not known and not admitted. *Quoad ultra* denied. Explained and averred that the pursuer's claims for financial provision are excessive.

PLEA-IN-LAW

The pursuer's claims for financial provision being unjustified by principle and being in any event excessive, decree therefor should not be pronounced.

IN RESPECT WHEREOF

Enrolled solicitor
159 St John Street
Dundee
Solicitor for the defender

c. Motion for order for provision of details of resources

SHERIFFDOM OF TAYSIDE, CENTRAL AND FIFE AT CUPAR

Court ref no C19/1994

MOTION FOR THE
PURSUER

in the cause

MRS SUSAN APPLEBY or WILKES (Assisted Person), residing at 1 The Grange, Cupar

PURSUER

against

ALEXANDER PETER WILKES, residing at 46 Shannon Street, Dundee

DEFENDER

The pursuer moves the court to order the defender to provide details of his resources.

4 June 1994   IN RESPECT WHEREOF

Enrolled solicitor
16 West Street
Cupar
Solicitor for the pursuer

d. Specification of documents

SHERIFFDOM OF TAYSIDE, CENTRAL AND FIFE AT CUPAR

SPECIFICATION OF
DOCUMENTS

in respect of which a commission and diligence is sought by the pursuer

in the cause

MRS SUSAN APPLEBY or WILKES (Assisted Person), residing at 1 The Grange, Cupar

PURSUER

against

ALEXANDER PETER WILKES, residing at 46 Shannon Street, Dundee

DEFENDER

1. All books of account, cash books and ledgers, VAT books, profit and loss accounts and balance sheets, and all other documents kept by or on behalf of APW Consultancy Services Ltd for the period 5 January 1987 to date, so that excerpts may be taken therefrom at the sight of the commissioner of all entries therein showing or tending to show the value of the defender's interest in the said company as at 5 January 1988 and as at the date hereof; and the defender's income from the said company as at the date hereof.

2. All returns, demand notices and receipts for income tax due by the defender since 5 April 1993 (except insofar as in the possession of the Inland Revenue).

3. All lists of investments, stock, share and debenture certificates and dividend counterfoils, bank account statements, building society passbooks, IOUs, bonds, deposit receipts, insurance and assurance policies,

pension plans and all other documents relative to the period 5 January 1987 to date so that excerpts may be taken therefrom at the sight of the commissioner of all entries showing or tending to show the extent and value of the moveable property in which the defender had an interest as at 5 January 1988 and has an interest at the date hereof.

4. All title deeds, back letters, valuations and like documentation for the period 5 January 1987 to date showing or tending to show the extent and value of the heritable property in which the defender had an interest as at 5 January 1988 and has an interest at the date hereof.

5. Failing principals, drafts, copies or duplicates of the above or any of them.

e. Joint minute of agreement

SHERIFFDOM OF TAYSIDE, CENTRAL AND FIFE AT CUPAR

JOINT MINUTE OF
AGREEMENT

in the cause

MRS SUSAN APPLEBY or WILKES (Assisted Person), residing at 1 The Grange, Cupar

PURSUER

against

ALEXANDER PETER WILKES, residing at 46 Shannon Street, Dundee

DEFENDER

MILLER for the pursuer and HANSON for the defender concurred in stating to the court that in the event of decree of divorce being pronounced and subject to the approval of the court, the parties have agreed and hereby agree as follows:

1. The defender shall dispone to the pursuer his right, title and interest in the heritable property at 1 The Grange, Cupar, and shall deliver to the pursuer within one month of the date of decree a valid disposition of his said right, title and interest in the said matrimonial home;

2. The defender shall repay the outstanding loan secured over the said heritable property in favour of The Sheffield Permanent Building Society within one month of the date of decree;

3. The defender shall pay to the pursuer a capital sum of TWENTY THOUSAND POUNDS (£20,000), with interest thereon at the rate of eight *per centum per annum* from the date of decree until payment;

4. The third, fourth, sixth and eighth craves of the initial writ shall be refused; and

5. The defender shall be liable for the expenses of the action as taxed.

The parties therefore craved and hereby crave the court to interpone authority hereto and to grant decree in terms hereof.

IN RESPECT WHEREOF

Enrolled solicitor
16 West Street
Cupar
Solicitor for the pursuer

Enrolled solicitor
159 St John Street
Dundee
Solicitor for the defender

6. BARTON v BARTON

Separation—Unreasonable behaviour—Protective measures—Matrimonial interdict—Power of arrest

a. Initial writ

SHERIFFDOM OF GRAMPIAN, HIGHLAND AND ISLANDS AT INVERNESS

INITIAL WRIT

in the cause

MRS IRENE LAWRENCE or BARTON, residing at 21 Vale Point, Inverness

PURSUER

against

ALAN DAVID BARTON, residing at 4 Amersham Road, Inverness

DEFENDER

The pursuer craves the court:

1. To separate the defender from the pursuer on the ground of the defender's behaviour.

2. To interdict the defender from molesting the pursuer by abusing her verbally, threatening her, putting her into a state of fear and alarm or distress or using violence towards her; and to grant interim interdict; and to attach a power of arrest to the said interdict and interim interdict.

3. To find the defender liable in the expenses of the action.

CONDESCENDENCE

1. The parties were married at Tain on 21 February 1979. Extract certificate of marriage is produced. They have no children.

2. The pursuer has been habitually resident in Scotland throughout the period of one year immediately preceding the raising of this action. She has been resident within the Sheriffdom of Grampian, Highland and Islands for a period exceeding 40 days immediately preceding the raising

of this action. She is unaware of any proceedings continuing in Scotland or elsewhere which are in respect of the marriage or are capable of affecting its validity or subsistence.

3. After their marriage the parties lived together until about 5 February 1994. Since then they have not lived together nor had marital relations.

4. The defender has behaved in such a way that the pursuer cannot reasonably be expected to cohabit with him. During the period of the parties' cohabitation he behaved violently towards her. He assaulted her on several occasions. In particular, in about early January 1994, he assaulted her by kicking and punching her in the matrimonial home. On or about 20 January 1993, he struck her in the face in the street outside the matrimonial home. On the said date of separation, he kicked her in the matrimonial home. As a result of the foregoing, the pursuer left him and now seeks decree of separation as first craved.

5. The pursuer also seeks orders as second craved. Following upon the parties' separation aforesaid, the defender has threatened the pursuer with violence. In particular, on or about 20 February 1994, he called at her present address and told her he was going to beat her up if she did not return to live with him. In these circumstances, the pursuer seeks interdict and interim interdict as craved, together with a power of arrest.

PLEAS-IN-LAW

1. The defender having behaved in such a way that the pursuer cannot reasonably be expected to cohabit with him, decree of separation should be granted as craved.

2. The pursuer having grounds to apprehend that the defender will molest her, is entitled to interdict and interim interdict as craved.

3. There being no circumstances to indicate that a power of arrest is unnecessary, such power should be attached to the aforesaid interdict and interim interdict.

IN RESPECT WHEREOF

Enrolled solicitor
19 Murray Street
Inverness
Solicitor for the pursuer

b. Minute of abandonment (OCR 23.1(1)(b))

SHERIFFDOM OF GRAMPIAN, HIGHLAND AND ISLANDS
AT INVERNESS

MINUTE OF
ABANDONMENT

for the pursuer

in the cause

MRS IRENE LAWRENCE or BARTON, residing at 21 Vale Point, Inverness

PURSUER

against

ALAN DAVID BARTON, residing at 4 Amersham Road, Inverness

DEFENDER

NORMAN for the pursuer stated to the court that the pursuer abandons this action.

IN RESPECT WHEREOF

Enrolled solicitor
19 Murray Street
Inverness
Solicitor for the pursuer

c. Motion for defender to be ordained to lodge an account of expenses

SHERIFFDOM OF GRAMPIAN, HIGHLAND AND ISLANDS
AT INVERNESS

Court ref no C9/1994

MOTION FOR THE
PURSUER

in the cause

MRS IRENE LAWRENCE or BARTON, residing at 21 Vale Point, Inverness

PURSUER

against

ALAN DAVID BARTON, residing at 4 Amersham Road, Inverness

DEFENDER

The pursuer moves the court to ordain the defender to lodge an account of expenses within 28 days and to remit the same when lodged to the Auditor of Court to tax and to report.

Part of process lodged with the motion:

Minute of abandonment

4 May 1994   IN RESPECT WHEREOF

Enrolled solicitor
19 Murray Street
Inverness
Solicitor for the pursuer

d. Motion for decree of dismissal

SHERIFFDOM OF GRAMPIAN, HIGHLAND AND ISLANDS
AT INVERNESS

Court ref no C9/1994

MOTION FOR THE
PURSUER

in the cause

MRS IRENE LAWRENCE or BARTON, residing at 21 Vale Point, Inverness

PURSUER

against

ALAN DAVID BARTON, residing at 4 Amersham Road, Inverness

DEFENDER

The pursuer moves the court to grant decree of dismissal.

Document lodged with the motion:

Receipt granted by defender for payment of his expenses.

24 August 1994   IN RESPECT WHEREOF

Enrolled solicitor
19 Murray Street
Inverness
Solicitor for the pursuer

7. JOHNSON v JOHNSON

Aliment (husband and wife)

a. Initial writ

SHERIFFDOM OF GLASGOW AND STRATHKELVIN
AT GLASGOW

INITIAL WRIT

in the cause

MRS JOAN ANDERSON or JOHNSON (Assisted Person), residing at 3 Barclay Avenue, Glasgow

PURSUER

against

JOHN JOHNSON, residing at 15 Cathcart Place, Irvine

DEFENDER

The pursuer craves the court:

1. To grant decree against the defender for payment to the pursuer of the sum of EIGHTY POUNDS (£80) per week, with interest at the rate of eight *per centum per annum* on each weekly payment from the due date until payment.

2. To find the defender liable in the expenses of the action.

CONDESCENDENCE

1. The pursuer resides at 3 Barclay Avenue, Glasgow. She has been so resident for more than three months immediately preceding the raising of this action. She is domiciled in Glasgow. She is in any event habitually resident there. This court accordingly has jurisdiction. The defender resides at 15 Cathcart Place, Irvine. To the knowledge of the pursuer no proceedings are pending before any other court involving the present cause of action and between the parties hereto. To the knowledge of the pursuer no agreement exists between the parties prorogating jurisdiction over the subject-matter of the present cause to another court.

2. The parties are married. The pursuer is in part-time employment as a cashier. Details of her income and outgoings will be produced. The defender is an electrician to trade. He is accustomed to earning about £280 per week net. When the parties cohabited, the defender normally gave the pursuer between about £100 and £150 per week for household bills and her personal expenses. In the circumstances, the sum sought as aliment is reasonable.

3. The defender refuses or at least delays to aliment the pursuer. This action is accordingly necessary.

PLEA-IN-LAW

The defender being obliged to provide reasonable support to the pursuer, decree should be pronounced as craved.

IN RESPECT WHEREOF

Enrolled solicitor
2 Gray Street
Glasgow
Solicitor for the pursuer

b. Motion for interim aliment

SHERIFFDOM OF GLASGOW AND STRATHKELVIN
AT GLASGOW

Court ref no C21/1994

MOTION FOR THE PURSUER

in the cause

MRS JOAN ANDERSON or JOHNSON (Assisted Person), residing at 3 Barclay Avenue, Glasgow

PURSUER

against

JOHN JOHNSON, residing at 15 Cathcart Place, Irvine

DEFENDER

The pursuer moves the court to grant an order against the defender for payment to her of interim aliment at the rate of £80 per week.

Documents lodged with the motion:

Statement of earnings
Statement of outgoings

14 June 1994   IN RESPECT WHEREOF

Enrolled solicitor
2 Gray Street
Glasgow
Solicitor for the pursuer

c. Motion for sist for legal aid

SHERIFFDOM OF GLASGOW AND STRATHKELVIN AT GLASGOW

Court ref no C21/1994

MOTION FOR THE DEFENDER

in the cause

MRS JOAN ANDERSON or JOHNSON (Assisted Person), residing at 3 Barclay Avenue, Glasgow

PURSUER

against

JOHN JOHNSON, residing at 15 Cathcart Place, Irvine

DEFENDER

The defender moves the court to sist the cause to enable him to apply for legal aid.

16 June 1994   IN RESPECT WHEREOF

Enrolled solicitor
14 Gloucester Road
Irvine
Solicitor for the defender

8. JONES v JONES

Aliment (husband and wife)—Variation of agreement on aliment

a. Initial writ (OCR 33.59(1))

SHERIFFDOM OF SOUTH STRATHCLYDE, DUMFRIES AND GALLOWAY AT DUMFRIES

SUMMARY APPLICATION UNDER THE FAMILY LAW (SCOTLAND) ACT 1985, section 7(2)

INITIAL WRIT

in the cause

JAMES JONES, residing at 3 Glebe Street, Dumfries

PURSUER

against

ANNE SMITH or JONES, residing at 46 Harper's Drive, Dumfries

DEFENDER

The pursuer craves the court:

1. To vary the agreement on aliment between the parties dated 10 January 1993 and that by reducing the amount of aliment payable by the pursuer to the defender thereunder to THIRTY POUNDS (£30) per week or such other sum as the court thinks fit.

2. To find the defender liable in the expenses of the action.

CONDESCENDENCE

1. The pursuer resides at 3 Glebe Street, Dumfries. He has been so resident for more than three months immediately preceding the raising of this action. He is domiciled there. He is in any event habitually resident there. This court has jurisdiction. The defender resides at 46 Harper's Drive, Dumfries.

2. The parties are married. By agreement dated 10 January 1993, the

pursuer agreed to aliment the defender at the rate of £90 per week. At that time, the pursuer earned about £300 per week net and had no other dependants. Since then there has been a material change of circumstances. The pursuer has suffered a reduction in earnings and has fathered a child by another woman. Reference is made to statement of earnings and birth certificate produced herewith. In these circumstances, and having regard to the pursuer's statement of outgoings produced herewith, the amount of aliment payable as aforesaid should be varied as craved.

PLEA-IN-LAW

There having been a material change of circumstances, the amount of aliment payable under the said agreement should be varied as craved.

IN RESPECT WHEREOF

Enrolled solicitor
1 Whitehouse Place
Dumfries
Solicitor for the pursuer

9. JACKSON v POLLOCK

Children—Parentage—Declarator of parentage

a. Initial writ (including minute of decree)

SHERIFFDOM OF LOTHIAN AND BORDERS AT EDINBURGH

INITIAL WRIT

in the cause

ALBERT ALAN JACKSON, residing at 46 Lyon Court, Edinburgh

PURSUER

against

JANICE POLLOCK, residing at 3 St Anthony's Mews, Edinburgh

DEFENDER

The pursuer craves the court:

1. To find and declare that the pursuer is the father of Peter Pollock, a child born to the defender on 1 June 1992.

2. To grant warrant to intimate this initial writ to Peter Pollock, residing at 3 St Anthony's Mews, Edinburgh, as a child who is affected by this action.

3. To find the defender liable in the expenses of the action.

CONDESCENDENCE

1. The pursuer resides at 46 Lyon Court, Edinburgh. The defender resides at 3 St Anthony's Mews, Edinburgh. The defender gave birth to a child, Peter Pollock, on 1 June 1992. Said child was born within the Sheriffdom of Lothian and Borders, namely at Edinburgh. Extract birth certificate is produced. This court accordingly has jurisdiction.

2. The pursuer is the father of the said child. From about February 1991 until shortly prior to the child's birth, the pursuer and the defender cohabited at 46 Lyon Court, Edinburgh. They regularly had sexual relations throughout the said period. To the knowledge of the pursuer,

the defender did not have such connection with any other man at the material time. On or about 20 March 1992, the defender acknowledged to the pursuer's mother at the latter's home that the pursuer was the father of the child. The defender has subsequently denied said parentage. She registered the identity of the child's father as unknown to her. This action is therefore necessary.

PLEA-IN-LAW

The pursuer being the father of the said child, is entitled to decree as craved.

IN RESPECT WHEREOF

                        Enrolled solicitor
                        1 George Street
                        Edinburgh
                        Solicitor for the pursuer

DAVIDSON for the pursuer, having considered the evidence contained in the affidavits and other document specified in the schedule hereto and being satisfied that upon the evidence a motion for decree in terms of the first crave may properly be made, moves the court accordingly.

IN RESPECT WHEREOF

                        Solicitor for the pursuer

SCHEDULE

1. Affidavit of the pursuer.
2. Affidavit of Mrs Maureen Jackson.
3. Birth certificate no 8 of process.

b. Affidavit of pursuer

SHERIFFDOM OF LOTHIAN AND BORDERS AT EDINBURGH

AFFIDAVIT

of the pursuer

in the cause

ALBERT ALAN JACKSON, residing at 46 Lyon Court, Edinburgh

PURSUER

against

JANICE POLLOCK, residing at 3 St Anthony's Mews, Edinburgh

DEFENDER

At Edinburgh the Sixteenth day of June Nineteen Hundred and Ninety Four in the presence of GEORGE DAVIDSON, Solicitor and Notary Public, 1 George Street, Edinburgh compeared ALBERT ALAN JACKSON, residing at 46 Lyon Court, Edinburgh, who being solemnly sworn depones as follows:

1. My full name is Albert Alan Jackson. I am 35 years of age, employed as a civil servant and reside at 46 Lyon Court, Edinburgh.

2. I commenced cohabiting with Janice Pollock, the defender in this action, at the foregoing address from about February 1991. We lived alone. Our relationship was sexual and we regularly had sexual relations together there. We lived together until May 1992 when our relationship deteriorated and the defender left. The defender gave birth to a child, Peter Pollock, on 1 June 1992 at Edinburgh. I refer to the extract of the entry in the Register of Births, no 8 of process, which I have signed as relative hereto.

3. I am the father of that child. To my knowledge, the defender did not associate with any other men at any time at which conception might

reasonably be held to have occurred nor, indeed, at any time during the period of our cohabitation. I am certain that I would have known had she done so. Since our separation she has taken to denying that I am the child's father. She has registered the identity of the child's father as unknown to her. I refer again to no 8 of process. Accordingly, I seek decree of declarator as craved.

All of which is truth as the deponent shall answer to God.

.... DEPONENT

.... NOTARY PUBLIC

c. Affidavit of witness

SHERIFFDOM OF LOTHIAN AND BORDERS AT EDINBURGH

AFFIDAVIT

of Mrs Maureen Jackson

in the cause

ALBERT ALAN JACKSON, residing at 46 Lyon Court, Edinburgh

PURSUER

against

JANICE POLLOCK, residing at 3 St Anthony's Mews, Edinburgh

DEFENDER

At Edinburgh the Sixteenth day of June Nineteen Hundred and Ninety Four in the presence of GEORGE DAVIDSON, Solicitor and Notary Public, 1 George Street, Edinburgh compeared MRS MAUREEN JACKSON, residing at 529 Kingsferry Road, Edinburgh, who being solemnly sworn depones as follows:

1. My full name is Mrs Maureen Jackson. I am 60 years of age, retired and I reside at 529 Kingsferry Road, Edinburgh. I am the mother of Albert Alan Jackson, the pursuer in this action.

2. I can confirm that my son lived with Janice Pollock at his house at 46 Lyon Court, Edinburgh for some time from early in 1991 until shortly before she gave birth to a son at the Simpson Memorial Hospital in Edinburgh in June 1992. I visited my son's house on a number of occasions and was well aware that they shared a bedroom. Miss Pollock showed no interest in any other men. She was devoted to my son. On 20 March 1992 she told me in my home that she was looking forward to having my son's child. So far as I am concerned, my son is the father of the child.

3. Unfortunately, shortly before the child's birth, my son and Miss

Pollock had a major disagreement and she left. I understand that she has since been saying that my son is not the child's father. I do not accept that.

All of which is truth as the deponent shall answer to God.

.... DEPONENT

.... NOTARY PUBLIC

10. HEPWORTH v HEPWORTH

Children—Custody Order—Access—Custody

a. Initial writ

SHERIFFDOM OF TAYSIDE, CENTRAL AND FIFE AT DUNFERMLINE

INITIAL WRIT

in the cause

JOHN HEPWORTH (Assisted Person), residing at 56 King Street, Perth

PURSUER

against

BRENDA BARNES or HEPWORTH, residing at 21 Gordon Terrace, Dunfermline

DEFENDER

The pursuer craves the court:

1. To find the pursuer entitled to access to Mary Josephine Hepworth and John James Hepworth, children of the marriage and under the age of 16 years, each alternate weekend between the hours of 6 pm on Friday and 6 pm on Sunday, and for two weeks during the said children's school summer holidays and for one week during each of their school Easter and Christmas holidays or during such other period or periods as the court thinks fit.
2. To grant warrant to intimate this initial writ to the said Mary Josephine Hepworth and John James Hepworth, both residing at 21 Gordon Terrace, Dunfermline, as children who are affected by this action.
3. To find the defender liable in the expenses of the action.

CONDESCENDENCE

1. The pursuer resides at 56 King Street, Perth. The defender resides at 21 Gordon Terrace, Dunfermline. The parties were married at Inverkeithing on 6 June 1980. They have two children: Mary Josephine

Hepworth, born 15 January 1981 and John James Hepworth, born 23 February 1983. The said children are habitually resident in the Sheriffdom of Tayside, Central and Fife. This court accordingly has jurisdiction. The pursuer is unaware of any proceedings continuing or concluded in Scotland or elsewhere which relate to the said children and of any proceedings continuing in Scotland or elsewhere which relate to the marriage of the parties.

2. After their marriage the parties lived together until about November 1992. Since then the said children have resided with the defender in the matrimonial home. Following upon the parties' separation, the pursuer was allowed access to the children on Saturday afternoons. Said access was much enjoyed by the children. In about early January 1994, the defender advised the pursuer that no further access was to be allowed. The pursuer is aware of no good reason why the defender should refuse him access. The pursuer has adequate accommodation for overnight stays by the children. He is well able to look after them. In the whole circumstances, it is in the best interests of the children that access be granted as craved.

PLEA-IN-LAW

It being in the best interests of the children that the defender should have access to them as craved, decree should be granted accordingly.

IN RESPECT WHEREOF

Enrolled solicitor
1 Pitt Street
Perth
Solicitor for the pursuer

b. Defences

SHERIFFDOM OF TAYSIDE, CENTRAL AND FIFE AT DUNFERMLINE

DEFENCES

in the cause

JOHN HEPWORTH (Assisted Person), residing at 56 King Street, Perth

PURSUER

against

BRENDA BARNES or HEPWORTH, residing at 21 Gordon Terrace, Dunfermline

DEFENDER

The defender craves the court:

1. To find the defender entitled to custody of Mary Josephine Hepworth and John James Hepworth, children of the marriage and under the age of 16 years.
2. To find the pursuer liable in expenses.

ANSWERS TO CONDESCENDENCE

1. Admitted. The defender is likewise unaware of any such proceedings.
2. Admitted that after their marriage the parties lived together until about November 1992. Admitted that since then the said children have resided with the defender in the said matrimonial home, under explanation that the defender seeks an award of custody in respect of them as craved. Admitted that for a period following upon the parties' said separation the pursuer was allowed access to the said children. The pursuer's state of awareness is not known and not admitted. *Quoad ultra* denied except insofar as coinciding herewith. Explained and averred that

the pursuer exercised access irregularly. He took to telephoning an excuse for non-attendance. The defender would have the children ready for access on each occasion. The pursuer's failures to appear caused the children distress. His said conduct alienated them. Further and in any event, on the occasions when the pursuer did arrive to collect the children, he had usually been drinking. The elder child told the defender that the pursuer's breath 'smelt funny'. The children do not now wish to see the pursuer. To require them to do so would be contrary to their best interests. In any event, the pursuer does not have suitable accommodation for overnight access. He lives in a one-bedroomed flat. In the circumstances, decree should not be pronounced as craved.

PLEAS-IN-LAW

1. It not being in the said children's best interests that the pursuer have access to them, decree therefor should not be pronounced as craved.

2. It being in the said children's best interests to be in the custody of the defender, decree therefor should be pronounced.

IN RESPECT WHEREOF

Enrolled solicitor
16 High Street
Dunfermline
Solicitor for the defender

c. Motion for warrant for intimation (OCR 33.15(2))

SHERIFFDOM OF TAYSIDE, CENTRAL AND FIFE AT DUNFERMLINE

Court ref no C18/1994

MOTION FOR THE DEFENDER

in the cause

JOHN HEPWORTH (Assisted Person), residing at 56 King Street, Perth

PURSUER

against

BRENDA BARNES or HEPWORTH (Assisted Person), residing at 21 Gordon Terrace, Dunfermline

DEFENDER

The defender moves the court to grant warrant to intimate the defences to Mary Josephine Hepworth and John James Hepworth, both residing at 21 Gordon Terrace, Dunfermline.

4 May 1994   IN RESPECT WHEREOF

        Enrolled solicitor
        16 High Street
        Dunfermline
        Solicitor for the defender

d. Motion for interim access (OCR 33.43(a))

SHERIFFDOM OF TAYSIDE, CENTRAL AND FIFE AT DUNFERMLINE

Court ref no C18/1994

MOTION FOR THE PURSUER

in the cause

JOHN HEPWORTH (Assisted Person), residing at 56 King Street, Perth

PURSUER

against

BRENDA BARNES or HEPWORTH (Assisted Person), residing at 21 Gordon Terrace, Dunfermline

DEFENDER

The pursuer moves the court to grant an order in his favour for interim access to Mary Josephine Hepworth and John James Hepworth, children of the marriage and under the age of 16 years, each alternate weekend between the hours of 6 pm on Friday and 6 pm on Sunday or during such other periods as the court thinks fit.

14 May 1994   IN RESPECT WHEREOF

Enrolled solicitor
1 Pitt Street
Perth
Solicitor for the pursuer

e. Motion for leave to appeal

SHERIFFDOM OF TAYSIDE, CENTRAL AND FIFE AT DUNFERMLINE

Court ref no C18/1994

MOTION FOR THE DEFENDER

in the cause

JOHN HEPWORTH (Assisted Person), residing at 56 King Street, Perth

PURSUER

against

BRENDA BARNES or HEPWORTH (Assisted Person), residing at 21 Gordon Terrace, Dunfermline

DEFENDER

The defender moves the court for leave to appeal the interlocutor dated 20 May 1994.

23 May 1994   IN RESPECT WHEREOF

Enrolled solicitor
16 High Street
Dunfermline
Solicitor for the defender

f. Motion for defender to be ordained to appear at the bar

SHERIFFDOM OF TAYSIDE, CENTRAL AND FIFE AT DUNFERMLINE

Cour ref no C18/1994

MOTION FOR THE PURSUER

in the cause

JOHN HEPWORTH (Assisted Person), residing at 56 King Street, Perth

PURSUER

against

BRENDA BARNES or HEPWORTH (Assisted Person), residing at 21 Gordon Terrace, Dunfermline

DEFENDER

The pursuer moves the court to ordain the defender to appear at the bar to explain her failure to obtemper the interlocutor dated 20 May 1994.

21 June 1994　　　　　　　　IN RESPECT WHEREOF

Enrolled solicitor
1 Pitt Street
Perth
Solicitor for the pursuer

g. Minute of variation (OCR 33.44(1)(a))

SHERIFFDOM OF TAYSIDE, CENTRAL AND FIFE AT DUNFERMLINE

MINUTE OF VARIATION

for the pursuer

in the cause

JOHN HEPWORTH (Assisted Person), residing at 222 Mayfield Avenue, Perth

PURSUER

against

BRENDA BARNES or HEPWORTH, residing at 21 Gordon Terrace, Dunfermline

DEFENDER

The pursuer craves the court:

To vary the interlocutor dated 4 August 1994 and that by finding the pursuer entitled to residential access to Mary Josephine Hepworth and John James Hepworth, children of the marriage and under the age of 16 years, each alternate weekend between the hours of 6 pm on Friday and 6 pm on Sunday; under reference to the undernoted statement of facts.

STATEMENT OF FACTS

1. By interlocutor dated 4 August 1994, the sheriff, after proof, found the defender entitled to custody of Mary Josephine Hepworth and John James Hepworth, children of the marriage and under 16 years of age, and found the pursuer entitled to access to the children each Sunday between the hours of 10 am and 6 pm. The sheriff held *inter alia* that the accommodation of the pursuer was unsuitable for residential access.

2. Since the said date there has been a material change of circumstances. The pursuer has now obtained accommodation suitable for residential access. Such comprises a three-bedroomed maisonette. He has regularly exercised access as allowed by the court, The children have greatly enjoyed said access. They have frequently expressed a desire to stay overnight with the pursuer. He is desirous to see the children for longer periods. He proposes residential access as craved. He has been unable to secure a response from the defender regarding his proposal. This minute is therefore necessary.

PLEA-IN-LAW

There having been a material change of circumstances and the access now sought being in the best interests of the said children, the said interlocutor should be varied as craved.

IN RESPECT WHEREOF

Enrolled solicitor
1 Pitt Street
Perth
Solicitor for the pursuer

11. BLANE v BLANE

Children—Custody order—Custody and delivery—Interdict against removal of child—Order to disclose child's whereabouts—Defender's whereabouts not known—Child's whereabouts not known

a. Initial writ

SHERIFFDOM OF LOTHIAN AND BORDERS
AT LINLITHGOW

INITIAL WRIT

in the cause

MRS SHARON BLANE (Assisted Person), residing at 4 Harriet Drive, Linlithgow

PURSUER

against

JOHN BLANE, whose whereabouts are not known

DEFENDER

The pursuer craves the court:

1. To find the pursuer entitled to custody of Amy Blane, child of the marriage and under the age of 16 years.
2. To ordain the defender to deliver the said child to the pursuer.
3. To grant warrant to intimate this initial writ to Mrs Martha Blane, residing at 4 Abbotsford Place, Linlithgow, mother and one of the next-of-kin of the defender.
4. To dispense with intimation to Amy Blane, a child who is affected by this action, whose whereabouts are not known.
5. To find the defender liable in the expenses of the action.

CONDESCENDENCE

1. The pursuer resides at 4 Harriet Drive, Linlithgow. She married the defender at Linlithgow on 5 May 1981. They have one child: Amy Blane, born 6 July 1984. The said child is habitually resident in the Sheriffdom of

Lothian and Borders. This court accordingly has jurisdiction. The pursuer is unaware of any proceedings continuing or concluded in Scotland or elsewhere which relate to the said child. The pursuer is unaware of any proceedings continuing in Scotland or elsewhere which relate to the marriage of the parties. The defender's whereabouts are not known and cannot reasonably be ascertained. He left the matrimonial home as hereinafter averred, taking the said child with him, and cannot be found. Enquiries with friends and neighbours have met with no success. The pursuer seeks warrant to intimate this initial writ to Mrs Martha Blane, his mother, designed in the third crave.

2. After their marriage the parties cohabited until about 15 May 1994, On that date, following upon an argument, the defender left, taking the said child with him. He told the pursuer that she would never see them again. The child has not returned to school. The pursuer does not know where the defender and the child have gone.

3. It is in the best interests of the said child to be in the custody of the pursuer. The pursuer has always looked after her. The standard of care offered by the pursuer to the child has always been high. The pursuer continues to live in the matrimonial home, which is clean and tidy. The child was happy and well settled there and at the local school, where she has many friends. The defender is a feckless and irresponsible man. Reference is made to the preceding order of condescendence. He has never been able to hold down a job for long. He acts before he thinks. He is unable to provide a proper and secure upbringing for a child. It is not in the best interests of the child to be in his custody. The pursuer accordingly seeks custody and delivery as craved.

PLEA-IN-LAW

It being in the best interests of the said child to be in the custody of the pursuer, decree therefor together with an order for delivery, should be granted as craved.

IN RESPECT WHEREOF

Enrolled solicitor
1 Main Street
Linlithgow
Solicitor for the pursuer

b. Motion for order to disclose child's whereabouts (OCR 33.23(1))

SHERIFFDOM OF LOTHIAN AND BORDERS AT LINLITHGOW

Court ref no C111/1994

MOTION FOR THE PURSUER

in the cause

MRS SHARON BLANE (Assisted Person), residing at 4 Harriet Drive, Linlithgow

PURSUER

against

JOHN BLANE, whose whereabouts are not known

DEFENDER

The pursuer moves the court to ordain Mrs Martha Blane, residing at 4 Abbotsford Place, Linlithgow, to appear at the bar to disclose to the court such information as she has which is relevant to the whereabouts of Amy Blane.

4 June 1994   IN RESPECT WHEREOF

Enrolled solicitor
1 Main Street
Linlithgow
Solicitor for the pursuer

c. Motion for interim interdict prohibiting removal of child from jurisdiction (OCR 33.24(1)(a))

SHERIFFDOM OF LOTHIAN AND BORDERS AT LINLITHGOW

Court ref no C111/1994

MOTION FOR THE PURSUER

in the cause

MRS SHARON BLANE (Assisted Person), residing at 4 Harriet Drive, Linlithgow

PURSUER

against

JOHN BLANE, residing c/o Jones, 5 Abbey Mount, Edinburgh

DEFENDER

The pursuer moves the court to grant interim interdict against the defender from removing Amy Blane, child of the marriage and under the age of 16 years, out of the control of the pursuer or furth of the Sheriffdom of Lothian and Borders.

14 December 1994 IN RESPECT WHEREOF

Enrolled solicitor
1 Main Street
Linlithgow
Solicitor for the pursuer

d. Motion for warrant for intimation or to dispense with intimation (OCR 33.7(6))

SHERIFFDOM OF LOTHIAN AND BORDERS AT LINLITHGOW

Court ref no C111/1994

MOTION FOR THE PURSUER

in the cause

MRS SHARON BLANE (Assisted Person), residing at 4 Harriet Drive, Linlithgow

PURSUER

against

JOHN BLANE, residing c/o Jones, 5 Abbey Mount, Edinburgh

DEFENDER

The pursuer moves the court to grant warrant to intimate the initial writ to Amy Blane, residing at 4 Harriet Drive, Linlithgow or to dispense with such intimation.

14 December 1994   IN RESPECT WHEREOF

Enrolled solicitor
1 Main Street
Linlithgow
Solicitor for the pursuer

12. BLACK v BLACK

Matrimonial home—Dispensation with spouse's consent to dealing

a. Initial writ (OCR 33.67(2))

SHERIFFDOM OF NORTH STRATHCLYDE AT KILMARNOCK

SUMMARY APPLICATION UNDER THE MATRIMONIAL HOMES (FAMILY PROTECTION) (SCOTLAND) ACT 1981, s 7

INITIAL WRIT

in the cause

ALFRED BLACK, residing at 21 Stockton Road, Kilmarnock

PURSUER

against

MRS MAVIS REYNOLDS or BLACK, residing at 12 Albert Drive, Kilmarnock

DEFENDER

The pursuer craves the court:

1. To grant decree dispensing with the consent of the defender to the sale of the heritable subjects at 21 Stockton Road, Kilmarnock by the pursuer to Arthur Connolly, residing at 10 Emmet Place, Ayr, in terms of missives dated 5, 8, 10 and 11 June 1994.
2. To find the defender liable in the expenses of the action.

CONDESCENDENCE

1. The pursuer resides in the heritable subjects owned by him at 21 Stockton Road, Kilmarnock. The pursuer's said subjects are a matrimonial home situated within the territory of this court. This court has jurisdiction. The defender resides at 12 Albert Drive, Kilmarnock.
2. The pursuer has concluded missives dated 5, 8, 10 and 11 June 1994

for sale of his said subjects to Arthur Connolly, residing at 10 Emmet Place, Ayr. The pursuer has repeatedly requested the consent of the defender to the said dealing. Reference is made to correspondence produced herewith. The defender has failed to answer these requests. There are no other steps which the pursuer could reasonably take to obtain an answer to his request for consent. In these circumstances, the defender has withheld her consent unreasonably and the pursuer is entitled to decree as craved.

PLEA-IN-LAW

The defender having withheld her consent unreasonably to a dealing, the pursuer is entitled to decree dispensing with said consent.

IN RESPECT WHEREOF

Enrolled solicitor
4 Whiteley Grove
Kilmarnock
Solicitor for the pursuer

IV HERITAGE PROCEEDINGS

1. THYME HOLDINGS LTD v ALLISONS' PAINT

Landlord and tenant—Declarator and removing—Irritancy of lease

a. Initial writ

2. BLACKSTONE PROPERTIES LTD v MARKET GARDENS LTD

Landlord and tenant—Sequestration and sale

a. Initial writ

3. NORTHERN BANK PLC v MURRAY

Heritable creditor—Declarator and ejection—Calling-up notice

a. Initial writ

4. CLARK v SPENCER

Common property—Declarator and division or sale—Heritable creditor

a. Initial writ

1. THYME HOLDINGS LTD v ALLISONS' PAINT

Landlord and tenant—Removing—Irritancy of lease

a. Initial writ

SHERIFFDOM OF NORTH STRATHCLYDE
AT KILMARNOCK

INITIAL WRIT

in the cause

THYME HOLDINGS LIMITED,
a company with its registered office
at 1 Albyn Place, Glasgow

PURSUERS

against

ALLISONS' PAINT, a firm having a place of business at 40 Love Street, Kilmarnock, and GEORGE ALLISON and ALEXANDER ALLISON both residing at 2 Lambert Drive, Kilmarnock, as partners of the said firm and as individuals

DEFENDERS

The pursuers crave the court:

1. To find and declare that the defenders, having allowed the rent in respect of the subjects hereinafter mentioned to remain unpaid for 21 days after 15 May 1994, being the day appointed for payment thereof, have in terms of the lease granted to them by the pursuers of the subjects situated at 40 Love Street, Kilmarnock, dated 16 August and 2 September and registered in the Books of Council and Session on 17 September, all dates in 1984, thereby incurred an irritancy of the said lease; that the said lease, with all that has followed thereon, is at an end, and that the parties thereto and their successors are no longer bound thereby; and that the pursuers are entitled to enter upon possession of the said subjects, and to dispone thereof at pleasure.

2. To ordain the defenders summarily to flit and remove themselves,

their family, dependants, servants and sub-tenants, with their goods, gear and whole belongings from the said subjects, and to leave the same void and redd, to the end that the pursuers may enter thereon and peaceably possess and enjoy the same, and that under pain of ejection.

3. To find the defenders liable in the expenses of the action.

CONDESCENDENCE

1. The pursuers are a company incorporated under the Companies Acts with its registered office at 1 Albyn Place, Glasgow. The defenders are a firm with a place of business at 40 Love Street, Kilmarnock and the partners thereof with a place of residence at the address in the instance. The present proceedings have as their object a tenancy of heritable property situated at 40 Love Street, Kilmarnock. This court has jurisdiction.

2. The pursuers are heritable proprietors of the shop premises forming and known as 40 Love Street, Kilmarnock, conform to disposition thereof in their favour by Leven Securities Ltd with consent therein mentioned dated 28 November and 15 December 1980 and recorded in the Division of the General Register of Sasines for the County of Kilmarnock on 14 January 1981. By lease between the parties dated 16 August and 2 September and registered in the Books of Council and Session on 17 September, all dates in 1984, the pursuers let the said premises to the defenders. The rent payable thereunder was £5,000 *per annum* payable by half-yearly instalments at Whitsunday and Martinmas in each year. In 1990 the rent was increased in accordance with the provisions of clause SIXTEENTH of the said lease to £10,000 per annum payable by half-yearly instalments of £5,000.

3. Clause SEVENTEENTH of the said lease provided *inter alia* that if at any time during the currency thereof the defenders should allow a half-year's rent to be in arrears for 21 days (whether demanded or not), then the landlords at their option by notice in writing might bring the said lease to an end. The defenders have not paid to the pursuers the half-yearly instalment of rent due at 15 May 1994. The pursuers accordingly exercised the option conferred on them by the said clause SEVENTEENTH by notice in writing to bring the said lease to an end. A copy of the notice sent to the defenders dated 10 June 1994 is produced and its whole terms held as repeated herein *brevitatis causa*.

4. Notwithstanding the terms of the said notice, the defenders have failed to remove from the said premises. The pursuers are accordingly under the necessity of raising the present action for declarator and removing.

PLEAS-IN-LAW

1. The defenders having incurred an irritancy of the said lease, decree of declarator should be pronounced in terms of the first crave.

2. The defenders having failed to remove from the said premises, decree of removing should be pronounced in terms of the second crave.

IN RESPECT WHEREOF

Enrolled solicitor
4 Chester Avenue
Kilmarnock
Solicitor for the pursuers

2. BLACKSTONE PROPERTIES LTD v MARKET GARDENS LTD

Landlord and tenant—Sequestration and sale

a. Initial writ

SHERIFFDOM OF NORTH STRATHCLYDE
AT CAMPBELTOWN

INITIAL WRIT

in the cause

BLACKSTONE PROPERTIES LIMITED, a company with a place of business at 4 George Square, Oban

PURSUERS

against

MARKET GARDENS LIMITED, a company with a place of business at 29 Low Street, Campbeltown

DEFENDERS

The pursuers crave the court:

To sequestrate and to grant warrant to officers of court to inventory and secure the whole stock, fittings, furniture, goods and other effects, so far as subject to the pursuers' hypothec, which are or have been in the premises occupied by the defenders at 29 Low Street, Campbeltown since 11 November 1993, in security and for payment to the pursuers (1) of the sum of SEVEN THOUSAND FIVE HUNDRED POUNDS (£7,500), being the annual rent thereof, due and payable at 11 November 1993 with interest thereon at the rate of eight *per centum per annum* from the said date until payment, and with expenses; and (2) of the like sum of SEVEN THOUSAND FIVE HUNDRED POUNDS (£7,500), being the current year's rent to become due and payable at 11 November 1994, with interest as aforesaid from the said date, and with expenses; and thereafter to grant warrant to sell by public roup the whole, or so much of the said sequestrated subjects as will satisfy and pay to the pursuers the said rents, interest and expenses (the date of 11 November 1994 being first come and bygone before granting warrant to sell for the rent then to become due, and interest and expenses); and to appoint payment to be made to the pursuer of the rents, interest, and expenses aforesaid, out of the proceeds of any sale or sales or out of any sums consigned to have the sequestration recalled; and to decern against the defenders for the said rents when due, interest and expenses, in the event of no sale taking place, or for such balance as may remain due to the pursuers after sequestration and sale, and after payment of expenses and all preferable claims therefrom; and, in the event of the subject of the hypothec being exhausted, or the premises being insufficiently furnished and hypothecated after any sale hereunder, to ordain the defenders to stock and replenish the said premises, so as to afford sufficient security for payment of any remaining rent payable, or to become payable as aforesaid; and, failing their doing so within such time and at the sight of such person as the court shall appoint, to grant warrant summarily to eject the defenders, and their goods, gear and effects, from the said premises; and to authorise the pursuers to relet the same for such periods and for such rents as may appear best; and to grant warrant to officers of court to break open, if necessary, shut and lockfast places for the purpose of carrying the warrants that may be granted into execution; and to decern against the defenders for payment of any balance of the said rents and expenses; that may be due by them and may not previously have been decerned for; and to grant warrant to arrest on the dependence of the action.

CONDESCENDENCE

1. The pursuers are a company incorporated under the Companies Acts with a place of business at 4 George Square, Oban. The defenders are a company incorporated under the Companies Acts with a place of business at 29 Low Street, Campbeltown. They are believed to be domiciled there. The present proceedings have as their object a tenancy of heritable property at 29 Low Street, Campbeltown. This court has jurisdiction.

2. By lease dated 4 July 1992, the pursuers let to the defenders the heritable subjects at 29 Low Street, Campbeltown at an annual rent of £7,500, payable on 11 November each year. The defenders have failed to make payment of the annual rent due at 11 November 1993. In respect that less than three months have elapsed since the said date, the pursuers are entitled to sequestration and sale and other remedies as craved in respect of payment of rent presently due and payable.

3. The defenders' said business has been unsuccessful. They have numerous creditors. Various effects belonging to them have been removed from the said subjects. The pursuers believe and aver that these items have been sold in order to raise moneys to pay the defenders' said creditors. In these circumstances, the pursuers are entitled to sequestration and sale and other remedies as craved in respect of security for rent due and payable on 11 November 1994.

PLEAS-IN-LAW

1. The defenders being in arrears in respect of rent presently due and payable, and being *vergens ad inopiam* and being in the course of removing

their effects, the pursuers are entitled to sequestration and sale and other remedies as craved in respect of payment of and security for rent.

2. In the event of the sequestrated effects being insufficient to meet the rent, the pursuers are entitled to warrant to replenish, eject and relet all as craved.

IN RESPECT WHEREOF

Enrolled solicitor
14 Henderson Street
Oban
Solicitor for the pursuers

3. NORTHERN BANK PLC v MURRAY

Heritable creditor—Declarator and ejection—Calling-up notice

a. Initial writ

SHERIFFDOM OF TAYSIDE CENTRAL AND FIFE
AT STIRLING

INITIAL WRIT

in the cause

NORTHERN BANK PLC, a company with its Head Office at Northern House, Halifax Road, Leeds

PURSUERS

against

HAMISH MURRAY and MRS MARY MURRAY, both residing at 125 Main Street, Stirling

DEFENDERS

The pursuers crave the court:

1. To find and declare that the pursuers have a right to enter into possession of the heritable subjects known as 125 Main Street, Stirling, being the subjects more particularly described in the standard security for all sums of principal and interest due and to become due by the defenders to the pursuers granted by the defenders in favour of the pursuers and recorded in the Division of the General Register of Sasines for the County of Stirling on 29 December 1988 and to receive and recover the rent of and for the said subjects or at least so much of the rent as shall satisfy and pay the pursuers all sums of principal and interest due to them under the said standard security and exercise in relation to the said subjects all other powers competent to a creditor in lawful possession of the security subjects by virtue of the Conveyancing and Feudal Reform (Scotland) Act 1970.

2. To grant warrant to officers of court summarily to eject the defenders, their family, dependants and servants with their goods, gear and whole belongings from the said subjects and to make the same void and

redd to the end that the pursuers may enter thereon and peaceably possess and enjoy the same.

3. To find the defenders liable in the expenses of the action.

CONDESCENDENCE

1. The pursuers are a company incorporated under the Companies Acts with its head office at Northern House, Halifax Road, Leeds. The defenders reside in heritable subjects at 125 Main Street, Stirling (hereinafter referred to as 'the subjects'). They are believed to be domiciled there. These proceedings have as their object rights *in rem* in the subjects, which are situated within the territory of this court. This court accordingly has jurisdiction.

2. The pursuers are creditors under the standard security for all sums of principal and interest due and to become due by the defenders to them granted by the defenders in favour of the pursuers and recorded in the Division of the General Register of Sasines for the County of Stirling on 29 December 1988. The defenders are the heritable proprietors of the subjects described in the said standard security, namely the subjects hereinbefore referred to.

3. On or about 15 March 1994 the pursuers served on the defenders a notice calling up the said standard security under and in terms of section 19 of the Conveyancing and Feudal Reform (Scotland) Act 1970. The calling-up notice, detailing the sums of principal and interest due by the defenders as at that date, is produced herewith and its terms held as repeated herein *brevitatis causa*. The said calling-up notice has not been complied with.

4. In these circumstances, the pursuers are entitled to enter into possession of the subjects and exercise all powers competent to a creditor in lawful possession of the security subjects and to that end to have the defenders ejected therefrom, all as craved.

PLEAS-IN-LAW

1. The defenders having failed to comply with a duly served calling-up notice, the pursuers are entitled to decree of declarator as first craved.

2. The defenders being in default in due payment of the principal after formal requisition, the pursuers are entitled to decree of ejection as second craved.

IN RESPECT WHEREOF

Enrolled solicitor
11 George Place
Stirling
Solicitor for the pursuers

4. CLARK v SPENCER

Common property—Declarator and division or sale—Heritable creditor

a. Initial writ

SHERIFFDOM OF LOTHIAN AND BORDERS AT EDINBURGH

INITIAL WRIT

in the cause

MARILYN CLARK, residing at 24 Harrison Drive, Edinburgh

PURSUER

against

JOHN SPENCER, residing at 24 Harrison Drive, Edinburgh

DEFENDER

The pursuer craves the court:

1. To find and declare that the pursuer is entitled to insist in an action of division or sale of All and Whole the subjects known as 24 Harrison Drive, Edinburgh, and described in the disposition granted by the trustees of William Ramsay in favour of Albert Cooper dated 9th, 12th and 17th and recorded in the Division of the General Register of Sasines applicable to the County of Edinburgh, now Midlothian, on the 21st, all days of May 1930; to divide the said subjects between the pursuer and the defender, or if the division of the said subjects is found to be impracticable or inexpedient, to find and declare that the same should be sold and the proceeds divided between the pursuer and the defender, and to grant warrant to sell accordingly; and to allocate the expenses of the sale and of this process between the pursuer and the defender.

2. To grant warrant to intimate this initial writ to the Sunderland Building Society, 1 Town Place, Sunderland, as the holders of a heritable security over the said subjects at 24 Harrison Drive, Edinburgh.

3. To find the defender liable in the expenses of the action to the extent of one-half thereof, or, in the event of his offering opposition hereto, in full.

CONDESCENDENCE

1. The parties reside at 24 Harrison Drive, Edinburgh. They are domiciled there. The present proceedings have as their object rights *in rem* in the said heritable property (hereinafter referred to as 'the subjects'), situated within the territory of this court. This court accordingly has jurisdiction. Warrant is sought to intimate this initial writ to the Sunderland Building Society, designed in the second crave, holders of a standard security over the subjects.

2. The parties are the *pro indiviso* heritable proprietors of the subjects by virtue of a disposition in their favour granted by Major Iain Harcourt on 5 June 1979 and recorded in the Division of the General Register of Sasines applicable to the County of Midlothian on 9 June 1979. The subjects are incapable of division. The pursuer seeks the sale thereof as craved. The parties have been unable to reach agreement on the sale of the subjects. This action is accordingly necessary.

PLEA-IN-LAW

The pursuer and the defender being *pro indiviso* proprietors of the subjects, the pursuer is entitled to insist in the present action.

IN RESPECT WHEREOF

Enrolled solicitor
22 Castle Drive
Edinburgh
Solicitor for the pursuer

V MISCELLANEOUS PROCEEDINGS

1. MURPHY v HAMILTON

Breach of interdict

a. Initial writ

2. KEATING v BANK OF WALES PLC

Suspension of charge

a. Initial writ

3. GRAY v STRATHKELVIN HEALTH BOARD

Recovery of documents

a. Initial writ

4. PORTER v JEDBURGH DISTRICT LICENSING BOARD

Local government—Licensing—Board acting contrary to natural justice

a. Initial writ

5. GEDDES v WEST HIGHLAND REGIONAL COUNCIL

Local government—Education—Refusal of placing request

a. Initial writ

6. SOUNDS GOOD LIMITED v LEITH DISTRICT COUNCIL

Local government—Control of pollution—Noise

a. Initial writ

7. MACTAGGART v GOVAN DISTRICT COUNCIL

Local government—Housing—Notice requiring works to be done

a. Initial writ

8. DOBBIE v THE SECRETARY OF STATE FOR SCOTLAND

Mental health—Discharge from short term detention in hospital

a. Initial writ

9. BLAKE v THE LORD ADVOCATE

Road traffic—Driving licence—Physical fitness of drivers

a. Initial writ

10. JOHNSTONE, PETITIONER

Trust—Appointment of new trustee

a. Petition

11. MARSHALL, PETITIONER

Trust—Removal of trustee

a. Petition

12. GRADY, PETITIONER

Trust—Completion of title to trust property by beneficiary of lapsed trust

a. Petition

13. ANDERSON, PETITIONER

Bankruptcy—Sequestration of individual—Apparent insolvency constituted by non-compliance with statutory demand

a. Petition

14. SOUTHERN BANK PLC, PETITIONERS

Bankruptcy—Sequestration of firm—Apparent insolvency constituted by expiry of days of charge without payment—Appointment of interim trustee before sequestration

a. Petition

15. GLOVER, PETITIONER

Bankruptcy—Sequestration of deceased debtor's estates

a. Petition

16. HARVEY, PETITIONER

Judicial factor—Curator bonis—Special powers—Dispensation with service upon incapax

a. Petition

17. DIXON, PETITIONER

Judicial factor—Winding-up of dissolved firm

a. Petition

18. TAIT, PETITIONER

Judicial factor—Deceased person's estates

a. Petition

19. INVERCLYDE PRODUCTS LIMITED, PETITIONERS

Company—Liquidation—Company resolving by special resolution to be wound up by the court

a. Petition
b. Note for leave to commence proceedings against company
c. Note for interim determination of amount of outlays and remuneration payable to liquidator

20. WESTERN BANK PLC, PETITIONERS

Company—Liquidation—Company unable to pay its debts as defined by non-compliance with statutory demand

a. Petition
b. Note for dispensation with settlement of list of contributories
c. Note for order for public examination of company officer

21. MANGROVE LIMITED, PETITIONERS

Company—Liquidation—Company unable to pay its debts as defined by expiry of days of charge without payment—Provisional liquidator

a. Petition

22. HAPPY DAYS LIMITED, PETITIONERS

Company—Administration order

a. Petition

23. BAXTER, PETITIONER

Company—Protection of members against unfair prejudice

a. Petition

24. JOHNSTONE MATTHEWS LIMITED, PETITIONERS

Company—Restoration of company name to register of companies

a. Petition

1. MURPHY v HAMILTON

Breach of interdict

a. Initial writ

SHERIFFDOM OF LOTHIAN AND BORDERS AT SELKIRK

INITIAL WRIT

in the cause

ELSPETH MURPHY, residing at
4 Crosby Road, Selkirk

PURSUER

against

JAMES HAMILTON, residing at
21 Tottenham Court, Selkirk

DEFENDER

The pursuer craves the court:

1. To ordain the defender to appear personally before the court on such day and at such hour as the court may appoint to answer for breach of interdict granted by this court on 10 January 1994; and, failing his appearance before the court as aforesaid, to grant warrant to officers of the court to apprehend the defender and bring him before the court to answer as aforesaid; and, on the charge being admitted or proved, to visit the defender with such punishment as to the court shall seem just.
2. To find the defender liable in the expenses of the action.

CONDESCENDENCE

1. The pursuer resides at 4 Crosby Road, Selkirk. The defender resides at 21 Tottenham Court, Selkirk. On 10 January 1994, this court granted interdict against the defender from molesting the pursuer by abusing her verbally, threatening her, putting her into a state of fear and alarm or distress or using violence towards her. The said order of the court was served on the defender on 12 January 1994. Execution of service is produced.

2. On or about 20 February 1994, the defender accosted the pursuer in the street outside her said place of residence. He abused her verbally and

threatened her with violence. In these circumstances, the defender is in breach of interdict and this action is necessary.

PLEA-IN-LAW

The defender being in breach of interdict, should be punished therefor.

IN RESPECT WHEREOF

Enrolled solicitor
1 Hope Road
Selkirk
Solicitor for the pursuer

Selkirk 13 March 1994

I do not intend to intervene and to that extent I concur in the foregoing writ.

'A. Smith'
Senior Procurator Fiscal Depute

2. KEATING v BANK OF WALES PLC

Suspension of charge

a. Initial writ

SHERIFFDOM OF GLASGOW AND STRATHKELVIN
AT GLASGOW

INITIAL WRIT

in the cause

JOHN ANDREW KEATING, residing at 49 Porteous Place, Glasgow

PURSUER

against

BANK OF WALES PLC, a company with its head office at 21 Swansea Place, Cardiff

DEFENDERS

The pursuer craves the court:

1. To suspend a pretended charge served by the defenders on the pursuer on 15 June 1994 given on a decree of this court for payment dated 10 January 1994 and extracted on 21 February 1994 and diligence following thereon.
2. To find the defenders liable in the expenses of the action.

CONDESCENDENCE

1. The pursuer resides at 49 Porteous Place, Glasgow. He has been so resident for at least three months immediately preceding the raising of this action. He is domiciled there. This court has jurisdiction over him. Decree was granted against him by this court on 10 January 1994, and extracted on 21 February 1994, for payment of the sum of £12,500, together with interest and expenses, to the defenders, who are a company incorporated under the Companies Acts with its head office at 21 Swansea Place, Cardiff.
2. On 15 June 1994 a pretended charge for payment of the said sum,

together with interest and expenses, was served by the defenders on the pursuer given on the said decree. However, on or about 11 May 1994, the pursuer had made payment in full to the defenders of all sums due to them, including such interest and expenses, as will be vouched. This application is therefore necessary.

PLEA-IN-LAW

The charger's claim having been satisfied, the said charge and diligence following thereon should be suspended as craved.

IN RESPECT WHEREOF

Enrolled solicitor
20 Marbert Road
Glasgow
Solicitor for the pursuer

3. GRAY v STRATHKELVIN HEALTH BOARD

Recovery of documents

a. Initial writ

SHERIFFDOM OF GLASGOW AND STRATHKELVIN
AT GLASGOW

SUMMARY APPLICATION UNDER THE ADMINISTRATION
OF JUSTICE (SCOTLAND) ACT 1972, s 1(1)

INITIAL WRIT

in the cause

MRS ELIZABETH MARTIN or GRAY, residing at 11 Coates Terrace, Linlithgow, suing as guardian of Lisa Gray, residing with her

PURSUER

against

STRATHKELVIN HEALTH BOARD, 10 March Street, Glasgow

DEFENDERS

The pursuer craves the court:

1. To grant an order for the recovery from the defenders of (a) all books of Glasgow District General Hospital relating to the child Lisa Gray, and in particular all reports, records, charts, x-ray photographs and other documents and films showing or tending to show the nature and extent of any condition from which the child was suffering while under treatment at the said hospital as an in-patient or as an out-patient at any time between 20 July 1986 and the present date; the nature and extent of all medical or surgical treatment given to the said child at any time during the said period, with particular reference to the operative procedures carried out in March 1990; and the effects of consequences of all such treatment upon the condition of the said child; and (b) failing principals, drafts, copies or duplicates of the above or any of them.

2. To find the defenders liable in expenses in the event of their offering opposition hereto.

CONDESCENDENCE

1. The pursuer resides at 11 Coates Terrace, Linlithgow. She sues as guardian of her daughter, Lisa Gray (hereinafter 'the child'), who was born on 20 July 1986 and who resides with her. The defenders are a health authority with its headquarters at 10 March Street, Glasgow. They are domiciled there. This court has jurisdiction.

2. Following the birth of the child in July 1986, it was discovered that she suffered from a heart defect, consisting of an open ductus which ought to have closed before birth. At that time the child was apparently happy, healthy and active, although the said defect gave rise to high blood and lung pressure. It was decided that when the child was aged four she should undergo open heart surgery with a view to correcting the said defect. On or about 12 March 1990, the said surgical operation was carried out by Mr Albert Smith at Glasgow District General Hospital. This was known to be a serious operation, involving the risk of failure or of the development of complications thereafter. When the said operation had been completed, the pursuer was informed by the said surgeon that all had gone according to plan. Thereafter, some two days later, the pursuer was informed that the child had suffered renal failure. This improved with treatment, but it was then discovered that the child had completely lost the use of her legs. The pursuer was informed that she would never walk again, and furthermore that her excessive blood pressure would require to be controlled by drugs. Thereafter the condition of the child's legs deteriorated, and certain deformities became apparent. In 1992 and 1993, the pursuer again sought medical advice to see if any improvement in the condition of the child's legs could be achieved by any further operative measures. Eventually, the child was re-admitted for this purpose to the said hospital in about February 1994. As a preliminary measure, a cardiac catheterisation was carried out. Shortly thereafter, a doctor at the said hospital disclosed to the pursuer that the said surgical measure had revealed that in the course of the open heart surgery in 1990 the main aorta had by mistake been tied off instead of the ductus. In this way, the blood supply to the lower part of the body of the child had been cut off, thus causing the paralysis of her lower limbs.

3. The pursuer intends to raise an action of damages against the defenders who were in 1990 in occupation and control of the said hospital and who were the employers of the said surgeon, Mr Albert Smith. The said proceedings will inevitably involve allegations of professional negligence against the said surgeon, who is now deceased. On the information available to her, the pursuer is confident that there exist good grounds for the action which she intends to raise, but she is reluctant to make specific and detailed allegations of professional negligence against the said surgeon without first having the benefit of expert advice in the light of all relevant facts and circumstances. For this purpose, the pursuer is desirous of obtaining an order for the recovery of the whole records of the said

Glasgow District General Hospital relating to the treatment received there by the child between 20 July 1986 and the present date. In particular, she seeks to recover the records of the said hospital relative to the operative treatment carried out as aforesaid by the said Mr Albert Smith in March 1990 and showing or tending to show the nature, extent and consequences thereof. The pursuer contends that the said documents relate to questions which may relevantly arise in proceedings which are likely to be brought.

PLEA-IN-LAW

The said hospital records relating to questions which might relevantly arise in proceedings which are likely to be brought, an order should be granted for their recovery, as craved.

IN RESPECT WHEREOF

Enrolled solicitor
5 Wemyss Place
Edinburgh
Solicitor for the pursuer

4. PORTER v JEDBURGH DISTRICT LICENSING BOARD

Local government—Licensing—Board acting contrary to natural justice

a. Initial writ

SHERIFFDOM OF LOTHIAN AND BORDERS AT JEDBURGH

SUMMARY APPLICATION UNDER THE LICENSING (SCOTLAND) ACT 1976, s 39(1)

INITIAL WRIT

in the cause

RAYMOND PORTER, residing at 19 Shore Street, Jedburgh

PURSUER

against

JEDBURGH DISTRICT LICENSING BOARD, 1 Low Street, Jedburgh

FIRST DEFENDERS

and

MRS JOANNA SMITH, residing at 42 Truro Court, Jedburgh

SECOND DEFENDER

The pursuer craves the court:

1. To reverse the decision of the first defenders made on 20 May 1994 to refuse the application by the pursuer for a new off-sale licence in respect of the premises at 12 Dryburgh Street, Jedburgh; and to grant the application; or to make such other order as the court thinks fit.

2. To find the defenders liable in expenses in the event of their offering opposition hereto.

CONDESCENDENCE

1. The pursuer resides at 19 Shore Street, Jedburgh. The first defenders are a licensing authority with its headquarters at 1 Low Street, Jedburgh. They are domiciled there. This court has jurisdiction. The second defender resides at 42 Truro Court, Jedburgh.

2. On 20 May 1994, at their quarterly meeting, the first defenders considered an application by the pursuer for a new off-sale licence in respect of the premises at 12 Dryburgh Street, Jedburgh. The second defender was an objector at that hearing and was the only other party who appeared.

3. On the said date, the first defenders refused the said application. In so doing, they purported to find that a statutory ground for refusal applied to the application, videlicet that set forth in section 17(1)(d) of the Licensing (Scotland) Act 1976, which so far as material provides: 'that, having regard to the facilities of the same or similar kind already available in the locality . . . the grant of an application would result in the overprovision of such facilities.' Thereafter, they issued to the pursuer a statement of reasons, a copy whereof is produced and its terms held as repeated herein *brevitatis causa*.

4. In arriving at their decision aforesaid, the first defenders acted contrary to natural justice. In their said statement of reasons, it is stated that 'in coming to their decision the Board had regard to their own knowledge of conditions in the area. . . .'. The first defenders did not at the said meeting divulge to the pursuer any such knowledge on their part. The pursuer was given no opportunity to counter or comment on the same. In these circumstances, the first defenders' decision should be reversed and the pursuer's application granted.

PLEA-IN-LAW

The first defenders in arriving at their decision having acted contrary to natural justice, the said decision should be reversed and the pursuer's application granted, as craved.

IN RESPECT WHEREOF

Enrolled solicitor
12 High Street
Jedburgh
Solicitor for the pursuer

5. GEDDES v WEST HIGHLAND REGIONAL COUNCIL

Local government—Education—Refusal of placing request

a. Initial writ

SHERIFFDOM OF GRAMPIAN, HIGHLAND AND ISLANDS AT OBAN

SUMMARY APPLICATION UNDER THE EDUCATION (SCOTLAND) ACT 1980, s 28F(1)

INITIAL WRIT

in the cause

FRANCIS GEDDES, residing at 21 Ackner Drive, Oban

PURSUER

against

WEST HIGHLAND REGIONAL COUNCIL, 121 Millard Street, Oban

DEFENDERS

The pursuer craves the court:

1. To reverse the decision of the defenders' appeal committee made on 30 June 1994 and refuse to confirm the decision of the defenders dated 19 May 1994 refusing the written request by the pursuer to them to place his child, Andrew John Geddes, in the school specified in the request, namely Rutherglen Primary School; and to require the defenders to give effect to the said placing request.

2. To find the defenders liable in expenses in the event of their offering opposition hereto.

CONDESCENDENCE

1. The pursuer resides at 21 Ackner Drive, Oban. The defenders are an education authority with its headquarters at 121 Millard Street, Oban. They manage Rutherglen Primary School, which is situated within the territory of this court. This court accordingly has jurisdiction.

2. On 19 May 1994, the defenders made a decision refusing the written request by the pursuer to them to place his child, Andrew John Geddes (hereinafter 'the child'), in the school specified in the request, namely the said school. The defenders purported to be satisfied that a ground of refusal specified in section 28A(3) of the Education (Scotland) Act 1980 existed, videlicet that set forth in paragraph (b), which so far as material provides that the duty to place the child does not apply: 'if the education normally provided at the specified school is not suited to the age . . . of the child'. Reference is made to the defenders' statement of reasons for their decision, which is produced and its terms held as repeated herein *brevitatis causa*. The pursuer thereafter referred the said decision to an appeal committee, which confirmed the defenders' decision on 30 June 1994.

3. The child was born on 2 January 1991. He is a gifted child. Reference is made to reports by educational psychologists produced herewith, the terms of which are held as repeated herein *brevitatis causa*. It is essential for his mental, educational and emotional development that he attend school at this stage, notwithstanding his tender years. He is able to benefit from the education normally provided at the said school. In these circumstances, no ground of refusal in respect of the placing request exists, and the said decision should not be confirmed. In any event, it is in all the circumstances inappropriate that the said decision should be confirmed.

PLEA-IN-LAW

There existing no ground of refusal in respect of the placing request, and in any event it being in all the circumstances inappropriate to do so, the said decision should not be confirmed.

IN RESPECT WHEREOF

Enrolled solicitor
1 Marr Road
Oban
Solicitor for the pursuer

6. SOUNDS GOOD LIMITED v LEITH DISTRICT COUNCIL

Local government—Control of pollution—Noise

a. Initial writ

SHERIFFDOM OF LOTHIAN AND BORDERS AT EDINBURGH

SUMMARY APPLICATION UNDER THE CONTROL OF POLLUTION ACT 1974, s 58(3)

INITIAL WRIT

in the cause

SOUNDS GOOD LIMITED, a company with its registered office at 10 Manfred Place, Leith, Edinburgh

PURSUERS

against

LEITH DISTRICT COUNCIL, Town Hall, Leith, Edinburgh

DEFENDERS

The pursuers crave the court:

1. To recall the notice served on the pursuers by the defenders on 5 July 1994 or to vary it in favour of the pursuers in such manner as the court thinks fit.
2. To find the defenders liable in expenses in the event of their offering opposition hereto.

CONDESCENDENCE

1. The pursuers are a company incorporated under the Companies Acts with its registered office at 10 Manfred Place, Leith, Edinburgh. The defenders are a local authority with its headquarters at Town Hall, Leith, Edinburgh. They are domiciled there. This court has jurisdiction.

2. On 5 July 1994 the defenders served on the pursuers a notice under section 58(1) of the Control of Pollution Act 1974 prohibiting the recurrence of an alleged nuisance, namely noise emanating from the pursuers' premises at 2 Maclaren Place, Leith, Edinburgh. The said notice is produced herewith and its terms held as repeated herein *brevitatis causa*.

3. The pursuers' said premises are a nightclub which the pursuers operate. The noise to which the notice relates is music played therein. Such is accordingly noise caused in the course of a trade or business. The best practicable means have been used to prevent or at any rate to counteract the effect of the noise. Substantial sums have been expended on soundproofing the premises. Reference is made to documentation produced herewith. The notice is in any event unreasonable in its extent. Prohibition of the recurrence of noise would effectively terminate the pursuers' business. In these circumstances, the said notice should be recalled. Alternatively the notice should be varied in favour of the pursuers by substituting for the prohibition of recurrence a requirement of abatement of nuisance or a restriction thereof in such terms as to the court seems proper, or in such other manner as the court thinks fit, all in terms of regulation 4 of the Control of Noise (Appeals) (Scotland) Regulations 1983.

PLEA-IN-LAW

The noise to which the notice relates being noise caused in the course of a trade or business and the best practicable means having been used for preventing or for counteracting the effect of the noise and the notice being in any event unreasonable in its extent, the said notice should be recalled or varied as craved.

IN RESPECT WHEREOF

Enrolled solicitor
1 Maybury Street
Edinburgh
Solicitor for the pursuers

7. MACTAGGART v GOVAN DISTRICT COUNCIL

Local government—Housing—Notice requiring works to be done

a. Initial writ

SHERIFFDOM OF GLASGOW AND STRATHKELVIN
AT GLASGOW

SUMMARY APPLICATION UNDER THE HOUSING
(SCOTLAND) ACT 1987, s 163(1)

INITIAL WRIT

in the cause

FREDERICK MACTAGGART, residing at 20 Ovenstone Road, Govan

PURSUER

against

GOVAN DISTRICT COUNCIL, 1 Royal Park Street, Glasgow

DEFENDERS

The pursuer craves the court:

1. To vary the notice served on the pursuer by the defenders on 10 August 1994 and that by deleting the period of three months specified therein as the period within which the works specified in the notice require to be executed and substituting therefor the period of twelve months or such other period as the court thinks fit.

2. To find the defenders liable in expenses in the event of their offering opposition hereto.

CONDESCENDENCE

1. The pursuer resides at 20 Ovenstone Road, Govan. The defenders are a local authority with its headquarters at 1 Royal Park Street, Glasgow. They are domiciled there. This court has jurisdiction.

2. On 19 August 1994 the defenders served on the pursuer a notice under section 162(1) of the Housing (Scotland) Act 1987 specifying works which in their opinion required to be executed to the pursuer's house at the said address to provide such means of escape from fire as the defenders considered necessary and requiring the pursuer to execute those works within a period of three months from the service of the notice. The said notice is produced herewith and its terms held as repeated herein *brevitatis causa*.

3. It is highly unlikely that the said works can be executed within the said period. The pursuer will require to obtain necessary consents and put the works out to tender. The works themselves are unlikely to be capable of speedy completion. In these circumstances, the time within which the works are to be executed is not reasonably sufficient for the purpose. A period of twelve months would be reasonable. The said notice should therefore be varied as craved.

PLEA-IN-LAW

The time within which the works specified in the notice are to be executed not being reasonably sufficient for the purpose, the said notice should be varied as craved.

IN RESPECT WHEREOF

Enrolled solicitor
10 Shamrock Place
Glasgow
Solicitor for the pursuer

8. DOBBIE v THE SECRETARY OF STATE FOR SCOTLAND

Mental health—Discharge from short term detention

a. Initial writ

SHERIFFDOM OF GRAMPIAN, HIGHLAND AND ISLANDS AT INVERNESS

SUMMARY APPLICATION UNDER THE MENTAL HEALTH (SCOTLAND) ACT 1984, s 26(6)

INITIAL WRIT

in the cause

JAMES IAN DOBBIE, at present an in-patient in the Royal Inverness Psychiatric Hospital, Inverness

PURSUER

against

THE SECRETARY OF STATE FOR SCOTLAND, St Andrew's House, Edinburgh

DEFENDER

The pursuer craves the court:

1. To order the discharge of the pursuer from detention in the Royal Inverness Psychiatric Hospital, Inverness.

2. To find the defender liable in expenses in the event of his offering opposition hereto.

CONDESCENDENCE

1. The pursuer is presently an in-patient in the Royal Inverness Psychiatric Hospital, Inverness (hereinafter 'the hospital'). The hospital being situated within this Sheriffdom, this court has jurisdiction. The defender is the Secretary of State for Scotland.

2. On 15 August 1994, the pursuer was admitted to the hospital in

pursuance of section 24 of the Mental Health (Scotland) Act 1984. After the expiry of 72 hours, he was detained in the hospital, purportedly in terms of section 26(1) of that Act.

3. The pursuer is not suffering from mental disorder of a nature and degree which makes it appropriate for him to be liable to be detained in a hospital for medical treatment. He is in a satisfactory state of mental health. In any event, it is not necessary for the health or safety of the pursuer or for the protection of other persons that he should receive such treatment. The pursuer is willing to attend the hospital on an out-patient basis. In these circumstances, the pursuer should be discharged from detention in the hospital.

PLEA-IN-LAW

The pursuer not suffering from mental disorder of a nature and degree which makes it appropriate for him to be liable to be detained in a hospital for medical treatment, and in any event it not being necessary for the health or safety of the pursuer or for the protection of other persons that he should receive such treatment, the pursuer should be discharged from detention in the hospital, as craved.

IN RESPECT WHEREOF

Enrolled solicitor
21 Queen's Road
Inverness
Solicitor for the pursuer

9. BLAKE v THE LORD ADVOCATE

Road traffic—Driving licence—Physical fitness of drivers

a. Initial writ

SHERIFFDOM OF NORTH STRATHCLYDE AT GREENOCK

SUMMARY APPLICATION UNDER THE ROAD TRAFFIC ACT 1988, s 100(1)

INITIAL WRIT

in the cause

COLIN ALFRED BLAKE, residing at 21 Clifford Road, Greenock

PURSUER

against

THE RIGHT HONOURABLE PETER JONES MP, Her Majesty's Advocate, Crown Office, 25 Chambers Street, Edinburgh representing the Secretary of State for Transport

DEFENDER

The pursuer craves the court:

1. To reverse the decision of the Secretary of State for Transport issued on 10 June 1994 to revoke the pursuer's driving licence.
2. To find the defender liable in expenses in the event of his offering opposition hereto.

CONDESCENDENCE

1. The pursuer resides at 21 Clifford Road, Greenock. This court has jurisdiction. The defender represents the Secretary of State for Transport (hereinafter 'the Secretary of State').
2. On 10 June 1994, the Secretary of State served notice in writing on the pursuer revoking the pursuer's driving licence with immediate effect.

The Secretary of State purported to be satisfied that the pursuer was suffering from a relevant disability, videlicet a non-prescribed disability likely to cause the driving of a vehicle by him in pursuance of a licence to be a source of danger to the public.

3. The decision of the Secretary of State aforesaid was unjustified and should be reversed. The pursuer is not suffering from any disability likely to cause the driving of a vehicle by him in pursuance of a licence to be a source of danger to the public, The pursuer is fit and healthy and well able to drive safely. In these circumstances, the decision to revoke the pursuer's licence should be reversed as craved.

PLEA-IN-LAW

The pursuer not suffering from any disability likely to cause the driving of a vehicle by him in pursuance of a licence to be a source of danger to the public, the decision to revoke his licence should be reversed.

IN RESPECT WHEREOF

       Enrolled solicitor
       1 Orchard Road
       Greenock
       Solicitor for the pursuer

10. JOHNSTONE, PETITIONER

Trust—Appointment of new trustee

a. Petition

SHERIFFDOM OF TAYSIDE, CENTRAL AND FIFE AT ALLOA

PETITION

of

EDWINA MARION ALICE JOHNSTONE, residing at 46 Barnton Place, St Andrews

for

Appointment of a new trustee to act under the trust disposition and settlement of the late Marvin Johnstone

The petitioner craves the court:

To appoint this petition to be intimated on the walls of court and to be served on Ruth Johnstone, residing at 61 Marlborough Street, London; to ordain her and all other parties interested to lodge answers, if so advised, within 21 days after intimation and service; thereafter, upon resuming consideration hereof, with or without answers and after such inquiry if any as may be thought necessary, to appoint John Thompson, Solicitor, 14 Queen Street, Alloa, or such other person as the court thinks fit, to be a trustee acting under the trust, disposition and settlement of the late Marvin Johnstone dated 21 May 1979 and registered in the Books of Council and Session on 10 June 1986, with all the powers incident to that office; and to find the petitioner entitled to the expenses of this petition and the procedure to follow hereon out of the trust estate.

CONDESCENDENCE

1. By trust, disposition and settlement dated 21 May 1979 and registered in the Books of Council and Session on 10 June 1986, Marvin Johnstone (hereinafter referred to as 'the truster') appointed John Blackie to be his trustee and conveyed to him his whole means and estate, heritable and moveable, real and personal, in trust for the purposes

therein specified. A copy of the said trust, disposition and settlement is produced. The truster died at Alloa on 10 November 1985. At that date, which was the date of the coming into operation of the trust, he was domiciled in the Sheriffdom of Tayside, Central and Fife. This court accordingly has jurisdiction.

2. The beneficiaries of the said trust estate are the petitioner and her sister, Ruth Johnstone, designed in the crave. There are no other persons with an interest therein.

3. The said John Blackie, having accepted office as sole trustee aforesaid, has disappeared for a period of at least six months. He was last seen in Alloa in late 1991. His whereabouts are not known. He has not assumed any other person to act as trustee. The petitioner is therefore under necessity of bringing this petition for appointment of a new trustee, in terms of the Trusts (Scotland) Act 1921, section 22. She respectfully suggests that John Thompson, Solicitor, designed in the crave, is a suitable person for the office of trustee.

PLEA-IN-LAW

The sole trustee of the said trust estate having disappeared for a period of at least six months, a new trustee should be appointed as craved.

IN RESPECT WHEREOF

Enrolled solicitor
14 Queen Street
Alloa
Solicitor for the petitioner

11. MARSHALL, PETITIONER

Trust—Removal of trustee

a. Petition

SHERIFFDOM OF TAYSIDE, CENTRAL AND FIFE
AT ARBROATH

PETITION

of

ALAN JOSEPH MARSHALL, residing at 5 St Mary's Place, Lenzie

for

Removal of a trustee acting under the trust deed of John Peters

The petitioner craves the court:

To appoint this petition to be intimated on the walls of court and to be served on Brian Maxwell, c/o Dunfermline Royal Psychiatric Hospital, Dunfermline, and Ivan Peters, residing at 42 Andover Street, Dunfermline; to ordain them and all other parties interested to lodge answers, if so advised, within 21 days after intimation and service; thereafter, upon resuming consideration hereof, with or without answers and after such inquiry if any as may be thought necessary, to remove the said Brian Maxwell from the office of trustee acting under the trust deed of John Peters dated 4 November 1979 and registered in the Books of Council and Session on 15 December 1979; and to find the petitioner entitled to the expenses of this petition and the procedure to follow hereon out of the capital of the trust estate.

CONDESCENDENCE

1. By trust deed dated 4 November 1979 and registered in the Books of Council and Session on 15 December 1979, John Peters (hereinafter referred to as 'the truster') appointed the petitioner and Brian Maxwell, designed in the crave, to be his trustees and conveyed to them certain property in trust for the purposes therein specified. A copy of the said trust deed is produced. The date of the coming into operation of the trust

was 4 November 1979. As at that date, the truster was domiciled in the Sheriffdom of Tayside, Central and Fife. This court accordingly has jurisdiction.

2. The sole beneficiary of the said trust is Ivan Peters, designed in the crave. There are no other persons with an interest therein.

3. The said Brian Maxwell has become incapable of acting as trustee aforesaid by reason of mental disability, conform to medical certificates produced herewith. The petitioner accordingly brings this petition for his removal from the office of trustee acting under the said trust deed, in terms of the Trusts (Scotland) Act 1921, section 23.

PLEA-IN-LAW

The said trustee having become incapable of acting as trustee by reason of mental disability, should be removed from the office of trustee as craved.

IN RESPECT WHEREOF

Enrolled solicitor
15 Abingdon Street
Arbroath
Solicitor for the petitioner

12. GRADY, PETITIONER

Trust—Completion of title to trust property by beneficiary of lapsed trust

a. Petition

SHERIFFDOM OF GRAMPIAN, HIGHLAND AND ISLANDS
AT DINGWALL

PETITION

of

PAMELA GRADY, residing at 14 Newton Street, Glasgow

for

Authority to complete title to property of George Peter Mackie's trust, now lapsed

The petitioner craves the court:

To appoint this petition to be intimated on the walls of court; to ordain all parties interested to lodge answers, if so advised, within 21 days after intimation; thereafter, upon resuming consideration hereof, with or without answers and after such inquiry if any as may be thought necessary, to authorise and grant warrant to the petitioner to complete a title in her own name to the heritable subjects All and Whole that dwellinghouse being the southmost flat on the ground floor of the tenement number 18 Blackstone Street, Dingwall in the County of Dingwall, being the dwelling-house described and disponed in the disposition by Andrew Maples in favour of George Peter Mackie dated 14 June 1959 and recorded in the Division of the General Register of Sasines for the County of Dingwall on 17 June 1959, together with all rights exclusive, common and mutual thereto, fixtures and fittings therein and parts and pertinents thereof described in the said disposition; and to find any person opposing this petition liable in expenses.

CONDESCENDENCE

1. By trust, disposition and settlement dated 30 June 1976 and registered in the Books of Council and Session on 10 December 1992, George

Peter Mackie (hereinafter referred to as 'the truster') appointed Alexander Forth to be his trustee and conveyed to him his whole means and estate, heritable and moveable, real and personal, in trust for the purposes therein specified. A copy of the said trust, disposition and settlement is produced. The truster died at Dingwall on 16 July 1992. At that date, which was the date of the coming into operation of the trust, he was domiciled in the Sheriffdom of Grampian, Highland and Islands. This court accordingly has jurisdiction.

2. The petitioner is the sole beneficiary of the said trust. There are no other persons with an interest therein.

3. The truster was at the date of his death proprietor of the heritable subjects All and Whole that dwelling-house being the southmost flat on the ground floor of the tenement number 18 Blackstone Street, Dingwall in the County of Dingwall, being the dwelling-house described and disponed in the disposition by Andrew Maples in favour of the truster dated 14 June 1959 and recorded in the Division of the General Register of Sasines for the County of Dingwall on 17 June 1959, together with all rights exclusive, common and mutual thereto, fixtures and fittings therein and parts and pertinents thereof described in the said disposition. The said Alexander Forth, having accepted office as sole trustee aforesaid, died on 15 August 1993 without having assumed any other person to act as trustee. The trust has therefore lapsed. The petitioner is desirous of completing title to the said heritable subjects in her own name. She therefore brings this petition for authority and warrant to do so, in terms of the Trusts (Scotland) Act 1921, section 24.

PLEA-IN-LAW

The petitioner being the sole beneficiary of a lapsed trust, should be granted the authority and warrant of the court to complete title to trust property in her own name, as craved.

IN RESPECT WHEREOF

Enrolled solicitor
1 Barnstable Road
Glasgow
Solicitor for the petitioner

13. ANDERSON, PETITIONER

Bankruptcy—Sequestration of individual—Apparent insolvency constituted by non-compliance with statutory demand

a. Petition

SHERIFFDOM OF GRAMPIAN, HIGHLAND AND ISLANDS AT ABERDEEN

PETITION

of

COLIN JOHN ANDERSON, residing at 3 Larbert Avenue, Aberdeen

for

Sequestration of the estates of Alan Meikle

The petitioner craves the court:

To grant warrant to cite Alan Meikle, residing at 20 Fortuna Court, Aberdeen, to appear before the court on such date as shall be specified in the warrant, being a date not less than six nor more than 14 days after the date of citation, to show cause why sequestration should not be awarded; to sequestrate the estates now belonging or which shall hereafter belong to the said Alan Meikle before the date of his discharge and declare the same to belong to his creditors for the purposes of the Bankruptcy (Scotland) Act 1985 and to appoint Lewis Brown, Chartered Accountant, 101 West Street, Aberdeen, or such other person as the court thinks fit, to be interim trustee on the said sequestrated estates with the powers and duties prescribed by the said statute and allow him to enter on the duties of his office upon a certified copy of the interlocutor appointing him; and to direct the expenses of this application to be expenses in the sequestration.

CONDESCENDENCE

1. The petitioner is a qualified creditor of Alan Meikle (hereinafter 'the debtor'), designed in the crave, conform to oath and voucher evidencing a

liquid debt of £2,940, produced herewith. The debtor was habitually resident in the Sheriffdom of Grampian, Highland and Islands within the year immediately preceding the date of presentation of this petition. This court accordingly has jurisdiction.

2. The debtor is apparently insolvent. On 5 July 1994 the petitioner served on him, by personal service by an officer of court, a demand in the prescribed form requiring him to pay the said debt or to find security for its payment. Execution of service is produced. Within three weeks after the date of service of the demand, the debtor had neither complied with the demand nor intimated to the petitioner, by recorded delivery, that he denied that there was a debt or that the sum claimed by the petitioner as the debt was immediately payable. The said apparent insolvency having been constituted within four months before the date of presentation of this petition, the petitioner is entitled to warrant to cite the debtor as craved and, subject to section 12(3) and (3A) of the Bankruptcy (Scotland) Act 1985, to sequestration of the debtor's estates in terms of that Act. The petitioners respectfully suggests that Lewis Brown, Chartered Accountant, 101 West Street, Aberdeen is a suitable person for the office of interim trustee. He satisfies the conditions set forth in section 2(3) of the said Act and a copy of the undertaking mentioned therein given by him is annexed to this petition.

PLEA-IN-LAW

The debtor's apparent insolvency being constituted within four months before the date of presentation of this petition, warrant to cite should be granted and thereafter sequestration of the debtor's estates should be awarded, as craved.

IN RESPECT WHEREOF

Enrolled solicitor
1 Hill Place
Aberdeen
Solicitor for the petitioner

14. SOUTHERN BANK PLC, PETITIONERS

Bankruptcy—Sequestration of firm—Apparent insolvency constituted by expiry of days of charge without payment—Appointment of interim trustee before sequestration

a. Petition

SHERIFFDOM OF NORTH STRATHCLYDE AT PAISLEY

PETITION

of

SOUTHERN BANK PLC, a company with its head office at 10 Burnbank Street, London

for

Sequestration of the estates of the firm of K & F Barclay and of Keith Barclay and Freda Barclay, as partners thereof and as individuals

The petitioners crave the court:

To grant warrant to cite the firm of K & F Barclay, Mucklemead Farm, Paisley and Keith Barclay and Freda Barclay, residing at the said address, as partners thereof and as individuals, to appear before the court on such date as shall be specified in the warrant, being a date not less than six nor more than 14 days after the date of citation, to show cause why sequestration should not be awarded; meantime, to appoint Terence Blake, Chartered Accountant, 11 East Street, Paisley, or such other person as the court thinks fit, to be interim trustee on the estates of the said firm and partners, as partners thereof and as individuals, with the powers and duties prescribed by the Bankruptcy (Scotland) Act 1985 and allow him to enter on the duties of his office upon a certified copy of the interlocutor appointing him; to sequestrate the estates now belonging or which shall hereafter belong to the said firm and partners, as partners thereof and as individuals, before the date of their discharge and declare the same to belong to their creditors for the purposes of the Bankruptcy (Scotland) Act 1985 and, failing appointment of the said Terence Blake or such other person as the court thinks fit as interim trustee before sequestration is awarded, to make such appointment upon the award of sequestration; and to direct the expenses of this application to be expenses in the sequestration.

CONDESCENDENCE

1. The petitioners are qualified creditors of the firm of K & F Barclay and Keith Barclay and Freda Barclay, as partners thereof and as individuals (hereinafter 'the debtors'), designed in the crave, conform to oath and decree in the sum of £12,694, produced herewith. The debtors had an established place of business in the Sheriffdom of North Strathclyde within the year immediately preceding the date of presentation of this petition. This court accordingly has jurisdiction.

2. The debtors are apparently insolvent. On 19 May 1994, charges for payment proceeding upon the said decree were duly served on the debtors (and in the case of the said partners, on them as partners and as individuals). The days of charge have expired without payment. The said apparent insolvency having been constituted within four months before the date of presentation of this petition, the petitioners are entitled to warrant to cite the debtors and, subject to section 12(3) and (3A) of the Bankruptcy (Scotland) Act 1985, the sequestration of the debtors' estates in terms of that Act. The petitioners respectfully suggest that Terence Blake, Chartered Accountant, 11 East Street, Paisley, is a suitable person for the office of interim trustee. He satisfies the conditions set forth in section 2(3) of the said Act and a copy of the undertaking mentioned therein given by him is annexed to this petition.

3. The petitioners seek the said appointment of an interim trustee before sequestration is awarded in terms of section 2(5) of the said Act. The assets of the said firm include livestock. The debtors have recently sold a substantial number of sheep. The petitioners are apprehensive that the debtors will dispose of their remaining stock. They therefore seek said appointment forthwith.

PLEAS-IN-LAW

1. The debtors' apparent insolvency being constituted within four months before the date of presentation of this petition, warrant to cite should be granted and thereafter sequestration of the debtors' estates should be awarded, as craved.

2. The appointment of an interim trustee forthwith being justified, such appointment should be made as craved.

IN RESPECT WHEREOF

Enrolled solicitor
1 Arthur Street
Paisley
Solicitor for the petitioners

15. GLOVER, PETITIONER

Bankruptcy—Sequestration of deceased debtor's estates

a. Petition

SHERIFFDOM OF LOTHIAN AND BORDERS
AT EDINBURGH

PETITION

of

PHILIP GLOVER, residing at 21 Quincy Road, Edinburgh, executor-nominate of the late John Glover by will and confirmation

for

Sequestration of the estates of the said John Glover

The petitioner craves the court:

To sequestrate the estates of the late John Glover, who resided latterly at 19 Campbell Street, Edinburgh and who died on 5 January 1994, and declare the same to belong to his creditors for the purposes of the Bankruptcy (Scotland) Act 1985 and to appoint Eric Harper, Chartered Accountant, 12 Nile Street, Edinburgh, or such other person as the court thinks fit, to be interim trustee on the said sequestrated estates with the powers and duties prescribed by the said statute and allow him to enter on the duties of his office upon a certified copy of the interlocutor appointing him; and to direct the expenses of this application to be expenses in the sequestration.

CONDESCENDENCE

1. The petitioner is the executor-nominate of the late John Glover, (hereinafter 'the deceased'), designed in the crave and who died on 5 January 1994, conform to will and confirmation produced herewith. The deceased was habitually resident in the Sheriffdom of Lothian and Borders within the year immediately preceding his said date of death. This court accordingly has jurisdiction.
2. The deceased's estate is absolutely insolvent and is likely to remain

so. The petitioner is accordingly entitled to sequestration of the deceased's estates in terms of the Bankruptcy (Scotland) Act 1985. The petitioner respectfully suggests that Eric Harper, Chartered Accountant, 12 Nile Street, Edinburgh is a suitable person for the office of interim trustee. He satisfies the conditions see forth in section 2(3) of the said Act and a copy of the undertaking mentioned therein given by him is annexed to this petition.

PLEA-IN-LAW

The deceased's estates being absolutely insolvent and being likely to remain so, sequestration should be awarded as craved.

IN RESPECT WHEREOF

Enrolled solicitor
10 Denby Drive
Edinburgh
Solicitor for the petitioner

16. HARVEY, PETITIONER

Judicial factor—Curator bonis—Special powers—Dispensation with service upon incapax

a. Petition

SHERIFFDOM OF NORTH STRATHCLYDE AT ROTHESAY

PETITION

of

CHARLES KEMP HARVEY, residing at 10 Vermont Grove, Rothesay

for

Appointment of a *curator bonis* to Mrs Olive Kemp or Harvey

The petitioner craves the court:

To appoint this petition to be intimated on the walls of court and to the Accountant of Court and to be served on Victor Albert Harvey, residing at 10 Abigail Drive, Linlithgow, Mrs Vera Harvey or Kent, residing at 19 Amberley Street, Liverpool and Gordon Harvey, residing at 20 Mountcastle Road, Greenock; and to dispense with service upon Mrs Olive Kemp or Harvey, at present an in-patient at Rothesay Royal Psychiatric Hospital; and to ordain all parties interested to lodge answers, if so advised, within 21 days after intimation and service; thereafter, upon resuming consideration hereof, with or without answers and after such inquiry if any as may be thought necessary, to appoint David Scott, Solicitor, 1 Moray Street, Rothesay, or such other person as the court thinks fit to be *curator bonis* to the said Mrs Olive Kemp or Harvey with the usual powers, he always finding caution before extract, and with special powers to sell the heritable subjects owned by the said Mrs Olive Kemp or Harvey at 1 Granton Street, Rothesay in such manner, at such price and on such terms and conditions as the Accountant of Court may approve, or otherwise as the court may direct, and upon payment of the sale price to grant a conveyance thereof to the purchaser containing all usual and necessary clauses; and to find the petitioner entitled to the expenses of this application and the procedure to follow hereon out of the estate of the said Mrs Olive Kemp or Harvey.

CONDESCENDENCE

1. Mrs Olive Kemp or Harvey (hereinafter referred to as 'the incapax'), designed in the crave, is now and has for some time been in such a mental condition as to be incapable of managing her own affairs or of giving instructions for their management, as appears from the medical certificates produced herewith. She is resident within the Sheriffdom of North Strathclyde. This court accordingly has jurisdiction.

2. The persons having an interest in the estate of the incapax are her children, namely the petitioner and Victor Albert Harvey, Mrs Vera Harvey or Kent and Gordon Harvey, all designed in the crave.

3. The incapax is possessed of estate, namely the heritable subjects owned by her at 1 Granton Street, Rothesay, valued at about £40,000, together with savings of about £500.

4. In the circumstances, it is necessary that a *curator bonis* be appointed to manage and administer the means and estate of the incapax. The petitioner respectfully suggests that David Scott, Solicitor, 1 Moray Street, Rothesay, is a suitable person for the office of *curator bonis*.

5. It further appears from the said medical certificates that the condition of the incapax is such that she is unlikely ever to be able to occupy the said heritable subjects again. If the subjects remain unoccupied, it is likely that they will deteriorate. In these circumstances, the petitioner respectfully suggests that it is expedient that the said subjects should be sold. Application is accordingly made for the *curator bonis* to have special power therefor, as craved.

6. It also appears from the said medical certificates that service of this petition on the incapax would be injurious to her health. The petitioner accordingly respectfully suggests that such service should be dispensed with, as craved.

PLEAS-IN-LAW

1. The incapax being incapable of managing her own affairs or of giving instructions for their management, a *curator bonis* should be appointed to manage and administer her means and estate, as craved.

2. It being expedient that the said heritable subjects be sold, special power therefor should be granted as craved.

IN RESPECT WHEREOF

Enrolled solicitor
1 Moray Street
Rothesay
Solicitor for the petitioner

17. DIXON, PETITIONER

Judicial factor—Winding-up of dissolved firm

a. Petition

SHERIFFDOM OF GRAMPIAN, HIGHLAND AND ISLANDS AT INVERNESS

PETITION

of

MRS IRENE DIXON, residing at 45 Pettigrew Road, Inverness

for

Appointment of a judicial factor on the dissolved firm of Black & Co

The petitioner craves the court:

To appoint this petition to be intimated on the walls of court and to the Accountant of Court; and to ordain all parties interested to lodge answers, if so advised, within 21 days after such intimation; thereafter, upon resuming consideration hereof, with or without answers and after such inquiry if any as may be thought necessary, to appoint Colin Todd, Solicitor, 1 Albany Street, Inverness, or such other person as the court thinks fit to be judicial factor with the usual powers on the estate of Black & Co, a now dissolved firm with a place of business at 29 Grange Street, Inverness; and to find the petitioner entitled to the expenses of this application and the procedure to follow hereon out of the partnership estate.

CONDESCENDENCE

1. The firm of Black & Co was dissolved by the death of one of its two partners, namely Arthur Black, on 16 June 1994. The said firm was formed under the law of Scotland. Its central management and control was exercised in Scotland. It had at date of dissolution aforesaid a place of business at 29 Grange Street, Inverness. It was domiciled there. This court has jurisdiction.

2. The petitioner is the former partner of the said Arthur Black in the said firm. She is the only person with an interest in the affairs of the said firm.

3. The said firm carried on business as debt collectors. The petitioner latterly played little part in the running of the firm's business and affairs by reason of disability. She is in poor health and unable to wind up the same. She therefore seeks the appointment of a judicial factor for such purpose. She respectfully suggests that Colin Todd, Solicitor, 1 Albany Street, Inverness, is a suitable person for the office of judicial factor.

PLEA-IN-LAW

The appointment of a judicial factor being necessary to wind up the business and affairs of the said dissolved firm, should be granted as craved.

IN RESPECT WHEREOF

Enrolled solicitor
1 Albany Street
Inverness
Solicitor for the petitioner

18. TAIT, PETITIONER

Judicial factor—Deceased person's estates

a. Petition

SHERIFFDOM OF TAYSIDE, CENTRAL AND FIFE
AT DUNFERMLINE

PETITION

of

WILLIAM FRANCIS TAIT, residing at 10 Abercorn Terrace, Derby

for

Appointment of a judicial factor on the estates of the late Francis David Tait

The petitioner craves the court:

To appoint this petition to be intimated on the walls of court and to the Accountant of Court, to be advertised in the Edinburgh Gazette in Form 3, and to be served on Mrs Alma Davidson or Tait, at present an in-patient in Dunfermline Royal Infirmary, Dunfermline, Bank of New England PLC, 1 Barnet Road, London and TGB Lagers Limited, 3 Tennant Street, Edinburgh; and to ordain them and all other parties interested to lodge answers, if so advised, within 21 days after such intimation, advertisement and service; thereafter, upon resuming consideration hereof, with or without answers and after such inquiry if any as may be thought necessary, to appoint Martin Jackson, Chartered Accountant, 21 Ives Road, Dunfermline, or such other person as the court thinks fit, to be judicial factor with the usual powers on the estates of the late Francis David Tait, who resided latterly at 46 Denheen Street, Dunfermline and who died on 21 June 1994; and to find the petitioner entitled to the expenses of this application and the procedure to follow hereon out of the said estates.

CONDESCENDENCE

1. The late Francis David Tait (hereinafter 'the deceased'), who resided latterly at 46 Denheen Street, Dunfermline, died intestate on 21 June

1994. The deceased resided and, in any event, carried on business within the Sheriffdom of Tayside, Central and Fife during the year immediately preceding the date of this petition. He also owned heritage situated within this Sheriffdom at the time of his death. This court has jurisdiction.

2. The petitioner is the son of the deceased and as such has an interest in the succession to the estate of the deceased. The only other person known to the petitioner as having an interest in the succession to the estate is the widow of the deceased, Mrs Alma Davidson or Tait, designed in the crave. She is also the personal representative of the deceased upon whom service falls to be made.

3. The only persons known to the petitioner as having an interest in the estate as creditors are Bank of New England plc and TGB Lagers Limited, designed in the crave, each of whom holds a standard security over the heritable subjects owned by the deceased, namely a public house known as 'The Gushing Tap' at 21 Fenton Street, Dunfermline.

4. The estate of the deceased so far as known to the petitioner, including heritable and moveable property, stock in trade, interest in business, and debts owed to and by the deceased, is as set forth in the appendix to this petition.

5. The estate of the deceased may be insolvent. It is necessary for the protection of the interests of the persons with an interest in the succession to the estate and the creditors of the estate that a judicial factor be appointed to administer the estate of the deceased, and in particular to manage the business of the said public house which was run by the deceased until his death. The value of the business as a going concern greatly exceeds its break-up value. The petitioner respectfully suggests that Martin Jackson, Chartered Accountant, 21 Ives Road, Dunfermline, is a suitable person for the office of judicial factor.

PLEA-IN-LAW

The appointment of a judicial factor being necessary to protect the interests of persons with an interest in the estate of the deceased, decree should be granted as craved.

IN RESPECT WHEREOF

Enrolled solicitor
21 Melville Street
Dunfermline
Solicitor for the petitioner

APPENDIX

Heritable estate	Estimated value
'The Gushing Tap', 21 Fenton Street, Dunfermline (including fixtures, fittings and stock)	£200,000

Moveable estate	
Royal National Bank Current Account	£ 200
Royal National Bank Deposit Account	£ 27,962
Savings Bank Premium Account	£ 13,000
National Savings Income Bonds	£ 12,000
	£253,162

Liabilities	
Bank of New England plc	£225,000
TGB Lagers Limited	£ 30,000
	£255,000

19. INVERCLYDE PRODUCTS LIMITED, PETITIONERS

Company—Liquidation—Company resolving by special resolution to be wound up by the court

a. Petition

SHERIFFDOM OF GLASGOW AND STRATHKELVIN
AT GLASGOW

PETITION

of

INVERCLYDE PRODUCTS LIMITED, a company registered under the Companies Acts with its registered office at 21 Flanders Place, Glasgow

for

A winding-up order

The petitioners crave the court:

To appoint this petition to be intimated on the walls of court and to be advertised in the Edinburgh Gazette and the Glasgow Echo newspaper; and to ordain all parties interested to lodge answers, if so advised, within eight days after such intimation and advertisement; thereafter, upon resuming consideration hereof, with or without answers and after such inquiry if any as may be thought necessary, to order that the petitioners be wound up by the court under the provisions of the Insolvency Act 1986; to appoint Archibald Fleming, Chartered Accountant, 21 Berman Street, Glasgow, or such other person as the court thinks fit, to be interim liquidator of the petitioners; and to find the expenses of this application to be expenses in the liquidation.

CONDESCENDENCE

1. The petitioners are a private limited company incorporated under the Companies Acts with its registered office at 21 Flanders Place, Glasgow. The share capital of the petitioners is £100, divided into 100 ordinary shares of £1 each, all of which are issued and are fully paid up. This court has jurisdiction.

2. The objects of the petitioners are to carry on business as suppliers of engineering products. The amount of the assets of the petitioners is about £75,000.

3. By special resolution dated 10 July 1994 the petitioners resolved that they should be wound up by the court. Copy resolution is produced herewith.

4. The petitioners respectfully suggest that Archibald Fleming, Chartered Accountant, 21 Berman Street, Glasgow, is a suitable person for the office of interim liquidator. He is qualified to act as an insolvency practitioner in relation to the petitioners.

PLEA-IN-LAW

The petitioners having resolved by special resolution to be wound up by the court, decree therefor should be granted.

IN RESPECT WHEREOF

Enrolled solicitor
21 Buccleuch Place
Glasgow
Solicitor for the petitioners

b. Note for leave to commence proceedings against company

SHERIFFDOM OF GLASGOW AND STRATHKELVIN
AT GLASGOW

NOTE

for GRAEME WALKER, residing at 101 Green Road Glasgow

in the liquidation of INVERCLYDE PRODUCTS LIMITED, a company registered under the Companies Acts with its registered office at 21 Flanders Place, Glasgow

for

Leave to commence proceedings

The noter craves the court:

To appoint this note to be served on Archibald Fleming, 21 Berman Street, Glasgow, liquidator of Inverclyde Products Limited (in liquidation) and to ordain him to lodge answers, if so advised, within 21 days after service; and thereafter, upon resuming consideration hereof, with or without answers and after such inquiry if any as may be thought necessary, to grant leave to the noter to commence proceedings in the Court of Session against the said Inverclyde Products Limited (in liquidation) and the said liquidator for reparation for loss, injury and damage sustained by the noter as a result of an accident which occurred on or about 10 May 1992.

CONDESCENDENCE

1. The noter resides at 101 Green Road, Glasgow. He was formerly employed by Inverclyde Products Limited (in liquidation), designed in the instance, of which Archibald Fleming, designed in the crave, is the liquidator.

2. On or about 10 May 1992 the noter was working in the course of his employment as a machine operator with the said company at their

premises at Alloa Street, Glasgow. At or about 11 am on the said date, the noter suffered an injury to his right ankle as a result of a fall on the said premises. Said fall occurred by reason of the noter coming into contact with oil which had been spilled on the floor by a fellow-employee. The noter contends that the said company was at fault and in breach of statutory duty and is liable to make reparation to him for loss, injury and damage arising out of the said accident. The said company was insured at the material time. In these circumstances, the noter seeks leave of the court to commence proceedings in the Court of Session against the said company and the said liquidator for reparation for loss, injury and damage sustained by the noter as a result of the said accident.

PLEA-IN-LAW

It being appropriate that the noter be given leave to commence proceedings aforesaid, decree should be granted as craved.

IN RESPECT WHEREOF

Enrolled solicitor
19 Whitelaw Place
Glasgow
Solicitor for the noter

c. Note for interim determination of amount of outlays and remuneration payable to liquidator

SHERIFFDOM OF GLASGOW AND STRATHKELVIN
AT GLASGOW

NOTE

for ARCHIBALD FLEMING, Chartered Accountant, 21 Berman Street, Glasgow, liquidator of Inverclyde Products Limited (in liquidation), a company with its registered office at 21 Flanders Place, Glasgow

in the liquidation of the said Inverclyde Products Limited

for

Interim determination of liquidator's outlays and remuneration

The noter craves the court:

To remit the business account incurred by the noter as liquidator of Inverclyde Products Limited (in liquidation) to his solicitors, to 30 November 1994, to the Auditor of Court for taxation and to authorise the noter to pay the taxed amount thereof; and to remit the account of the noter's intromissions as liquidator, to 30 November 1994, to Adam Jones, Chartered Accountant, 11 Alva Place, Glasgow, or such other person as the court thinks fit, to audit the same and suggest a suitable sum for payment of remuneration for the noter as liquidator to the said date and, upon consideration thereof, to determine the said sum or such other sum as the court thinks fit to be the remuneration to be paid to the noter as liquidator to the said date and to authorise him to take credit therefor; and to find the expenses of this application to be expenses in the liquidation.

CONDESCENDENCE

1. The noter is the liquidator of Inverclyde Products Limited (in liquidation) (hereinafter 'the company'), designed in the instance.

2. Following upon his appointment as liquidator, the noter has carried out the duties of his said office. No liquidation committee has been established. It appears that civil proceedings are to be raised against the company and that it is therefore likely to be some time before the liquidation can be concluded. In these circumstances, the noter seeks an interim determination of outlays (including the business account incurred to his solicitors) and remuneration payable to him for the period to 30 November 1994, as craved.

PLEA-IN-LAW

It being appropriate that an interim determination of outlays and remuneration payable to the noter be made, decree should be pronounced as craved.

IN RESPECT WHEREOF

Enrolled solicitor
21 Buccleuch Place
Glasgow
Solicitor for the noter

20. WESTERN BANK PLC, PETITIONERS

Company—Liquidation—Company unable to pay its debts as defined by non-compliance with statutory demand

a. Petition

SHERIFFDOM OF LOTHIAN AND BORDERS
AT EDINBURGH

PETITION

of

WESTERN BANK PLC, a company with its registered office at 12 Marchmont Place, Glasgow

for

An order to wind up Fleetco Limited

The petitioners crave the court:

To appoint this petition to be intimated on the walls of court, advertised in the Edinburgh Gazette and the Edinburgh Times newspaper and to be served on Fleetco Limited, a company with its registered office at 5 Broxburn Street, Edinburgh; and to ordain all parties interested to lodge answers, if so advised, within eight days after such intimation, advertisement and service; thereafter, upon resuming consideration hereof, with or without answers and after such inquiry if any as may be thought necessary, to order that the said Fleetco Limited be wound up by the court under the provisions of the Insolvency Act 1986; to appoint Kenneth Patrick, Chartered Accountant, 11 Fort Street, Edinburgh, or such other person as the court thinks fit to be interim liquidator of the said company; and to find the expenses of this application to be expenses in the liquidation.

CONDESCENDENCE

1. Fleetco Limited is a private limited company (hereinafter referred to as 'the company') incorporated under the Companies Acts with its registered office at 5 Broxburn Street, Edinburgh. The share capital of the company is £1,000, divided into 1,000 ordinary shares of £1 each, all of which are issued and are fully paid up. This court has jurisdiction.

2. The objects of the company are to carry on business as grocers, greengrocers, fruit and vegetable merchants and florists. The amount of the assets of the company is about £25,000.

3. The company is unable to pay its debts. On 21 January 1994, the petitioners served on the company, by leaving it at its registered office, a written demand in the prescribed form requiring the company to pay the sum of £4,500 then due to the petitioners. Copy written demand, duly docquetted, is produced. The company has for three weeks thereafter neglected to pay the sum or to secure or compound for it to the reasonable satisfaction of the petitioners. In these circumstances, the petitioners are entitled to an order that the company be wound up by the court under the provisions of the Insolvency Act 1986. The petitioners respectfully suggest that Kenneth Patrick, Chartered Accountant, 11 Fort Street, Edinburgh, is a suitable person for the office of interim liquidator. He is qualified to act as an insolvency practitioner in relation to the company.

PLEA-IN-LAW

The company being unable to pay its debts, should be wound up as craved.

IN RESPECT WHEREOF

Enrolled solicitor
1 Trainer Place
Edinburgh
Solicitor for the petitioners

b. Note for dispensation with settlement of list of contributories

SHERIFFDOM OF LOTHIAN AND BORDERS AT EDINBURGH

NOTE

for KENNETH PATRICK, Chartered Accountant, residing at 11 Fort Street, Edinburgh, liquidator of Fleetco Limited (in liquidation), a company with its registered office at 5 Broxburn Street, Edinburgh

in the liquidation of the said Fleetco Limited

for

An order dispensing with settlement of a list of contributories

The noter craves the court:

To dispense with the settlement of a list of contributories.

CONDESCENDENCE

1. The noter is the liquidator of Fleetco Limited (in liquidation), (hereinafter 'the company'), designed in the instance.

2. The share capital of the company is fully paid up. There is no prospect of any surplus being available for the contributories of the company. It not being necessary to make calls on or adjust the rights of contributories aforesaid, the noter seeks dispensation with the settlement of a list of contributories as craved.

PLEA-IN-LAW

It not being necessary to make calls on or adjust the rights of contributories of the company, the settlement of a list of contributories should be dispensed with, as craved.

IN RESPECT WHEREOF

Enrolled solicitor
1 Trainer Place
Edinburgh
Solicitor for the noter

c. Note for order for public examination of company officer

SHERIFFDOM OF LOTHIAN AND BORDERS
AT EDINBURGH

NOTE

for KENNETH PATRICK, Chartered Accountant, residing at 11 Fort Street, Edinburgh, liquidator of Fleetco Limited (in liquidation), a company with its registered office at 5 Broxburn Street, Edinburgh

in the liquidation of the said Fleetco Limited

for

An order for public examination

The noter craves the court:

To direct that a public examination of Joseph Struthers, residing at 1 Fortune Drive, Livingston, shall be held on a day appointed by the court and to ordain the said Joseph Struthers to attend on that day and be publicly examined as to the promotion, formation or management of Fleetco Limited (in liquidation), or as to the conduct of the said company's business and affairs, or his conduct or dealings in relation to the said company.

CONDESCENDENCE

1. Joseph Struthers, designed in the crave, is a director of Fleetco Limited (in liquidation) (hereinafter referred to as 'the company'), designed in the instance. The noter is the liquidator of the company.

2. In the course of his duties the noter has ascertained the existence of certain irregularities in the management of the company and the conduct of its business and affairs by the said Joseph Struthers. Certain aspects of said Joseph Struthers' conduct and dealings in relation to the company

have given rise to concern. The noter therefore seeks an order for the public examination of the said Joseph Struthers, as craved.

PLEA-IN-LAW

The noter being entitled to an order for the public examination of the said officer of the company, such order should be granted as craved.

IN RESPECT WHEREOF

Enrolled solicitor
1 Trainer Place
Edinburgh
Solicitor for the noter

21. MANGROVE LIMITED, PETITIONERS

Company—Liquidation—Company unable to pay its debts as defined by expiry of days of charge without payment— Provisional liquidator

a. Petition

SHERIFFDOM OF TAYSIDE, CENTRAL AND FIFE
AT KIRKCALDY

PETITION

of

MANGROVE LIMITED, a company with its registered office at 2 Mountcastle Street, Birmingham

for

An order to wind up Colby Travel Limited

The petitioners crave the court:

To appoint this petition to be intimated on the walls of court, advertised in the Edinburgh Gazette and the Kirkcaldy Post newspaper and to be served on Colby Travel Limited, a company with its registered office at 21 High Street, Kirkcaldy; and to ordain them and all other parties interested to lodge answers, if so advised, within eight days after such intimation, advertisement and service; meantime, to appoint Richard Robinson, Chartered Accountant, 101 Nevis Street, Kirkcaldy, or such other person as the court thinks fit to be provisional liquidator of the said company with all the usual powers necessary for the preservation of the assets of the company and particularly the powers specified in Part II of Schedule 4 to the Insolvency Act 1986, and that until the appointment of an interim liquidator hereinafter craved or the dismissal of this petition, whichever is the earlier; and thereafter, upon resuming consideration hereof, with or without answers and after such inquiry if any as may be thought necessary, to order that the said Colby Travel Limited be wound up by the court under the provisions of the Insolvency Act 1986; to appoint the said Richard Robinson, or such other person as the court thinks fit to be interim liquidator of the said company; and to find the expenses of this application to be expenses in the liquidation.

CONDESCENDENCE

1. Colby Travel Limited is a private limited company (hereinafter referred to as 'the company') incorporated under the Companies Acts with its registered office at 21 High Street, Kirkcaldy. The share capital of the company is £20,000, comprising 20,000 ordinary shares, of which 10,000 have been issued and are fully paid up. This court has jurisdiction.

2. The objects of the company are to carry on business as a general commercial company and in particular as a travel agency. The amount of the assets of the company is to the petitioners unknown.

3. The company is unable to pay its debts. On 15 January 1994, a charge for payment proceeding upon a decree in favour of the petitioners for payment of the sum of £15,690, with interest and expenses, was duly served on the company. Extract decree and execution of charge are produced. The days of charge have expired without payment. In these circumstances, the petitioners are entitled to an order that the company be wound up by the court under the provisions of the Insolvency Act 1986. The petitioners respectfully suggest that Richard Robinson, Chartered Accountant, 101 Nevis Street, Kirkcaldy, is a suitable person for the office of interim liquidator. He is qualified to act as an insolvency practitioner in relation to the company.

4. The petitioners seek the appointment of a provisional liquidator with all the usual powers necessary for the preservation of the assets of the company and particularly the powers specified in Part II of Schedule 4 to the Insolvency Act 1986 and that until the appointment of an interim liquidator aforesaid or the dismissal of this petition, whichever is the earlier. The company continues to trade and takes bookings and cash from the public. Sums received can easily be applied or disposed of to the prejudice of creditors. The company has other creditors who are pressing for payment and may seek to attach assets of the company. It is important to preserve the goodwill of the business of the company. In these circumstances, it is expedient that the company be brought under the immediate control of a provisional liquidator. The petitioners respectfully suggest that the said Richard Robinson is a suitable person for the office of provisional liquidator. He is an insolvency practitioner, duly qualified under the said Act of 1986 to act as liquidator and consents so to act. To the knowledge of the petitioners, there is no receiver for the company nor has a liquidator been appointed for the voluntary winding up of the company.

PLEAS-IN-LAW

1. The company being unable to pay its debts, should be wound up as craved.

2. There being grounds for the appointment of a provisional liquidator, such appointment should be made as craved.

IN RESPECT WHEREOF

Enrolled solicitor
10 Castle Place
Kirkcaldy
Solicitor for the petitioners

22. HAPPY DAYS LIMITED, PETITIONERS

Company—Administration order

a. Petition

SHERIFFDOM OF GLASGOW AND STRATHKELVIN
AT GLASGOW

PETITION

of

HAPPY DAYS LIMITED, a company with its registered office at 2 Carpenter Street, Glasgow

for

An administration order

The petitioners crave the court:

To appoint this petition to be intimated on the walls of court and to Bank of New France plc, 101 Duke Street, Manchester, Graham Smythe, Chartered Accountant, 11 Armour Place, Glasgow, the registrar of companies and the Keeper of the Register of Inhibitions and Adjudications, and otherwise as the court thinks fit; and to ordain all parties interested to lodge answers, if so advised, within 21 days after such intimation; and thereafter, upon resuming consideration hereof, with or without answers and after such inquiry if any as may be thought necessary, to make an administration order in relation to the petitioners, and to appoint the said Graham Smythe, or such other person as the court thinks fit, to be the administrator of the petitioners, for the purposes of (a) the survival of the petitioners, and the whole or any part of their undertaking, as a going concern; and (b) the approval of a voluntary arrangement between the petitioners and their creditors under Part 1 of the Insolvency Act 1986.

CONDESCENDENCE

1. The petitioners are a company incorporated under the Companies Acts with its registered office at 2 Carpenter Street, Glasgow. Their share capital is £100, comprising 100 ordinary shares of £1 each, all of which have been issued and are fully paid up. This court has jurisdiction.

2. The petitioners are unable to pay their debts. In the year to 31 January 1993, they suffered a trading loss of £42,050. In the ensuing year to 31 January 1994, they suffered a further trading loss of £55,291. Audited accounts for the said years are produced. Trading losses are continuing. The petitioners have suspended payments to their creditors. Copy correspondence is produced. Reference is also made to the report hereinafter mentioned.

3. The assets of the petitioners comprise the heritable subjects in which they operate, together with fixtures, fittings and stock-in-trade, and items of moveable property, with a total value of about £220,000, all as more fully described in the Schedule produced herewith. The petitioners' liabilities total about £195,000, as more fully set forth in the said Schedule, the terms of which are held as repeated herein *brevitatis causa*.

4. There is a security held by a creditor of the petitioners, namely a floating charge over the assets of the company in favour of Bank of New France plc, designed in the crave. The said security confers power on the holder to appoint a receiver. No receiver has been appointed.

5. No steps have been taken for the winding up of the petitioners.

6. A report has been prepared under rule 2.1 of the Insolvency (Scotland) Rules 1986 and is produced.

7. The petitioners expect to be achieved by the making of an administration order the purposes specified in section 8(3)(a) and (b) of the Insolvency Act 1986, videlicet – (a) the survival of the petitioners, and the whole or any part of their undertaking, as a going concern; and (b) the approval of a voluntary arrangement between the petitioners and their creditors under Part 1 of the Insolvency Act 1986. As the said report discloses, additional capital is available from members of the petitioners in the event that an administration order were to be made. The business of the petitioners is stated therein to be viable if it can survive its short term difficulties. Several creditors of the petitioners are longstanding and loyal customers. Further, the value of the petitioners' assets would be substantially less upon a cessation of trading than their value upon the basis of continued trading; and the petitioners' liabilities would be increased significantly by employees' claims upon a cessation. In the whole circumstances, the petitioners seek the making of an administration order in relation to themselves, and the appointment of an administrator, for the purposes hereinbefore set forth and as specified in the crave in terms of section 8 of the said Act.

8. The petitioners respectfully suggest that Graham Smythe, designed in the crave, is a suitable person for the office of administrator. He is qualified to act as an insolvency practitioner in relation to the company.

PLEA-IN-LAW

The company being unable to pay its debts, and the making of an administration order being likely to achieve the purposes specified, such order should be granted as craved.

IN RESPECT WHEREOF

Enrolled solicitor
21 Comyn Place
Glasgow
Solicitor for the petitioners

23. BAXTER, PETITIONER

Company—Protection of members against unfair prejudice

a. Petition

SHERIFFDOM OF NORTH STRATHCLYDE AT KILMARNOCK

PETITION

of

COLIN ARTHUR BAXTER (Assisted Person), residing at 21 Compton Grove, Kilmarnock

for

Relief in respect of unfair prejudice relative to the conduct of the affairs of Blackbird Limited

The petitioner craves the court:

To appoint this petition to be intimated on the walls of court and to be served on Blackbird Limited, a company with its registered office at 20 Firestone Road, Kilmarnock, William Laing, residing at 42 Ayr Road, Kilmarnock and Mrs Wilma Laing, residing at 42 Ayr Road, Kilmarnock; and to ordain them and all other parties interested to lodge answers, if so advised, within 21 days after such intimation and service; thereafter, upon resuming consideration hereof, with or without answers and after such inquiry if any as may be thought necessary, (i) to order that general meetings of the said company shall be called in order to transact the business of the annual general meeting of the company for each of the financial years ending 31 July 1990, 31 July 1991, 31 July 1992 and 31 July 1993; (ii) to require the said company to call an annual general meeting in each financial year of the company's future existence; (iii) to authorise civil proceedings to be brought in the name and on behalf of the company by the petitioners against Laing Limited, a company with its registered office at 42 Ayr Road, Kilmarnock and the said William Laing and Mrs Wilma Laing for the recovery of all sums paid by the said Blackbird Limited to the said Laing Limited; (iv) to appoint Alan Dick, Chartered Accountant, 3 Bell Place, Kilmarnock or such other person as the court thinks fit to prepare accounts of the said Blackbird Limited for each of the financial years ending 31 July 1990, 31 July 1991, 31 July 1992 and 31 July 1993, following upon completion of the said civil proceedings and to the extent that the same are successful; and (v) to require the said Blackbird Limited to refrain from making any further payments to the said Laing Limited or to any other company in which the said William Laing or Mrs Wilma Laing have an interest; and to find the said William Laing and Mrs Wilma Laing liable in the expenses of this petition.

CONDESCENDENCE

1. Blackbird Limited (hereinafter 'the company') is a company incorporated under the Companies Acts with its registered office at 20 Firestone Road, Kilmarnock. The nominal and issued share capital of the company is £100, comprising 100 ordinary shares of £1 each. This court has jurisdiction.

2. The petitioner is a member of the company and has been since its inception in 1989. He holds 40 shares. Of the remaining shares, 30 are held by William Laing, designed in the crave, and 30 by his wife, Mrs Wilma Laing, also designed in the crave. The petitioner and the Laings are directors of the company. There are no other persons with an interest in the company.

3. Throughout the period of the petitioner's membership of the company, he has received no notice of any general meeting of the company. So far as he is aware, no such meeting has ever taken place. The petitioner has received no notice of any meeting of the board of directors. So far as he is aware, no such meeting has ever taken place.

4. During the financial years to 31 July 1990, 31 July 1991, 31 July 1992 and 31 July 1993 the sums of £29,500, £35,000, £39,000 and £40,000, respectively, were paid by the company to Laing Limited, designed in the crave, a company wholly owned by William Laing and Mrs Wilma Laing, for 'management services'. No such services have been provided to the company. The company has not authorised any such payment at a meeting of its board of directors or at a general meeting, so far as the petitioner is aware.

5. In the foregoing circumstances, the company's affairs have been conducted in a manner which is unfairly prejudicial to the interests of the petitioner. His shares have been substantially devalued. He seeks orders for giving relief in respect of the foregoing matters complained of in terms of sections 459 and 461 of the Companies Act 1985.

PLEA-IN-LAW

The company's affairs having been conducted in a manner which is unfairly prejudicial to the interests of the petitioner, orders for relief should be granted as craved.

IN RESPECT WHEREOF

Enrolled solicitor
1 Craigs Road
Kilmarnock
Solicitor for the petitioner

24. JOHNSTONE MATTHEWS LIMITED, PETITIONERS

Company—Restoration of company name to register of companies

a. Petition

SHERIFFDOM OF GLASGOW AND STRATHKELVIN
AT GLASGOW

PETITION

of

JOHNSTONE MATTHEWS LIMITED, a company with its registered office at 21 St Peters Place, Glasgow

for

An order restoring company name to register of companies

The petitioners crave the court:

To appoint this petition to be intimated on the walls of court and to be served on the Lord Advocate and the registrar of companies and to be advertised in the Edinburgh Gazette and the Glasgow Mail newspapers; to ordain any parties interested to lodge answers hereto, if so advised, within 21 days after intimation, service and advertisement; thereafter, upon resuming consideration hereof, with or without answers and after such inquiry if any as may be thought necessary, to order that the name of the petitioners be restored to the register of companies and to direct the registrar of companies to advertise such order in his official name in the Edinburgh Gazette; and to authorise the expenses of this application and of the procedure following thereon including the expenses to be paid to the registrar to be paid out of the first and readiest funds of the company.

CONDESCENDENCE

1. The petitioners are a company incorporated under the Companies Acts with its registered office at 21 St Peters Place, Glasgow. The share capital of the petitioners is £100, comprising 100 ordinary shares of £1 each, all of which are issued and are fully paid up. This court has jurisdiction.

2. On 12 March 1994 the name of the petitioners was struck off the register of companies by the registrar. At that time the petitioners were carrying on business, purchasing materials and selling manufactured goods, conform to documentation produced herewith. The petitioners therefore seek an order that their name be restored to the register of companies in terms of the Companies Act 1985, section 653.

PLEA-IN-LAW

The petitioners having been carrying on business at the time of the striking off, an order that their name be restored to the register of companies should be granted as craved.

IN RESPECT WHEREOF

Enrolled solicitor
1 Frederick Road
Glasgow
Solicitor for the petitioners

Index

A mensa et thoro, 251–255
Abandonment,
  spouse, 233–238
  See also DIVORCE; SEPARATION
Abatement of nuisance. *See* NUISANCE
Access rights, 268–277
  See also CHILDREN
Accident,
  road traffic, 52–66
  tenement (common stair), 67–73
  work, 74–103
Ad factum praestandum,
  hire-purchase agreement, 177–196
  missives (buyer's action), 175–176
  missives (seller's action), 169–174
Address unknown. *See* WHEREABOUTS UNKNOWN.
Administration order,
  company, 354–356
  See also COMPANY
Adultery, 205–217
  See also DIVORCE; SEPARATION
Affidavit,
  pursuer, 236–237, 264–265
  pursuer (OCR 33.27), 222–223
  supplementary (pursuer), 229–230
  supplementary (witness), 231–232
  witness, 126–127, 238, 266–267
  witness (OCR 33.27), 224–225
Alcohol licence,
  refusal of application, 308–309
Aliment,
  spouse, 256–259, 260–261
  variation of agreement, 260–261
  See also FINANCIAL PROVISION; MATRIMONIAL HOME
Annoyance. *See* NUISANCE
Answers,
  third party notice (OCR 20.5), 60–61
Appointment,
  curator bonis (incapax), 332–333
  judicial factor, 7–9, 332–338
  provisional liquidator, 351–353
  trustee, 320–321
  trustee (interim), 326–329
Apportionment,
  plea, 104–121
Arrears. *See* DEBT; RENT ARREARS

Arrest, power of. *See* POWER OF ARREST
Arrested funds, 154–156
Asbestosis, 104–121
  See also DERMATITIS
Assets, sequestration. *See* BANKRUPTCY

Bank loan,
  debt, 34–40
  guarantee, 34–40
  See also IOU
Bankruptcy,
  deceased person's estate, 330–331
  expiry of days of charge without payment, 328–329
  firm, 328–329
  individual, 326–327
  interim trustee (appointment), 326–329
  non-compliance with statutory demand, 326–327
  sequestration of assets, 326–331
  See also COMPANY; DEBT
Behaviour. *See* UNREASONABLE BEHAVIOUR
Beneficiary of lapsed trust. *See* TRUST
Breach of contract,
  hire-purchase agreement, 177–179
  missives (buyer's action), 175–176
  missives (seller's action), 169–170
  professional services, 133–137
  restrictive covenant, 180–182
  sale of goods, 24–33
  See also CONTRACT; CONVEYANCING
Breach of interdict, 301–302
  See also INTERDICT
Breach of statutory duty,
  accident at work, 74–103
  occupational disease, 104–132

Calling-up notice,
  ejection from heritable property, 293–294
Capital sum, 205–217, 241–250
  See also FINANCIAL PROVISION; MATRIMONIAL HOME

363

Charge,
  suspension of, 303–304
Children,
  access rights, 268–277
  custody and delivery, 278–282
  custody order, 218–232, 268–282
  declarator of parentage, 262–267
  interdict preventing removal, 278–282
  local authority care, 239–240
  order to disclose whereabouts, 280
  school placement request, 310–311
  whereabouts unknown, 278–282
Clubs,
  nuisance, 183–197
Common property,
  division or sale, 295–296
Company,
  administration order, 354–356
  liquidation. *See* LIQUIDATION OF
    COMPANY
  protection of members interests, 357–358
  registration, 359–360
  See also BANKRUPTCY
Compensation. *See* DAMAGES
Competency,
  plea, 169–174
Completion of title. *See* TRUST
Condescendence and claim (OCR 35.11(1)), 159–160
Condescendence and list, (OCR 35.4(2)), 166–167
Consent to dealing (dispensing with),
  matrimonial home, 283–284
  See also CONVEYANCING
Contract,
  breach of. *See* BREACH OF CONTRACT
  implied, 19–23
Contributory negligence,
  plea, 93–103
Control of noise pollution, 312–313
  See also NUISANCE
Conveyancing,
  consent to dealing (dispensing with), 283–284
  missives (buyer's action), 175–176
  missives (seller's action), 169–174
Counterclaim (OCR 19.1),
  loss and damages, 28–30
Court reckoning and payment,
  executry, 149–153
  partnership, 146–148
Curator bonis (incapax),
  appointment, 332–333
  judicial factor, 332–333
  special powers, 332–333
  See also MENTAL HEALTH

Custody and delivery,
  children, 278–282
  See also CHILDREN
Custody order, 218–232, 268–282
  See also CHILDREN

Damages,
  negligence, 52–145
  provisional, 74–82
  reparation, 24–33, 52–145, 177–179
Death,
  declarator, 7–9
  declarator (seven years disappearance), 10–11
  road traffic accident, 52–66
Debt,
  bank loan, 34–40
  collection. See recovery below
  deceased, 330–331
  hire of services, 19–23
  hire-purchase, 177–179
  IOU, 41–51
  recovery, 19–51, 154–156, 177–179
  sale of goods, 24–33
  See also BANKRUPTCY; PAYMENT
Deceased debtor, 330–331
  See also BANKRUPTCY; DEBT; ESTATE OF DECEASED
Declarator,
  death, 7–9
  death (seven years disappearance), 10–11
  dissolution of partnership, 5–6
  division or sale of common property, 295–296
  parentage, 262–267
  repossession of heritable property, 293–294
  servitude, 3–4
Defences,
  accident at work, 96–97
  child access, 270–271
  court reckoning and payment (executry), 151
  custody order, 270–271
  damages, 55–56, 96–97, 108–109
  debt, 43
  divorce (adultery), 207–208
  divorce (five year action), 244–245
  missives (seller's action), 171–172
  nuisance, 188–189
  occupational disease, 108–109
  personal injury, 96–97, 108–109
  road traffic accident, 55–56
Defences (OCR 19.1),
  sale of goods, 28–30

Delivery,
child into custody, 278–282
debt (hire-purchase), 177–179
repossession of vehicle, 177–179
Dermatitis, 122–132
See also ASBESTOSIS
Desertion, 233–238
See also DIVORCE; SEPARATION
Determination of parentage, 262–267
Diligence,
suspension of, 303–304
Disability,
driving licence revoked, 318–319
Disappearance. See WHEREABOUTS UNKNOWN
Discharge from detention,
mental health, 316–317
Disease. See OCCUPATIONAL DISEASE
Disposition of trust property. See TRUST
Dissolution of partnership,
court reckoning and payment, 146–148
declarator, 5–6
Division or sale,
common property, 295–296
declarator, 295–296
Divorce,
adultery, 205–217
children in care, 239–240
custody order, 218–232
desertion, 233–238
exclusion order, 218–232
financial provision order, 205–217
five years non-cohabitation, 241–260
matrimonial interdict, 218–232
property order, 218–232
two years non-cohabitation and defender's consent, 239–240
unreasonable behaviour, 218–232
See also FINANCIAL PROVISION; SEPARATION
Documents,
recovery, 305–307
specification (OCR 28.2(2)), 88–89, 247–248
Domestic relations. See CHILDREN; DIVORCE; SEPARATION
Drink licence,
refusal of application, 308–309
Driving licence,
fitness to drive, 318–319
revocation, 318–319
Duty of reasonable care,
employer's, 74–132
local authority, 67–73
professional, 133–145
road driver, 52–66

Education,
school placement request, 310–311
Ejection from heritable property,
calling-up notice, 293–294
declarator, 293–294
See also HERITABLE PROPERTY
Employer's liability, 74–132
See also LIABILITY
Engineering construction,
personal injury, 74–82
See also PERSONAL INJURY
Equipment and plant,
safety, 74–132
Estate of deceased,
bankruptcy, 330–331
court reckoning and payment (executry), 149–153
judicial factor (appointment), 336–338
Eviction,
tenant, 287–289
See also LANDLORD AND TENANT
Evidence, written. See AFFIDAVIT
Exception,
plea, 169–174
Exclusion order, 218–232
See also DIVORCE; INTERDICT; ORDER
Executry,
court reckoning and payment, 149–153
Expenses, *passim*
Extraordinary removing, 287–389

Fatal accident, 52–66
Financial provision,
aliment, 256–261
capital sum, 205–217, 241–250
orders, 205–217
periodical allowance, 241–250
transfer of property, 241–250
See also DIVORCE; MATRIMONIAL HOME; SEPARATION
Firm,
bankruptcy, 328–329
dissolved (winding-up), 334–335
See also BANKRUPTCY
Fitness for purpose,
sale of goods, 24–33
Fitness to drive,
licence revoked, 318–319
Five years non-cohabitation, 241–260
See also DIVORCE; SEPARATION
Foreign currency, 19–23
Fund,
arrestment of, 154–156
in medio, 157–168
Furthcoming, 154–156

Guarantee,
bank loan, 34–40

Hazardous substances,
control of, 104–132
Health hazards,
control of, 104–132
Health, mental. *See* MENTAL HEALTH
Heritable creditor,
holders of security, 295–296
repossession, 293–294
See also HERITABLE PROPERTY
Heritable property,
completion of title, 324–325
creditor, 293–296
missives (buyer's action), 175–176
missives (seller's action), 169–174
repossession, 293–294
rights *in rem*, 3–4, 283–284, 293–296
survey (negligence), 133–137
See also HERITABLE CREDITOR; JUDICIAL FACTOR
Hire of services,
debt, 19–23
Hire-purchase,
debt, 177–179
Hospital records,
recovery, 305–307
Housing,
local authority, 314–315
notice requiring works, 314–315
Husband and wife. *See* DIVORCE; SEPARATION

IOU,
debt, 41–51
Illness, mental, *See* MENTAL HEALTH
Implement (contractual obligation),
missives (buyer's action), 175–176
missives (seller's action), 169–174
Implied contract,
hire of services, 19–23
See also BREACH OF CONTRACT
***In rem*, 3–4, 283–284, 293–296**
See also HERITABLE PROPERTY
Incapacity, mental. *See* CURATOR BONIS (*INCAPAX*); MENTAL HEALTH
Incidental order, 205–217
See also INTERDICT; ORDER
Indebtedness. *See* DEBT
Indemnity,
plea, 104–121
Individual,
bankruptcy, 326–327
See also BANKRUPTCY
Industrial disease. *See* OCCUPATIONAL DISEASE

Infidelity, 205–217
See also DIVORCE; SEPARATION
Initial writs,
(OCR 33.59(1)), 83–85
with minute for decree, 218–221, 233–235, 262–263
See also specimen writs under subject
Injunction. *See* INTERDICT
Injury, personal. *See* PERSONAL INJURY
Inspection of tenement, 67–73
See also NEGLIGENCE
Insolvency. *See* BANKRUPTCY
Interdict,
ad interim, 180–200, 218–232, 251–255
breach of, 301–302
matrimonial, 218–232, 251–255
nuisance, 183–197
passing off, 198–200
removal of child, 278–282
restrictive covenant, 180–182
See also ORDER; POWER OF ARREST
Interest charge,
from prior to citation, 41–51, 177–179
from prior to citation (different rates), 133–137
from prior to citation (variable rates), 34–40
Interim interdict, 180–200, 218–232, 251–255
See also INTERDICT; ORDER; POWER OF ARREST
Intromissions,
executry (court reckoning and payment), 149–153
partnership (court reckoning and payment), 146–148
Irretrievable breakdown of marriage. *See* DIVORCE

Joint and several liability, 34–40
See also LIABILITY
Joint minute,
admissions, 91–92
agreement, 70
agreement (OCR 33.26), 249–250
settlement (extra-judicial), 80–81
See also MINUTE
Joint motion,
decree in terms of joint minute of settlement, 82
decree of absolvitor and expenses against pursuer as assisted person, 72
See also MOTION
Judicial factor,
appointment, 7–9, 332–338
curator bonis, 332–334

Judicial factor—contd
  estate of deceased, 336–338
  winding up of dissolved firm, 334–335
Judicial separation. See SEPARATION

Landlord and tenant,
  eviction, 287–289
  irritancy of lease, 287–289
  rent arrears, 287–292
  sequestration and sale, 290–292
Lease,
  irritancy of, 287–289
  See also LANDLORD AND TENANT
Liability,
  employer's, 74–132
  joint and several, 34–40
  occupier's, 67–73
  professional, 133–145
  vicarious, 138–145
  See also NEGLIGENCE
Licensing board,
  acting contrary to natural justice, 308–309
  refusal of application, 308–309
Liquidation of company,
  expiry of days of charge, 351–353
  non-compliance with statutory demand, 345–350
  provisional liquidator, 354–356
  special resolution, 339–344
  unable to pay debts, 345–353
  See also COMPANY
Liquor licence,
  refusal of application, 308–309
List of witnesses (OCR 9.14(1)), 100
Loan from bank. See BANK LOAN
Local authority,
  children in care, 239–240
  housing (notice requiring works), 314–315
  licensing board, 308–309
  noise control, 312–313
  school placement request, 310–311
Losses. See DAMAGES

Maintenance. See ALIMENT
Manual handling operation,
  personal injury, 83–92
  See also PERSONAL INJURY
Matrimonial home,
  consent to dealing (dispensing with), 283–284
  transfer of property, 241–250
  transfer of tenancy, 218–232
  See also FINANCIAL PROVISION

Matrimonial interdict,
  divorce, 218–232
  separation, 251–255
  See also INTERDICT; ORDER; POWER OF ARREST
Matrimonial property. See FINANCIAL PROVISION
Medical liability, 138–145
  See also LIABILITY; NEGLIGENCE
Medical records,
  recovery, 305–307
Mental health,
  discharge from detention, 316–317
  removal of trustee, 322–323
  See also CURATOR BONIS (INCAPAX)
Merchantable quality,
  sale of goods, 24–33
Minor. See CHILDREN
Minute,
  abandonment (OCR 23.1(1)(a)), 71
  abandonment (OCR 23.1(1)(b)), 253
  acceptance of tender, 142
  admission of liability, 87
  amendment, 128
  amendment (answers), 131
  amendment (crave), 173
  amendment (instance), 37
  decree (with initial writ), 218–221, 233–235
  sist, adoption and amendment (OCR 36.6), 62–63
  sist (mandatory), 22
  sist (representative) (OCR 25.1), 48
  tender, 141
  tender (Houston tender), 118–119
  tender (Williamson tender), 65–66
  transference (OCR 25.2), 161–162
  variation (OCR 33.44(1)(a)), 276–277
  withdrawal of defences, 51
  withdrawal of tender, 120–121
  See also JOINT MINUTE
Misrepresentation of goods,
  interdict, 198–200
  See also INTERDICT
Missives,
  consent to dealing (dispensing with), 283–284
  implement (buyer's action), 175–176
  implement (seller's action), 169–174
Motion,
  amendment in terms of minute, 38
  amendment in terms of minute of amendment and answers, 132
  approval of condescendence of fund (OCR 35.13(2)), 168
  commission and diligence to recover documents, 90

Motion—*contd*
commission to examine a witness (OCR 28.10), 102
decree in terms of minutes of tender and acceptance of tender, 143
decree of dismissal, 255
defender to be ordained to appear at the bar, 275
defender to be ordained to disclose information anent identity of potential witness, 116–117
defender to be ordained to lead at diet of proof, 217
defender to be ordained to lodge an account of expenses, 254
defences to be received late, 186–187
discharge of diet of proof, 103
document to be admitted as evidence without calling maker as witness (OCR 29.3(2)), 101
evidence of witness to be received by way of affidavit (OCR 29.3(1)), 125
incidental order *pendente lite* (OCR 33.49(1)), 214
interim access (OCR 33.43(a)), 273
interim aliment (OCR 33.58(1)), 258
interim custody (OCR 33.43(a)(ii)), 228
interim interdict prohibiting removal of child from jurisdiction (OCR 33.24(1)(a)), 281
interim order suspending occupancy rights (OCR 33.69(1)(b)), 226–227
interim payment of damages (OCR 36.9), 79
leave to appeal, 274
minute of amendment to be received and answered, 129
minute of amendment to be received and for amendment, 174
minute of sist, adoption and amendment to be received, 64
modification of assisted person's liability for expenses, 73
order for inspection and photographing of property, 99
order for proof (OCR 37.4(1)), 9
order for provision of details of resources, 246
order for service of third party notice (OCR 20.1), 57
order to disclose child's whereabouts (OCR 33.23(1)), 280
prorogation of time to lodge answers, 130
pursuer(s) ordained to find caution (OCR 27.2), 31–32, 148

Motion—*contd*
pursuer(s) ordained to sist mandatory, 21
pursuer(s) ordained to submit to medical examination, 78
pursuer(s) solicitor has withdrawn from acting to appear or be represented at specified diet (OCR 24.2), 190–191
recall of arrestment, 23
recall of sist, 137
reference to oath (OCR 29.1(1)), 47
sist for legal aid, 259
sist for negotiation, 136
sist of mandatary, 23
sist of minuter as pursuer, 50
summary decree disposing of merits (OCR 17.2), 77
summary decree in terms of craves (OCR 17.2), 40
transference of cause against representative of defender's estate, 163
warrant for intimation (OCR 33.15(2)), 272
warrant for intimation or to dispense with intimation (OCR 33.7(6)), 282
See also JOINT MOTION
Moveable property,
arrested funds, 154–156
multiplepoinding, 157–168
sequestration and sale, 290–292
Multiplepoinding,
party holding fund, 157–163
party not holding fund, 164–168

Necessary services,
personal injury, 83–92
Negligence,
contributory (plea), 93–103
driver, 52–66
employer, 74–132
local authority, 67–73
medical, 138–145
professional, 133–145
See also LIABILITY
Noise control, 312–313
See also NUISANCE
Note,
adjustments, 39, 44, 86, 192–193, 209
dispensation with settlement of list of contributories, 347–348
interim determination of amount of outlays and renumeration payable to liquidator, 343–344
leave to commence proceedings against company, 341–342

Note—*contd*
  objections to accounts, 152–153
  objections to Auditor's report (OCR 32.4), 144–145
  order for public examination of company officer, 349–350
Notice of non–admission (OCR 29.14(2)(a)), 216
Notice to admit,
  document (OCR 29.14(1)(b)), 112–113
  fact (OCR 29.14(2)), 215
Notice requiring works,
  local authority housing, 314–315
Nuisance,
  interdict, 183–197
  noise control, 312–313

Occupancy rights, 218–232
  See also MATRIMONIAL HOME
Occupational disease,
  asbestosis, 104–121
  dermatitis, 122–132
Occupier's liability, 67–73
  See also LIABILITY; NEGLIGENCE
Order,
  administration, 354–356
  child custody, 218–232
  disclosure of child's whereabouts, 278–282
  exclusion, 218–232
  financial provision, 205–217, 241–250
  incidental, 205–217, 241–250
  property, 218–232
  See also INTERDICT; POWER OF ARREST

Parentage,
  declarator, 262–267
Parental access, 268–277
  See also CHILDREN
Partnership,
  court reckoning and payment, 146–148
  dissolution (declarator), 5–6
Passing off, 198–200
  See also INTERDICT
Paternity,
  declarator of parentage, 262–267
Payment,
  accident at work, 74–103
  accident in tenement, 67–73
  bank loan, 34–40
  court reckoning (executry), 149–153
  court reckoning (partnership), 146–148
  damages, 24–33, 52–145
  furthcoming, 154–156

Payment—*contd*
  hire of services, 19–23
  IOU, 41–51
  medical negligence, 138–145
  multiplepoinding, 157–168
  occupational disease, 104–132
  personal injury, 67–132, 138–145
  professional negligence, 133–145
  proof of, 41–51
  sale of goods, 24–33
  See also DEBT
Periodical allowance, 241–250
  See also FINANCIAL PROVISION
Personal injury,
  accident at work, 74–103
  accident in tenement, 67–73
  damages, 67–132, 138–145
  medical negligence, 138–145
  necessary services, 83–92
  occupational disease, 104–132
  professional negligence, 67–132
Personal loan,
  IOU, 41–51
  See also BANK LOAN
Personal services,
  relatives of deceased, 52–66
Petition,
  administration order, 354–356
  bankruptcy (deceased person), 330–331
  bankruptcy (firm), 328–329
  bankruptcy (individual), 326–327
  beneficiary of lapsed trust, 324–325
  curator bonis (appointment), 332–333
  estate of deceased, 336–338
  liquidation of company, 339–350
  restoration of company name, 359–360
  shareholder (unfair prejudice), 357–358
  trustee (appointment), 320–321
  trustee (removal), 322–323
  winding-up (dissolved firm), 334–335
Physical fitness of driver,
  driving licence revoked, 318–319
Plant and equipment,
  safety, 74–132
Plea,
  apportionment, 104–121
  competency, 169–174
  contributory negligence, 93–103
  exception, 169–174
  indemnity, 104–121
  prescription, 183–197
  relevancy of defence(s), 34–40, 83–92
  retention, 24–33
  time bar, 93–103
  writ or oath, 41–51

Pollution,
noise control, 312–313
See also NUISANCE
Power of arrest, 251–255
See also INTERDICT; ORDER
Prescription,
plea, 183–197
Presumption of death, 7–9. 10–11
Primary education,
school placement request, 310–311
Pro indiviso,
division or sale, 295–296
Professional negligence, 133–145
See also LIABILITY; NEGLIGENCE
Proof of payment, 41–51
See also PAYMENT
Property,
order, 218–232
specification (OCR 28.2(2)), 98
survey (negligence), 133–137
transfer, 241–250
Protection measures,
divorce, 218–232
separation, 251–255
Protection of members interests,
company shareholder, 357–358
Protective equipment,
occupational disease, 104–132
Provisional damages, 74–82
See also DAMAGES
Provisional liquidator,
appointment, 351–353
See also LIQUIDATION OF COMPANY
Pupil. See CHILDREN

Reasonable care. See DUTY OF
REASONABLE CARE
Record (OCR 9.11), 45–46, 194–197, 211–213
Recovery (debt). See DEBT
Recovery of documents, 305–307
Register of companies,
restoration of name, 359–360
See also COMPANY
Relevancy of defence(s),
plea, 34–40, 83–92
Removal of child,
interdict preventing, 278–282
See also CHILDREN; INTERDICT
Removal of tenant,
rent arrears, 287–289
See also LANDLORD AND TENANT
Removal of trustee,
mental disability, 322–323
See also TRUST; TRUSTEE
Rent arrears,
removal of tenant, 287–289

Rent arrears—*contd*
sequestration and sale, 290–292
See also DEBT
Reparation. See DAMAGES
Reponing note (OCR 8.1(1), 26–27
Repossession,
declarator of ejection, 293–294
heritable creditor, 293–294
Requisition. See DEBT
Restoration of company name,
register of companies, 359–360
Restrictive covenant,
interdict, 180–182
See also INTERDICT
Retention,
plea, 24–33
Return of goods. See DELIVERY
Right of way,
declarator of servitude, 3–4
Road traffic,
accident, 52–66
driving licence, 318–319
fitness to drive, 318–319
See also LIABILITY; NEGLIGENCE

Safety at work,
plant and equipment, 74–132
See also PERSONAL INJURY
Sale of goods,
fitness for purpose, 24–33
merchantable quality, 24–33
sequestration for rent, 290–292
Sale of house. See CONVEYANCING
School placement request, 310–311
Security for rent due,
sequestration and sale, 290–292
See also LANDLORD AND TENANT
Seizure of moveable property,
rent arrears, 290–292
See also LANDLORD AND TENANT;
MOVEABLE PROPERTY
Separation,
matrimonial interdict, 251–255
unreasonable behaviour, 251–255
See also DIVORCE; FINANCIAL
PROVISION
Sequestration (bankruptcy). See
BANKRUPTCY
Sequestration and sale,
rent arrears, 290–292
See also LANDLORD AND TENANT
Servitude,
right of way (declarator), 3–4
Shareholder in company,
unfair prejudice to interests, 357–358
See also COMPANY

Specific implement. *See* IMPLEMENT (CONTRACTUAL OBLIGATION)
Specification,
 documents (OCR 28.2(2)), 88–89, 247–248
 matters (OCR 28.2(2)), 114–115
 property (OCR 28.2(2)), 98
Sport,
 nuisance, 183–197
Statutory duty. *See* BREACH OF STATUTORY DUTY
Suicide,
 declarator of death, 7–9
 See also DEATH
Supplementary affidavit. *See* AFFIDAVIT
Survey of heritable property,
 professional negligence, 133–137
 See also HERITABLE PROPERTY; LIABILITY; NEGLIGENCE
Suspension of charge, 303–304
Suspension of diligence, 303–304

Tenancy transfer, 218–232
 See also LANDLORD AND TENANT
Tenant. *See* LANDLORD AND TENANT
Termination of partnership,
 court reckoning and payment, 146–148
 declarator, 5–6
Third party notice, 58–59, 110–111
 answers (OCR 20.5), 60–61
Time bar,
 plea, 93–103
Traffic,
 right of way, 3–4
 See also ROAD TRAFFIC
Transfer,
 property, 241–250
 tenancy, 218–232
Trust,
 beneficiary of lapsed trust, 324–325
 completion of title, 324–325
 disposition of property, 324–325
 See also TRUSTEE

Trustee,
 appointment, 320–321
 appointment (interim), 326–329
 removal, 322–323
 whereabouts unknown, 320–321
 See also TRUST
Two year action, 239–240
 See also DIVORCE; SEPARATION

Unfaithfulness, 205–217
 See also DIVORCE; SEPARATION
Unpaid debt. *See* DEBT
Unreasonable behaviour, 218–232, 251–255
 See also DIVORCE; SEPARATION

Variation on agreement,
 aliment, 260–261
 See also FINANCIAL PROVISION
Vicarious liability, 138–145
 See also LIABILITY

Whereabouts unknown,
 child, 278–282
 defender, 34–40, 154–156, 233–238, 278–279
 husband, 7–9
 relative, 10–11
 trustee, 320–321
Winding-up,
 company (expiry of days of charge), 351–353
 company (non-compliance with statutory demand), 345–350
 company (special resolution), 339–344
 firm (dissolved), 334–335
Witness,
 list (OCR 9.14(1)), 100
Work,
 accident, 74–103
 occupational disease, 104–132
 safety, 74–132
Writ or oath,
 plea, 41–51
Writings. *See* DOCUMENTS

Young persons. *See* CHILDREN